Uncommon Sense:
Effective Critical Thinking and Decision-Making in a Complex World

Lisa Weisman-Davlantes, Psy.D, MFT

Pearson Learning Solutions, 501 Boylston Street, Suite 900,
Boston, MA 02116
A Pearson Education Company
www.pearsoned.com

Printed in the United States of America

1 2 3 4 5 6 7 8 9 10 V092 16 15 14 13

000200010271789811

MT

ISBN 10: 1-269-40570-5
ISBN 13: 978-1-269-40570-6

Table of Contents

About the Author

Dr. Lisa Weisman-Davlantes, MFT has been a Lecturer in the psychology department at California State University, Fullerton since 2002, teaching such courses as Reasoning and Problem Solving, Human Sexuality, Developmental Psychology, and Psychology of Gender.

Before that she taught at various community colleges in Southern California. She has also been a licensed marriage and family therapist since 1990 and has extensive experience treating diverse individuals, couples, groups, and children.

Acknowledgments

As with any long-term project, there are so many supportive people to thank for their cheerleading skills, patience, and unwavering loyalty. I am blessed to have so many wonderful, loving role models. I told God that I wanted to write a book, He said okay, and sent me all of you to guide me.

First, thank you Charles and Rochelle Weisman (my parents) for teaching me the value of an education, whether academic, life experience, or good old-fashioned common sense. Your names in this book and your influence on my life now make you immortal.

To Karen Dancey, sister and fellow college instructor, no one can make me laugh as long and as hard as you do, and Lord knows we have had to call on humor many times over the years!

Mr. Bruce Himes, president of Western Water Works Supply Company in Chino Hills, California, your quest for knowledge is truly admirable, and your encouragement and recognition of this project were great motivators. You deserve an honorary Ph.D in Psychology.

Dr. Jack Mearns, chair of the CSUF Psychology Department, thank you for your sensitive, respectful collaboration and problem solving skills, as well as your calming influence. You encouraged me to teach Psych. 110 the way I saw fit, and recommending new course instructors to discuss my ideas and methods is the highest compliment I can receive.

Dr. MaryAnn Larson, my dear friend and colleague since 1990, if it wasn't for your constant nagging about becoming a psychology instructor, I never would have believed that I could or should be teaching. That phone call in 1995 about the open faculty position at Fullerton College changed my life. I am forever indebted to you.

My amazing students over so many years must also be thanked, but in particular, my personal minions, Reinalyn Echon, Stephanie Waidner, and Catherine Pineda have lifted my spirits when I was discouraged, listened to me vent frustration on various topics, and demonstrated that critical thought is indeed alive and well in the student population. Steph, I promised I would be done before you graduated, so maybe now you will forgive and forget that B-almost-an-A you earned in my class?! You all believe that I have motivated you to do your best, even in the face of opposition, but the inspiration has been reciprocal.

Cynthia Bruns, CSUF librarian and all-around expert of remarkable, useful knowledge, thank you for demonstrating EndNote. You saved me a lot of time and grief.

My bus-stop gal-pals Stacey Campbell, Melissa Compani, Susan Dunham, and Grace Hagman, have been my lifeline and personal cheerleaders in every part of my life. I only hope that I have waved my pom-poms for you as much as you have for me. Wait, that didn't sound right...

Christine Galvez, MFT, your sense of humor and endless supply of hysterical personal stories have entertained me for hours. Your love, insight, and articulate demonstrations of critical thinking make me strive to be like you. You have chosen the right profession.

Victoria Chamberlin and Iain MacDonald of Pearson Publishing, the two of you have been like a breath of fresh air. You care about the students and instructors, and encouraged me to finish this book from the first time we discussed it. Your enthusiasm rekindled the spark in me, and having a deadline for publication didn't hurt either!

Meg Tiedemann, project manager extraordinaire from Pearson, from the first contact with you, I felt excited, supported, and respected. Your positive energy shines in every email and I am glad to say, it is contagious! If you are ever in Southern California, lunch is on me!

Last but certainly not least, I have to lovingly acknowledge my wonderful family, starting with my husband, Jim, who told me 19 years ago that we would journey on a magic carpet ride. You have been right since day one, even though a colleague told you after we married that you would never win another argument. I gladly concede and I look forward to many more adventures with you, my best friend and soul-mate.

Cameron and Victoria, you are the true impetus for this book. Parents are children's first teachers, but you have been my perpetual instructors and reason to continue learning, growing, and trying to improve the world we live in. I love you.

Introduction

Spending two years of my life thinking about, planning, organizing, and creating a finished product seems like a long time. When I reflect further, I realize that this book has taken me a lifetime to complete. Yet as I was writing and gathering information, I realized that I would never truly finish the task because continual learning is the core of critical thinking.

I became a Marriage and Family Therapist for many reasons; I wanted to forever guide, assist, teach, and learn about others as well as myself. After I taught my first college class and thus began the second phase of my career-life, I never dreamed that the course I despised teaching the most at Cal State Fullerton, Psychology 110—Reasoning and Problem Solving (aka Critical Thinking), would one day become my favorite.

Instructors can become bored teaching the same subjects, semester after semester, yet this has not been the case for me when spearheading the critical thinking course. Each grading period there is always new information; social and media events, a new group of students with differing opinions and beliefs, and a lecturer just as eager to learn from them as I hope they are from me. I finally took their advice and wrote a book containing many of the examples and stories discussed and laughed about in class. I truly hope you all enjoy and learn from them.

****

As for the information within, keep in mind throughout each chapter that this book is about you. You will most definitely find friends and relatives in these pages, but it is always easier to be critical about someone else's personality quirks and mistakes than our own. This is not an excuse to feel superior to others because the descriptions of poor critical thought apply to them. Be ever-cognizant of how they apply to you. Recognize your own decision-making and thought processes and utilize the theories and examples to aid in your self-growth, not to criticize and judge others.

The book is broken down into three sections. First, we will explore the roots of critical thinking. We are taught about critical thinking skills in college courses, but what always seems lacking is theoretical information on how those skills are first shaped and learned. What factors play a part in our future ability to choose wisely, believe firmly, and question constantly?

In the second part of the book, we will analyze critical thought that we attempt to utilize in the real world, examining the influences of higher education, technology, politics, religion, and the media. Last but not least, we will discuss how to apply all these theories and influences at work, in relation-ships, and the way we manage money.

There will be a few themes throughout: these include accountability, char-acter and integrity, empathy, social/communication skills, and the practical applications of such. Without practical application, we are largely unable to assign relevance to information studied. Reading this book won't necessar-ily make you wiser, but deeper awareness and practice of critical thinking skills will. Much of what you will read may seem like common sense, yet knowing about common sense and practicing it are two different things. Hence, the title of this book. . . .

Part I
Roots of Critical Thinking

What Does it Mean to be a Critical Thinker?

"Critical thinking is a desire to seek, patience to doubt, fondness to meditate, slowness to assert, readiness to consider, carefulness to dispose and set in order; and hatred for every kind of imposture."
—*Francis Bacon (1605)*

You've probably heard the term "critical thinking" before, but what does this actually mean? We all think, though it seems at times that some don't, but what is the difference between thinking and critical thinking? Here are a few definitions:

1. "Critical thinking is the process by which we test claims and arguments and determine which have merit and which do not. In other words, critical thinking is a search for answers, a quest" (Ruggiero, 2012).

2. "Critical thinking is the systematic evaluation or formulation of beliefs, or statements, by rational standards" (Vaughn, 2008, p.4).

3. "When we take a position on an issue, we assert or claim something. The claim and the thinking on which it's based are subject to rational evaluation. When we do that evaluating, we are thinking critically" (Moore & Parker, 2004).

Here is my definition: Critical thinking is an ongoing process that involves the utilization of thought, emotion, and intuition in order to gather information and arrive at logical, sound conclusions regarding people, events, and beliefs.

As you can see, there can be varied definitions of critical thinking (CT) and they are all correct. CT is something to be learned and practiced throughout one's life. "Critical thinking is not about what you think, but how you think" (Vaughn, 2008, p.4). Thinking involves the endless stream of thoughts running through your head, the constant chatter in your mind that narrates your daily experiences. For many, this is viewed as unimportant background noise. For effective thinkers, this process demands constant attention because it tells us how we feel, what we believe, and it influences our decisions and how we treat others.

Paying attention to the patterns of our thoughts helps us decide what we believe and what we are correct in believing. This involves "an openness to other points of view, a tolerance for opposing perspectives, a focus on the issue at hand, and fair assessment of arguments and evidence" (Vaughn, 2008, p. 7). We must intimately and painfully know ourselves, the good, the bad, and the ugly.

REQUIREMENTS AND GOALS OF CRITICAL THINKING

> Many highly intelligent people are poor thinkers. Many people of average intelligence are skilled thinkers. The power of the car is separate from the way the car is driven.
>
> —*Edward deBono*

Ruggiero (2012) noted that CT entails a search for answers. You don't have to possess a special academic degree to achieve enlightenment or be a critical thinker, but you need to meet the following requirements (Ruggiero, 2012; Moore & Parker, 2004):

1. Careful reading, listening, and observation of self and others.
2. Questioning, deeper investigation of self, others, problems.
3. The ability to spot relevant vs. irrelevant information in oral and written communication.
4. 3 Types of Intelligence (Sternberg, 1985, 1996)
   a. Education (Analytical/Academic)
   b. Experience (Creativity)
   c. Common sense (Practical)
5. Openness, tolerance, and interest in new ideas.
6. Empathy
7. Practice!!
8. Mental discipline, self-control, and self-awareness.
9. Ability to anticipate your own and others' needs and emotions
10. Ability to anticipate events and consequences.
11. Accepting full responsibility for your thoughts, feelings, and actions.
12. Curiosity.

There are also goals of CT that we need to strive for, in order to make us effective thinkers (Ruggiero, 2012; Moore & Parker, 2004):

1. The bottom line of CT = finding the truth.
2. Form opinions based on fact/study.

3. Using thought, feeling, and intuition in making decisions.

4. Challenge/question established ideas, develop a degree of skepticism.

5. Educate oneself and others.

6. Gain knowledge/understanding = growth and change.

7. Know your biases.

8. "Consider the source"—pay attention to your sources of information.

We will examine each requirement and goal in depth, but first you need to know that as humans, we tend to overestimate our social and cognitive skills, as well as our level of self-awareness (DeAngelis, 2003; Ludwig, 2010; Olson, Zanna, and Dunning, 2011). That said, understand that you will attempt to brush past some of the concepts in this book as common sense or "stuff I already know." If you approach the material within in this fashion, I guarantee you will not learn anything and feel like you wasted your time and money on this book.

Common sense, according to the Merriam-Webster dictionary, means "sound and prudent judgment based on a simple perception of the situation or facts" (Merriam-Webster Inc., 2013). Simple perceptions, such as "slow down when driving your vehicle during a rainstorm" or "look both ways before you cross the street" may seem like yesterday's news. Everybody knows these ideas are practical and obvious . . . or do they? How many times have you seen people driving at alarming speeds on the highway during a downpour? How often do you see someone cross the street in front of your vehicle, eyes on their cell phone, and never even glance at you? Just because we determine that ideas belong in the realm of common sense does not mean that these concepts automatically become a routine part of our life. Critical thought focuses on putting these seemingly banal ideas into practice. This means thinking about what you are doing, saying, and feeling and the possible effects your words and actions have on yourself and others—every waking moment.

Socrates noted that "The only true wisdom is in knowing you know nothing." If you're not going to listen to Socrates, you won't heed anyone's advice. If that's the case, return the book, drop the class, continue on the same path, and wonder why you don't have what you want in your life.

To those of you still with me, let's discuss the requirements of CT. We first need to carefully read information, including instructions, listen to conversations, and observe ourselves as well as others. Again, focus on what you do and say, and how you affect others. Pay attention to what others do and say and how they affect you. Really pay attention. That means hearing what is actually being said, instead of focusing on what you will say next. Take note of how often you interrupt others and their facial reactions when you do. Notice when you are silently criticizing someone without knowing much about them or why they behaved as they did. It is certainly easier to be critical about others than about ourselves. Many times, we read but do not understand or truly think about instructions. Some don't want to follow or read instructions, then wonder why the bookcase-in-a-box doesn't get constructed properly, why they earn failing grades on term papers, or why machined airplane parts fail when tested. One of my biggest peeves as an instructor is that students don't read/follow instructions. I typically get this response when I explain the directions to them for the umpteenth time: "Oh. I didn't see that." Sometimes they actually have the nerve to tell me that the "rules" are not in the syllabus or assignment prompt. I must admit, I enjoy getting the paper out and pointing to the exact sentence they overlooked.

Questioning and deeper investigation are next on the list. The first question to ask yourself is: Do I want to be a more effective thinker? I would suppose this is your goal, due to the fact that you are reading this book. However, wanting and doing are two separate things. Some people are taught not to think "too much" while growing up. Some are also taught not to question authority or the status quo. As juror #6 said in the movie *Twelve Angry Men* (starring Henry Fonda), "Me? I'm just a working man. My boss does the supposing." Some of us are content to remain ignorant or are taught that we should be. The problem I see with this is that allowing others to think for you sometimes leads to disaster. Think back to high school, when "everybody" was supposedly involved in one activity or another. "Geez Dennis, everybody smokes pot! You're such a straight edge!" If Dennis has high self-esteem and has been taught to think for himself instead of following the crowd, he'll laugh off his peers' attempts to pressure him to conform. It will hurt a bit, yes, but he will understand that it will hurt more if he follows someone else's path.

Don't be afraid to ask questions, even of the most revered authorities. Ask respectfully, and you should get some intelligent, well-thought responses. How do you ask respectfully, you inquire? Here's an example of what not to do:

A few years ago, at the beginning of a new semester, a student asked me if I thought the field of psychology was truly valid and useful in people's lives or just a bunch of hooey. Mind you, this was shortly after I enthusiastically and painstakingly discussed background information on myself, including my education and occupational experience, which incorporated half my life-span to that point. Immediately after the student asked the question, I noticed other students' reactions. Some laughed and shook their heads, others had open mouths and looks of horror on their young faces. What did these students know that the questioner didn't? They knew that his "question" was nothing more than an arrogant slap in the face to me and my profession. At least I got to use his "question" to explain more about therapy and the field in general, as well as how NOT to ask questions of authority figures. The moral of the story is, if you really want to learn about someone or something, don't mock the person, situation, or profession. Don't prejudge. You may think you're being witty and clever, but the person you are mocking has heard it all before and will have little if any tolerance for your disrespectful, judgmental attitude.

Moving on, how does one distinguish what is relevant vs. irrelevant in a claim or argument? Let's use a personal, everyday example. You are approaching your significant other in an assertive (= respectful) way to discuss how he leaves the wet towel on the floor after his daily shower.

She: "Honey, I'd really appreciate it if you would pick up your wet towel after your shower and drape it over the shower door."

He: "You know, you always leave the toothpaste tube on the counter, with the top off, after you brush your teeth!"

Many of us then continue in a round-robin kind of argument of "No I don't," "Yes you do," etc. The original argument quickly becomes lost in the battle and the recipient of the criticism has successfully changed the subject and turned the conversation (and responsibility) away from himself. Thus, 'he' has introduced irrelevant information and 'she' has fallen for it. As "She" becomes more aware of how "He" manipulates the situation (usually unconsciously), she can see the change coming and say something like this: "Wait; right now we are talking about you and the towel." He most likely will try again to change the topic, but she can repeat her mantra until he either gives in and listens, or gives up and leaves the room.

Learn to recognize the relevant vs. irrelevant information you read about in newspapers and magazines, as well as the speeches and statements made by politicians or CEOs accused of unethical business practices. How much information is "filler," and doesn't add any important facts to the story or answer the question? We will discuss this more later on.

Sternberg's Triangular Theory of Intelligence (1985, 1996) also serves us well as critical thinkers. Sternberg stated that there are three kinds of knowledge we must possess in order to be thought of as intelligent; education, experience, and common sense. We all know people who are highly educated, but possess poor social or survival skills. Some have great common sense, but not much formal education. Others learn from experience and know how to "read" people and situations, but don't speak using proper grammar and wording. Sternberg noted that when we have a nice balance of the triangle, we tend to be more successful and confident.

If you have this nice balance, you will more likely be open to and interested in new ideas and ways of doing things, and more tolerant of those who are different from you. Notice how quickly or how often you mock someone or something that is different from you, your beliefs, or your way of life. You will come off as sarcastic, arrogant, and closed-minded, like the psychology-question-asking student described earlier. I love it when people mock my profession ("Oh, you're a shrink?! Do you analyze everyone?"), then change their tune and ask genuine, knowledge-seeking questions after one of my snappy comebacks. It feels like a victory, a chance to educate and help someone be just a bit more open. We tend to fear what we don't understand or know, so mocking others who are different is a way to deal with that fear and insecurity. Sometimes we are afraid that being "open" means being forced to change our opinions. Being open can lead to modifying your beliefs, but it can also mean just listening and learning without criticism or praise.

Being a great listener who is open to new ideas also involves **empathy**. Empathy entails being able to truly comprehend someone else's experience, cognitively, emotionally and physically. This idea is the origin of popular sayings such as "Put yourself in someone else's shoes," or "Walk a mile in my shoes." Empathy helps us to focus on someone else and connect on a deeper level. It is different than sympathy, which is feeling sorry for someone's misfortune or feeling glad that

> empathy—Identification with and understanding of someone else's experience, cognitively, emotionally and physically.

they won an award. Empathy contains more emotional and cognitive depth. Here's the difference: Sympathy: "I am so sorry that you broke your leg. How awful for you!" Empathy: "Boy, it must have been awful breaking your leg during the baseball game, being scared, in pain, and wondering when the ambulance would arrive." Empathy allows us to truly experience another's situation and assists in connecting with that person. The positive effects of empathy include better relationships (we all want to be understood and valued) and less judgment. If I can put myself in someone else's shoes, I am more likely to understand the steps leading up to their decisions and less likely to criticize and negatively judge them.

Another requirement of CT is practice. Some people are naturally better at the requirements of effective thinking than others, but we all must practice and use our skills every day, throughout our lives, in order to master our thoughts, feelings, opinions, and beliefs. That means being involved with the outside world on a regular basis. This includes reading, listening, asking questions, showing genuine interest in others, and learning new things. Don't interrupt, stop thinking about what you are going to say next, and allow for some silence in order to process information and ask or respond to the next question. Put the phone, iPod, iPad, and Nintendo DS away and have a face-to-face conversation with another person.

The last three requirements go hand-in-hand. Being wholly responsible for what you do, say, and feel involve self-discipline, self-control, and self-awareness. If you are disciplined and self-aware, you will have a stronger ability to anticipate your own as well as others' needs and emotions and in turn you will be better able to anticipate events and consequences. You will be acutely aware of your biases, strengths and weaknesses, think of others as well as yourself, and know when to speak, when to listen, and when to say no. Since critical thinking at its best involves being able to stop yourself before you make a poor choice, the mantra of "personal responsibility" will resonate throughout this book.

Above all, critical thinkers are curious. They want to know why people behave the way they do (including themselves). Why were certain decisions made and not others? How do we come to embrace certain beliefs? They are constantly seeking knowledge and truth. They want answers, but recognize that they may not find them, or that the answers may change with time and the discovery of new information. They are not comfortable with the status quo and believe that they and others can and should change for the better. They seek self-awareness and growth, even if it is painful. I've found over the years that the best critical thinkers tend to be positive and people-oriented. The latter doesn't necessarily mean that one is extroverted, it just means that one is aware of and interested in others. Critical thinkers don't take information at face value; they engage in research to find the answer. They typically won't be comfortable with one person's assessment of another. They want to meet the individual in question and make their own decision about that person's skills or character.

How do CT'ers become so independent and self-confident? Their focus on the goals of effective thinking are all-encompassing. So now that we've explored the necessary factors in becoming/being a critical thinker, let's focus on the goals of all this practice. First, the goal of CT is to find the truth (Ruggiero, 2012). In order to find the truth some steps must be taken, in no particular order, to get to the truth. We may not like what we find, but we must be open to it. We must realize that the truth of a person, event, or situation could go against everything we have been taught to believe, or everything we have experienced, but we still must be open and accepting. Critical thinkers want to find the correct information and are willing to incorporate this new knowledge, even if it means changing long-standing views of people, religion, politics, education, medicine, business, and how the natural world functions.

Seeking, and many times finding, the truth first depends on our ability to establish opinions based on fact and study. Humans tend to believe that their strongest opinions are based on fact, then realize when questioned that they haven't a clue how they came to believe that opinion or where the information came from. In order to find this out about yourself or someone else, all you have to do is ask one simple question: Where did you get that information? Watch the stuttering and stammering begin, sometimes turning into frustration and subject-changing. That means paying attention to this process in yourself as well as Aunt Minnie. We all have long-standing opinions without correct background information. As Ruggiero (2012) states, the mind is an opinion factory. It operates 24/7, even when you're asleep. I liken it to the stock market ticker at the bottom of the screen on CNBC, with one exception. The stock market ticker actually changes with time, novel information and new cognitive demands. Some people's "opinion ticker" stays the same their whole life, even when presented with more innovative and practical information. In psychological jargon, this is called **mental set**. Mental set happens when we do

> **mental set**—Using or trusting the same beliefs or problem solving techniques over time, even when new information or more effective methods are available.

or believe the same thing over time, even when better, more effective ways of believing or doing are available. Think of Grandpa being unwilling to use a computer because he's never used one. "I've been doing without it for 60 years. Why should I change now?" Along with this typically comes **functional fixedness**, which is an inability to see new uses for familiar items. You see an example of this when someone stubs their toe and runs to find some ice.

> **functional fixedness—** Inability to consider new uses for familiar items.

If there is no ice in the freezer, the person afflicted with functional fixedness won't think to use the bag of frozen peas as an ice pack. He/she will mutter and complain that there is no ice. The bottom line with mental set (MS) and functional fixedness (FF) is that we are stuck in doing and believing the same things and no new information is allowed to penetrate our cerebral walls.

An important goal that will be discussed in more detail in this book will be your ability and comfort in utilizing thought, feeling, and intuition in your decisions and social interactions. Americans especially are still taught that emotion is bad, and intuition is a touchy-feely therapy concept. You are born with feelings, and someone teaches you along the way that these emotions are not okay, invalid, or they make you weak. We are taught not to feel, not to listen to the internal thoughts and sensations in our bodies. We are taught only to make decisions based on pure logic (whatever that actually is) and not let our feelings "interfere." You will see in this book that we need to utilize logic, emotion, and intuition in order to make the best decisions.

Critical thinkers must also challenge established ideas and have a degree of skepticism. This does not mean you should necessarily be cynical. Skepticism has to do with asking questions, delving deeper into various subjects, sales pitches, and people. Skepticism is the same as not taking something at face value. Cynicism is completely different; it is negative and based on feelings of paranoia and insecurity. There is a feeling that someone is out to get you, to cheat you out of your money, or their intentions are suspect. Being cynical leads to these conclusions quickly, while being skeptical helps you keep an open mind in determining whether you are getting a good deal or not.

Challenging ideas is easy for some, incredibly difficult, even painful, for others. Again, some of us have been taught not to question—at home, in school or religious organizations, and at our place of employment. Some people don't like being questioned, even on the simplest topics, and regardless of how respectfully you pose the question: "Gee Grandma, how come you smoke cigarettes but tell me not to?" "Why do you keep going out to lunch every day when you say you can't afford your mortgage payment?" "Why do you have a $400 cell phone when you can't afford books for your college classes?" "Why do you complain about the price of gasoline when you drive a large SUV?" You get the idea. These are legitimate questions that can be asked in the gentlest of ways . . . only to be met with anger, hostility, and possibly attempts to change the subject to questions about your life. We don't want to be reminded that we are inconsistent in our words and actions. We like our opinions and beliefs and don't want to have to think about whether they are valid or not. We feel uncomfortable when we are told that we are the creators of our destiny; that we have control over our thoughts, feelings and actions. It's so much easier to complain and blame someone or something else for our decisions. This does not mean you should refrain from questioning yourself, others and the world. Just be respectful and gentle in your approach, and be prepared for an occasional backlash when you hit a nerve.

During a brief stint teaching budding therapists at a private graduate school, I challenged and questioned students' beliefs about everything, but mostly about how to deal with therapy clients. Some graduate clinical psychology students are a special breed. They know just enough knowledge to be dangerous, and have just enough clinical experience to believe they are expert therapists. I quickly found that they didn't like their clinical and theoretical views challenged. This was a curious state of affairs to me because, after all, isn't therapy (for both therapist and client) about challenging one's beliefs and opinions, thus leading to more effective behavioral choices? I didn't see a problem until my department chair called a meeting with me to discuss my teaching strategy. He noted that my style was iconoclastic. At the time, I wasn't quite sure about the definition of that word, but I knew from his tone of voice that it was not a compliment. I raced to the dictionary on my return home that day to find the definition of iconoclast (Webster's Dictionary, 1989):

1. A breaker or destroyer of images, esp. those set up for religious veneration.
2. One who attacks cherished beliefs, traditional institutions, etc. as being based on error or superstition.

In all fairness, I wasn't that harsh; I have always been questioning but respectful of others' opinions and beliefs, but apparently some students became distressed when I challenged them to think outside their comfortable, albeit arrogant, boxes. Suffice it to say that I found another, more tolerant institution as my place of employment, and to this day, I warn students that I will question their most cherished beliefs about themselves, their religious and political views, and how the world functions.

Two of the most important goals of critical thinking involve knowledge. Educating yourself and others leads to understanding and change. While you are questioning, investigating, and concluding, remember that you are doing all this in order to find the truth and grow as a person. As you grow and share your knowledge, others can and will flourish too, if they are open to doing so. A word of caution needs to be said here: Don't get into an argument just to show someone up or "win." Don't use your new-found knowledge to "prove" your point. We don't educate others by screaming at them or trying to convince them that we have better ideas. People change very slowly, over time, with experience and self-aware-ness. No one is going to change long-standing beliefs after one conversa-tion with you, so take your ego out of the mix, casually state what you believe to be true and back it up with valid, researched information. Then let the chips fall where they may. Expect others to disagree, and then get to know them better by asking questions about their principles. You will learn about yourself, too. It feels good to win an argument but what do you really gain? A few minutes (or a few days, weeks, or even years) of one-up-man-ship and possibly a lifetime of resentment and loss of respect from the other person.

Ideas about educating ourselves lead to the need for awareness of our bi-ases—and please don't tell me you aren't biased, because you are. If you are alive and human, you believe in and act in accordance with certain stereo-types and prejudices—against certain ethnicities, races, religions, political and sexual orientations, social and economic statuses, ad nauseum. Many of us profess that we don't believe the stereotypes, but our actions and words show and speak differently. How often do you laugh at the ethnic joke or ut-ter it yourself? It's okay—it's typical and human.

We also fall prey to a concept called the **confirmation bias**, which states that we tend to seek information that agrees with our viewpoint, while automatically rejecting data that does not fit our experience. Many of us associ-ate mostly (or only) with people who agree with our ideologies or fit with our lifestyle. It is certainly safe to stay within our comfort zone, rarely being chal-lenged intellectually or emotionally, but we typically aren't open to discovering much about ourselves and our choices when we constantly feel secure that our preferences are correct.

> confirmation bias— Tendency to seek information that agrees with our views, while automatically rejecting data that does not fit our experience.

Accept that we are all biased, in both positive and negative ways, and you can then focus on the partialities that you dislike and change them. In the process, you become a clearer, more effective decision-maker, and isn't this the most important part of the journey you have thus far undertaken?

Last but certainly not least, consider the source. Your parents probably said this to you many times while you were growing up and questioning why your schoolmates told you all kinds of incorrect information about life, sex, drugs, significant others, etc. These wise adults were trying to teach you to get your information from people who had more experience and educa-tion than your 14 year old best friend. This same lesson holds true through-out life. If you want specific medical information, do you ask your gardener, or do you call your doctor? Pretty obvious answer, but you'd be surprised how many people get their information through third party sources, rather than asking an expert outright. When a rumor is being spread about some-one, do you ask the subject of the rumor about the truth of the accusation, or feel your BFF's word (or *US magazine's*) is as good as gold?

CHANGE AND GROWTH: NATURE VS. NURTURE

Man is not what he thinks he is, but what he thinks, he is.

—*Elbert Hubbard*

By now you might be thinking one of two things. Either, "Wow, this is exciting stuff!" or "This sounds like a lot of work!" It is exciting and it can be hard work, but it is rewarding. Critical thinking is not something you are born with (nature); it is learned behavior (nurture). Some are naturally better than others, but they need to hone their skills as much as the next person. The ability to think critically aids in problem-solving, active learning, and intelligent self-improvement (Vaughn, 2008). It results in better decisions, less stress and chaos in your life, and better relationships.

As you can see from the lists of requirements and goals, being a critical thinker involves a strong sense of self. If you didn't grow up with this, you can develop it as an adult. It involves feeling good about your decisions and thought processes, having morals/ethics, and trusting that you can and will take good care of yourself and your life. Ruggiero (2012) notes that being an effective thinker depends on mental discipline. Do you know what you want and don't want in your life? Do you have self-control? Can you express emotions without getting out of control? Can you pass up junk food when you've decided not to eat it? What about using drugs and alcohol? Can you be faithful in a relationship regardless of the temptation to stray? What rules do you live by? Are they rules you decided for yourself or did someone/something give you those rules? What are you goals in life? What is your purpose for being on earth?

Serious questions indeed! This book will help you to answer these and many more questions, if you do the work. You must read, reflect, be uncomfortable, and grow. This takes time. It won't involve a few weeks of effort, but a lifetime of continued self-exploration and growth. The more you grow, the more others can grow with you. You may think or may have even been told that you don't have the intelligence to do better, whether that is academically, cognitively, or financially, but you do. Teachers and therapists know this concept well. As a therapist, I was told that my clients would only advance to the level of my personal growth. Thus, if I was unable to solve my own problems and move forward, they would not either. This action-reaction is true in all areas, no matter your profession or station in life. Students, clients, children, or employees will only improve to the level of functioning of their mentors. This is true for growing a business too. If you want others to learn and improve, you must do so first. Be the role model who talks the talk and walks the walk. Being a role model will be another ongoing theme in this book.

As role models 24/7, there is always someone watching how we respond to various situations. If you grow and change, those who love you or work with you must do likewise, lest they get left behind. Others will be anxious about any changes you make and attempt what I call "change-back" behavior. Say I spray all my students' hair a nice, bright shade of blue and send them on their way. Family and friends will be uncomfortable and demonstrate this discomfort by making comments such as, "What on earth did you do? How could you let that crazy professor do this to you?!" After some time goes by (the amount depending on how upset others are and how one handles the change-back pressure), I decide to change the students' hair to a fiery orange. When they arrive home, someone will undoubtedly say, "Gee, I liked the blue hair better." What's the lesson here? When a change first occurs, many people will protest, some more loudly and longer than others. After awhile, they get used to the change. They have to, or they will risk losing the person they care about. Relationships depend on our ability to change and accept change in those we love. Some relationships don't survive the modifications and end. Sometimes the change is so daunting that another person has enough power to prevent the change. I remember a colleague years ago who was obese and wanted to lose weight. According to her, her husband announced that if she lost weight he would divorce her. She didn't call his bluff and she didn't lose the weight. They both lost out on some necessary modifications for her health and their relationship growth.

To clarify, I am speaking of changes that don't negatively affect someone else, like an affair or lying. If I change something in or for myself, like my hairstyle, my car, my major in college, or where I choose to live, I am not hurting anyone; others just have to get used to my doing something different.

Politicians and others in power also rely on our ability to adapt to change. When a rule or law is first amended or created, they expect some people to complain and protest. If enough do, then they have to be concerned about the outcome and their careers. They know that after the law is passed, we tend to accept the change, move on and forget about our original issues with the legislation. We become complacent, that is until the next threat of change presents itself.

As critical thinkers, we cannot become complacent (not for too long, anyway) because then we stop focusing on what we believe is important. In today's society, there is so much information from so many sources, it is nearly impossible to pay attention to everything going on around us, so we block out the news that is overwhelming or not directly affecting our daily lives. I was surprised that with the media coverage of the 2010 BP oil spill in the Gulf of Mexico, there was not a lot of discussion in my social circle about the extent of the devastation. It was a tragedy of overwhelming proportions, but happened far away from our home state, and it hadn't personally affected us yet. If there had been a shortage of seafood and/or the prices soared in restaurants and grocery stores, then we would have been angry. When I watched a documentary on the destruction of sea life in the region, I was finally furious and terribly sad. These kinds of reactions are normal, human responses to things we cannot control. However, as an effective thinker, I can and should focus on this situation; it affected us all and we need to cry out for sanctions against the offenders and ways to prevent accidents like this from ever happening again. Issues like these become even bigger political bouncing balls and we need to be fully informed in order to make the best decisions.

Know that we are all guilty at one time or another of following the "Do as I say, not as I do" way of living our lives. "Cigarettes are bad for you," we smugly announce as we take the next drag in front of our children. "If you use drugs or alcohol I'll kick you out of the house," we scream, as we reach into the refrigerator for our next beer. This is also referred to as a **double-standard**. I have one set of rules for me and another for you. We all know that actions speak louder than words; thus, in all areas of our lives we must pay attention to what we are doing and what we want to teach others. That is, if you

> **double-standard—**
> Having one set of rules for oneself and different rules for others.

want to be a more effective thinker, have more control over your life, and rid yourself of chaos (that of others as well as your own). You will make mistakes—probably every single day, if you are human—but that's the name of the game. Make a mistake, reflect and decide what you will do next time a similar situation arises, and put your plan into action. Always be prepared to mess up and learn. Of course, this is easier said than done for many of us.

Along these lines, people are great at "knowing" their strengths—even if others disagree—but we tend to deny or ignore our weaknesses. Oops . . . I mean "challenges," in politically correct (PC) vernacular. As I stated earlier in this chapter, research has shown time and again that we tend to overestimate our social skills and positive behaviors, while completely ignoring the negative effects on ourselves or others. Here is an example of this self-denial in action:

> A friend on Facebook, who is very controlling, wrote that she couldn't believe people could be so controlling of others. "Let people make their own decisions," she demanded (still trying to control . . .).

We accuse others of behaving the same way we do, except we don't recognize our own behavior, or believe that our actions are not similar or not as offensive as others'. Effective thinkers make this kind of mistake less often because they pay attention to what they think, say, and do, and how others respond to them. They are more open to change and more willing to modify their thoughts, feelings and behaviors over time.

I find it amazing that some of us don't have a clue about who we are. In therapist-speak, this is due to a combination of defense mechanisms called denial and projection. Whatever you find uncomfortable in yourself, you dislike in others. Many times, we aren't even aware that we possess a certain projected characteristic, let alone that we don't like that about ourselves. How about the person who goes to the same few restaurants repeatedly, verbalizes the same catch-phrases or jokes for years, and refuses to change their schedule or the way they do things? This is a person who is comfortable but stuck, like a broken record; the stylus gets stuck in one place and it takes physical effort to move it forward. For those who are younger and don't know what a record is, it's like a scratch on a CD with a verse of music that repeats until you either smack the CD player (my solution) or push a button to move forward to the next track. Either way you look at it, like a broken record or a scratched CD, when one is made aware of the repetition, that person has a choice. Change and grow, or stay and stagnate. Sadly, many choose to stay and stagnate.

Some are afraid to change. Self-exploration means there will be some emotional pain. You might find out that after so many arguments over the years, you really are very controlling, condescending, stubborn, or aloof. So what? Make a conscious effort to change. Find out why you are the way you are, the costs and benefits of such, and modify what you wish. Becoming more self-aware has many benefits: less stress, better, closer relationships, less arguing and conflict, and improved physical health. All these benefits for very little cost and emotional pain. Ah yes, but this is like therapy, and Americans in general are still very uncomfortable about introspection. "Aw, you think too much, you get confused. You know what I mean?" claimed juror #10 in *Twelve Angry Men*. When we don't think enough, we harm ourselves and our society. Think of road rage, drive-by shootings, government spending. "Thinking enough" entails focusing on the here-and-now effects as well as the distant consequences of our decisions. Distant can mean 5 minutes from now or 5 years from now, ad infinitum. We need to pay attention to the consequences for ourselves, as well as for others. When we scream and display hand gestures at the driver who cut us off, we are not thinking of the consequences. We are running on pure emotion: fear, anger, pride. Only after the other person demonstrates his/her own proficiency at sign language, can we begin to realize that the situation could get out of hand and have a more drastic conclusion. Even so, some of us are fueled even more by the offender's response in kind, and emotion continues to overrule logic. So what do we do? We follow the person at breakneck speed down the highway, of course! Screaming and cursing all the way, oblivious to others in our path, and running on auto pilot. And for what? To win. To be "right." "I'll show him!" you mutter to yourself as you zip in and out of traffic lanes to keep up with the perpetrator, while your blood pressure shoots skyward and your stress hormone, cortisol, builds up in your system like a backed-up commode. Not a pretty picture you say? It isn't. Studies have shown that continual, highly charged emotional incidents like the one described above can keep your cortisol levels high long after the events are over. Heightened levels of cortisol affect many organs and functions of the body (Dickerson, Gruenewald, & Kemeny 2009; Lazarus, 1991). According to Dr. Ellen Weber (2008), and others (Gottfried, 2012; Kemeny & Shestyuk, 2008) cortisol:

- Lowers immune system functioning
- Slows thinking and can even shrink the hippocampus (an important brain area in regard to memory)
- Leads to blood sugar imbalances
- Raises blood pressure
- Weakens muscle tissue
- Decreases bone density
- Increases abdominal fat

The critical thinker in this case understands the possible and definite consequences and decides either beforehand or just as the rage is beginning to build, that it's not worth the effort to become so angry or hold onto years-long grudges directed at loved ones. Do we experience frustration? Yes. Is the continual hostility and lashing out at the world worth your life or someone else's? Absolutely not.

I know what you're thinking and the answer is "yes." Yes, you (and others) can learn to think before you speak or act. You can learn to focus on consequences, you can put yourself in the shoes of others and understand how they feel or how they might react to what you do. You have to want to. If you already do these things well (according to you, of course), you can refine these skills. Quite frankly, your personal and professional success depend on these people skills = effective thinking and decision making. You won't be perfect; you will make mistakes. That is our job every day on this planet—to make mistakes and learn from them. The only perfect people are dead. They have reached their highest level of functioning and no longer need to be concerned with self-improvement. Keep in mind that self-improvement leads to world improvement. You become a kinder, happier, intellectually and emotionally stronger, more industrious person and then you teach others how to do the same by example. There is no age restriction in one's ability to do this and no college courses are necessary.

THE JOURNEY

> The road of life twists and turns and no two directions are ever the same. Yet our lessons come from the journey, not the destination.
>
> —*Don Williams, Jr.*

How do you begin your personal quest for truth, justice, and the American way? Alright, how do you commence your personal expedition in search of more effective critical thinking and decision making skills? This is the basis of this book. It will demonstrate that training in critical thinking begins at home, with your parents, continues with schooling and peer relationships, and how it can become distorted by various influences, "authorities," and media outlets if we aren't observing closely enough. It follows us in our life-long journey as we discover our abilities and the world, develop empathy and memory skills, and learn to socialize with others. Studying the diverse topics in this book will lead to insight into these developmental processes and show you how to utilize the information discovered in order to become a critical thinker. More importantly, it will teach you how you became who you are today. Once you know about yourself, what influenced you growing up, and what (and who) continues to manipulate you, you can more easily change what you don't like and strengthen what you do enjoy about your-self. You have a choice. Learn about yourself and your surroundings and ultimately make wiser choices, or continue to react without taking into ac-count all the variables needed to make healthy decisions. Will you continue to blame others for your personality characteristics or your status in life or will you resolve to take charge and re-create yourself? I think you know by now which side of the coin leads to more productivity and personal success in the long run, so let's begin . . .

Accountability: If You Mess Up, Fess Up!

2

You may make mistakes, but you are not a failure until you start blaming someone else.

—Anonymous

Accountability; our present society's four-letter word. This will be an ongoing theme in this book. As a culture, we are sorely lacking in this area. We are teaching our children to want, whine, and wantonly point the finger at someone/something else when they fail. As Rabbi Schmuley Boteach stated on his television show *Shalom in the Home* in 2006, "We are teaching our children how to have, not how to be."

"The public education system isn't helping my child." What are you doing as a parent? "That baseball coach criticized my son." So? How are you helping your child improve and grow? We are afraid to discipline or direct our kids. We don't want to raise our voices to them. We don't want to hurt their feelings by pointing out their mistakes or inappropriate behavior. We don't want to make them feel guilt, shame, embarrassment, or accountability. If we don't comment on their behavior and don't induce some appropriate difficult feelings when necessary (we'll get to that later), they become spoiled brats. And more importantly, if we don't guide our offspring this way, someone else will, and that person will be less patient, loving, and accepting of that child and his/her behavior.

WOULD YOU LIKE SOME CHEESE WITH THAT WHINE?

The girl who can't dance says the band can't play.

—Jewish proverb

As a college instructor, I have many stories about guiding other people's offspring. At the Cal State level a few years back, a student was having a very emotionally difficult semester and was flunking all her classes. She mentioned that she wanted to quit mid-term and go back home. I couldn't agree more and discussed the university procedures necessary to do so. She thanked me and I didn't see her again for about 5 weeks, when she appeared on the day of the final exam. I was incredibly busy that morning and didn't think much of her sudden appearance in class. She failed my course, as well as all her others, but a curious thing happened. A few months later, when the next semester began, I received a packet from the university president's office, with letters from the student, her guidance counselor at her new college, and her therapist, all asking me to grant her a reprieve. Her mother originally wrote to the university president, asking for his support. Would the professors please change her daughter's grades to W (withdrawal, with no academic penalty)? Her parents threatened to sue the university if the grades were not modified. All her other professors did so, according to the Admissions representative I spoke with, but I didn't need to. I didn't change her grade.

Now some of you are reading this exclaiming, "Yeah, baby!" and others are horrified that I didn't help this poor kid. Why didn't I change her grade, you ask? For many reasons. First of all, I did help her, though she and all her enablers may not ever realize it. I wanted to help her recognize and own her mistakes, get up, brush herself off, and start anew. You can't truly start over in any area of life if you've never owned up to your role in your downfall. She needed to feel the embarrassment, anger, depression, and eventual pride in her own emotional and psychological strength. It would make a great story later to her children and those she hoped to teach someday as an educator. Picture these two conflicting scenarios:

"Hey kids, when I was in college I crashed and burned one semester, didn't take care of my needs, didn't listen to practical advice that would've helped me make some healthy decisions. I flunked all my classes and returned home, embarrassed and sad. I sought the help of a therapist and a guidance counselor at the local community college. I enrolled in classes there for the next year and increased my grade point average. It was really stressful having to start all over again, but I worked hard, and I learned more about myself and what I really wanted in my life. I was so excited when I was accepted to another four-year university closer to home, where I was a much better and more mature student."

VS.

"Hey kids, when I was in college I crashed and burned one semester, didn't take care of my needs, didn't listen to practical advice that would've helped me make some healthy decisions. I flunked all my classes and returned home, embarrassed and sad. I sought the help of a therapist and a guidance counselor at the local community college. I asked them and my mom to write letters to the president of the university and my former professors, asking if they would please change my failing grades due to my inability to take care of myself. I even wrote a letter to the one professor who wouldn't change my grade, but she refused to respond. Luckily, the other professors gave me a break, and I felt relieved, but I was still angry at the one instructor who wouldn't help me. In fact, my parents seriously discussed suing her and the university. Because of this instructor, my grade point average was too low for me to transfer to another 4-year university. I had to spend 6 more months at a junior college building my academic record before I could even apply to another university!"

Hopefully, the second scenario sounds pathetic to you. If not, listen up. The bottom line of the first scenario is that the student experienced and dealt with confusion and pain. She grew. In the second, she is angry and blaming someone else for her problems. The second scenario doesn't lead to a strong ending, a lesson learned, or a teachable moment to pass on to others. The second scenario keeps us feeling like victims of life, professors, people who are mean, etc. This kind of "poor me" thinking slithers its way into all kinds of arenas: intimate and professional relationships, parenting, politics, education, and the list goes on. It is a lack of critical thinking, combined with our present culture of narcissism, that prevents people from growing, changing, and being fully responsible for their thoughts, feelings, and actions. They are what keep us tethered to houses we can't afford, cars and clothes that are too expensive, and the overall pressure to "keep up with the Jones'." They lead us to believe that our children need to be constantly busy with extra-curricular activities, that we should defend their poor behavior and performance at school, and that average sports skills will and should lead to full-ride scholarships to prestigious universities.

Unfortunately, lack of effective thinking skills, along with narcissism and poor coping skills (that is, how you handle emotions and stress), also have strong connections to the cult of perfection in Western society. Women—and now men—are rushing in droves to plastic, oh sorry, "cosmetic" surgeons, who will fix all their perceived physical flaws with the single wave of a credit card. Women believe they must have large breasts in order to attract a man, and men think they need to shave their chests while growing hair on their scalp in order to be with a woman. Whatever happened to ego strength? This involves the ability to persevere and feel good about yourself in the face of challenge, fear, failure, or large-nose jokes by your siblings. We are giving up ourselves to others and to trends, in order to fit in, keep up (there's that phrase again), win. We all want to be unique, as long as we are like everyone else. Or as the character Frank Burns stated in the 1970s television show *M*A*S*H*, "I don't mind individuality, as long as we're doing it all together."

Being fully responsible for your life begins at home, with your parents. When you are two years old and gleefully exploring everything in your house, the car, any store, or your own body, parents have a responsibility to shape your behavior. No one likes to see a child run amuck in a retail store or restaurant while his parents ignore the obvious danger to his safety, and the sensibilities of others. Children need to understand that their behavior impinges upon others, and parents need to utilize appropriate parenting skills. Junior needs to be told what he did and how it affected another person, so he can think about and change his actions as he develops and matures. Children are responsible for their conduct; parents are responsible for teaching them self-control and empathy. We need to know that our behavior has an effect on others. It is not all about us: what we want, how we feel, what someone else did to us. When we understand that our deeds affect other people, we develop empathy. As discussed in chapter one, this is a deeper understanding of what others might be experiencing. Empathy prevents us from hurting others because we know what it feels like (or might feel like) to be treated poorly, and we don't want others to treat us that way either. This leads to the development of a conscience, or moral guide, that useful, nagging voice inside your head that says, "Don't do that; it isn't right." Effective parenting leads to the development of empathy and a conscience, which help us become better critical thinkers because we will be less impulsive in our actions. We will think about what is going on in our lives and in our own minds and make changes for the better.

Accountability, empathy, and the possession of a conscience aid in every area of our lives. We tend not to think of work or co-workers as part of this relationship cycle, but we need to. People with full time jobs spend most of their lives with others outside their families. It isn't enough to have an occupation, return home, and begin again the next day. We need to have productive, positive relationships with supervisors and colleagues. We need to be part of the decision-making process, even in some small way, in order to feel functional on the job. Whatever coping and decision-making skills you learned as a child, you will bring into your place of employment. If you can't handle your own finances, what makes you think you can balance the books at work? If you don't get along with those you live with and don't like yourself, how do you expect to perform adequately with a group of people you don't know very well?

Before you can become an effective critical thinker, you must become an individual; a responsible individual. As stated in Ruggiero's (2012) book, Beyond Feelings: A Guide to Critical Thinking, becoming an individual is not something we are born with, but is acquired or earned by realizing that we are always influenced by others and circumstances. Thus, we must be vigilant of who we are, how we respond and why, and how we can improve in the future. As Mahatma Gandhi said, "Be the change you wish to see in the world." Critical thinking begins with each one of us, in our own minds. The first step to becoming a critical thinker is self-awareness: knowing who you are, what you want, how you feel, what you believe, and what your purpose is. Start asking yourself what you need, what you want, how you feel, and why you respond the way you do. How did you come to believe your most treasured values? What is the running dialogue in your head in regard to yourself, others, and the world? Are your thoughts positive, negative, or neutral, and how often does each category dominate? Self-awareness is key to being an individual and accepting full responsibility for yourself. There is a reciprocal relationship here; being accountable leads to greater self-awareness, and self-awareness leads to greater accountability. Who are you? Whatever you have in your heart is what you see in the world.

Critical thinking and self-awareness leading to personal responsibility, begin with **introspection** and **metacognition**. Introspection is paying attention to how you feel, believe, and behave. Metacognition is thinking about how you think. When we focus on what we feel and how we think, we have the ability to become more **mindful**.

> **introspection**—Paying attention to how you feel, believe, and behave.

How does one become more mindful? First, listen to what you are saying to yourself about yourself, others, and the world in general. Do you ever ask "What do I need today?" Many people will laugh at this question, thinking it ridiculous, unimportant, or useless. Try it now. What do you need today, right now? Do you need to stay home because you are feeling ill? Do you need to exercise? Do you need to confront a colleague? Do you need to get that proposal done for work? Do you need some quiet time for yourself? Here are some other questions to guide you:

> **metacognition**—Thinking about how you think.

> **mindful**—Being attentive to and aware of ourselves and our needs.

1. What do you want in your life?
2. What do you believe about God, other people, yourself?
3. What is the role of money in your life?
4. What is your purpose on Earth?
5. What kind of work do you want to do?
6. What kinds of relationships do you want to have?
7. What are your priorities, values?
8. What kinds of ethics or rules of conduct do you have for yourself? Others?
9. What are your strengths? Weaknesses?
10. What bothers you about others?
11. What bothers others about you?
12. How do you treat people? How do they typically treat you?
13. What makes you happy, angry, sad, worried, embarrassed?
14. What kind of student/employee are you?

15. What kind of lover are you?

16. What kind of parent are you? How do your kids do in the world?

17. What kind of friend are you?

18. What kind of driver are you?

19. Are you able to listen to and think about new ideas, even ones that are completely against what you believe?

20. How judgmental are you about other people? Self?

21. What do you do and say when you are angry?

22. Can you verbally and physically express love?

23. Do you arrive on time to appointments?

24. How do you keep your home?

25. What do you like to do in your leisure time?

26. What do you want others to know about you?

27. What kind of a role model do you want to be to others?

28. What is it like to be friends with you?

29. What is it like to be in an intimate relationship with you?

30. What is it like to have you for a parent?

31. What is it like to have you for a boss? Employee? Teacher?

32. What is it like for strangers to interact with you?

33. How do you treat salespeople?

34. How often are you using your cell phone while driving, in stores and restaurants?

Obviously, you need to answer each question completely and honestly—the good, the bad, and the ugly. We aren't taught to take time to explore ourselves; we aren't taught that this is necessary and important and directly connected to the quality of our relationships and decision-making skills. We expect others to get to know us, but we don't take the time to do that for ourselves. Then we get angry when our needs aren't met, as if others have some sort of crystal ball or special insight into what we need and want. You have to recognize what you need and want AND learn to ask for it. This will save you, your colleagues, and your loved ones much grief.

Self-awareness is not a destination, it is a journey. Since you are human and ever-changing, self-awareness is dynamic as well. Sometimes you will be painfully aware of who you are and what you want—especially when you suffer a loss. Loss and pain (physical or emotional) force us to pay attention to ourselves, to be "selfish." As far as I am concerned, there are two kinds of selfish: 1. Needing to meet your own needs before that of others is positively selfish. It results in a favorable outcome. 2. Not caring about anyone else's needs/feelings is narcissistically selfish. It results in a negative outcome.

We don't change unless we are in pain. We don't learn unless we make mistakes. If you do something just right the first time, do you try to change the procedure the next time you attempt it? No, why should you? It's already perfect. However, when we make mistakes, it is an opportunity to change direction, learn something new and more effective, and become a better person. Missteps are embarrassing, which causes us emotional pain. This pain forces us to pause and think about what we are doing. The idea is not to stop making mistakes, though you don't want to make the same errors over and over again. This is where a good book or therapist can help. The idea is to stumble, deal with the pain you caused yourself and/or others, and devise and carry out a plan to prevent that particular blunder from happening again. The "devising-and-carrying-out-a-plan" part is where humans tend to fail.

Occasionally, I had therapy clients who were divorcing or newly divorced. They would present seeking guidance in regard to their emotional pain and new social status. I always asked them to explore their role in the perpetuation and end of the relationship, including working through some interfering childhood issues of anger, control, and trust. Of course, it is so much easier to focus on their ex-spouse's gaffes than their own, but they worked through this. Then would come the $1,000,000 question: "So, what will you do to prevent this kind of relationship (or issue) from happening again?" The clients who became most self-aware had a plan—they knew what went wrong. More importantly, they knew where <u>they</u> went wrong, and had grown enough to know why they would not choose the same type of person next time. However, those who didn't complete the difficult task of increased self-awareness would answer in this way: "I'm just not ever going to do that again!" Red flags waving, warning lights and buzzers going off! Saying that you'll never behave a certain way again is not enough. It doesn't involve enough pain or enough introspection for you to realize how your behavior affected yourself and others. It doesn't include looking at long-standing patterns of feelings and opinions about yourself and others. See the difference?

Say you have a friend who is chronically late and apologizes profusely each time. For added measure, she throws in some "reasons" (aka excuses) why she was late. How many times do you sympathize with her before you stop listening to and believing her? She doesn't change her behavior, and it becomes a negative part of your relationship, especially as she declares, "Well, you know, I'm always late! I'll be late to my own funeral!" Dr. Phil McGraw (2000) stated that being late is arrogant. It sends many messages about you. First, you cannot manage your time. Second, that you don't care about other people's schedules. It also demonstrates that you aren't willing to change your behavior and that your schedule seems to be more important than another's. Finally, it shows that you make commitments that you do not keep. Understand that you will not be viewed as dependable, trustworthy, or capable of getting the job done. Now, there are some people who just cannot seem to organize their schedules, stay on task, and arrive at their destination on time. They still need to try to overcome this fault if they want to have successful personal and professional relationships. Waving the behavior off as, "This is just the way I am!" is not good enough.

SNAP OUT OF IT! STOP DEFENDING, START ATTENDING

> Your attitude, not your aptitude, will determine your altitude.
> —*Zig Ziglar*

How do you respond when you commit an error? Do you feel bad? Do you attack and criticize yourself? Do you immediately place blame outside yourself? Can you laugh at and admit your foibles, decide where you went wrong, and develop a new plan of action? As you can guess, the latter traits are the mark of a critical thinker; a mature person who takes responsibility for his/her missteps.

Accountability also has implications in the workplace. If you claim ownership of what you do, say, think, and feel, you are more likely to be a productive employee, co-worker, or manager. You will set high standards of performance, ethics, and service for yourself and expect the same from others. When you and others fall short you will demand and expect solutions, not excuses.

When we know ourselves, in all our beauty and ugliness, we have more self-control. You know those people who say whatever comes to mind? Whatever is in their head comes out their mouth, with no 7-second delay to stop and think: "Should I say this? I might hurt this person's feelings," or "Maybe I don't have enough information to answer this question." These people are reactors, not critical thinkers. They consistently speak to others inappropriately and when their victims protest, they accuse the recipients of being too sensitive. They are completely unaware of their effect on others, even when they are told directly. They are not self-aware and are afraid to be. I've always found it interesting to tell people about my first career as a therapist. Those that are comfortable with themselves are excited and ask in-depth questions about the profession. They embrace self-growth. Those who are more insecure usually begin with a smarmy comment about my being a "shrink," or that psychology is not a real science and it's a bunch of hooey. My reply goes something like this: Those that argue against psychology and therapy the loudest are usually the ones that need it the most. They tend to avoid me like the plague afterward. Hmmm…I wonder why?

If you are comfortable with yourself and continually question and analyze your thoughts, beliefs, actions and motives, then you can more easily utilize what I call the crucial triangle of critical thought: logic, emotion, and intuition. We will discuss this trio at length later on. Just know for now that you must use all sides of this triangle in order to be a fully functioning, mature, effective thinker.

CHAOS OR CONTROL? INTERNAL VS. EXTERNAL LOCUS OF CONTROL

> I believe that we are solely responsible for our choices, and we have to accept the consequences of every deed, word, and thought throughout our lifetime.
>
> —*Elisabeth Kubler-Ross*

Finally, what is your **locus of control**? Locus of control is a personality trait studied by Julian Rotter (1954, 1966). Rotter claimed that the likelihood of choosing a certain behavior depends on two factors: (1) the expectation of accomplishing the goal and (2) the personal value of that goal (Zimbardo, Jonhson, & Weber, 2006). According to Rotter, our decisions depend greatly on our locus of control, or our belief about our ability to control events in our lives. Those

locus of control—Our belief about our ability to control events in our lives.

with an internal locus of control believe that they have the power to change their lives. When they succeed, they believe it is because of their hard work. When they fail, it is due to lack of planning or sufficient effort. These people tend to be happier, responsible, socially successful, and physically healthy.

On the other hand, those who ascribe to an external locus of control tend to be more depressed, stressed, and ill (Lefcourt, 1982). When they succeed, they believe it is due to luck. When they fail, it's because someone or something got in their way. They see themselves and expect to be viewed as victims of fate. "Poor me! These things always happen to me!" They accept little, if any, responsibility for anything that happens in their lives. Hence, they are unhappier and tend to often be physically sick.

How do we become more responsible? First and foremost, resolve to make changes in your life. Write down what is going right and what is wrong in your life. What is occurring that makes your daily journey smooth? Conversely, what leads to experiencing pain and difficulty? Only focus on your actions, not your teachers', bosses', or relatives'. Has more than one supervisor (or loved one) talked with you about the same attitude or behavior? Does your life tend to feel rushed and chaotic, or well-paced and controlled?

If you are struggling in relationships, answer these three questions, each on a separate piece of paper: What do I absolutely want and need in a relationship? What will I refuse to allow in my life? What can I live with and accept in a relationship? Be incredibly picky about what you want and don't want in another person, right down to eye color, height, specific personality characteristics, etc. Then look back at your lists and figure out what you are getting. Are you putting up with poor, even abusive behavior when you said you wouldn't? Are you settling for less than what you truly want? Are you focusing too much on body part sizes or salary requirements as determinants for companionship? Have you lost relationships due to similar issues? You should see some patterns and yes, it will hurt.

Second, if you mess up, fess up! As Mark Twain stated, "When in doubt, tell the truth." In order to fess up, you must be able to see your strengths and weaknesses. You must be comfortable with yourself. This is going to sound like incredibly corny psychobabble, but I truly believe that we cannot fully love another person until we love ourselves first. Love involves caring for another, warts and all, and making a commitment to be kind, caring, and present. If you can't do that for yourself, you can't expect someone else to do that for you. Plus, you will become involved with relationships and jobs out of desperation and need, instead of freedom and want. You'll always be chasing after the perfect person or job and never find what you are seeking.

You begin to love yourself by being mindful, allowing yourself to experience confusion and discomfort, setting a course of action, and following through. Notice how you feel when someone criticizes you. Be aware of what excuses you use to cover up your mistakes or avoid telling someone what you truly think or feel. Stop defending your behavior and start attending to yourself and others.

MASLOW'S HIERARCHY OF NEEDS

What a man can be, he must be.

—*Abraham Maslow*

When you begin to meet your basic needs, you can focus on other, loftier goals, like those in Maslow's Hierarchy of Needs (1970). Maslow proposed that our basic needs must be met in order to concentrate on "higher" needs for self-growth. **Self-actualization** is the goal, and a lifelong journey of fulfilling our potential and finding purpose in our lives. As you may guess, self-actualized people take responsibility for their lives, have an internal locus of control, and tend to be excellent critical thinkers.

> **self-actualization—**
> A goal and lifelong journey of fulfilling our potential and finding purpose in our lives.

Here's how this plays out in real life: A few years ago Jim went back to school when he had enough discretionary cash to pay for it. However, he was recently reminded that his mortgage payment—the 5 year fixed rate that the lending company said was a great idea and he thought it was manageable—on the home loan is about to change to a 25 year adjustable. His mortgage payment is now increasing from an affordable $900 per month to an outrageous $2500 per month. He is so concerned with meeting his family's safety and biological needs that he can't focus on school, nor does he want to. His wife, Joan, is no longer interested in her volunteer work, where she gets great pleasure assisting others. She is now anxious to find a full-time job to help support the family.

What Maslow figured out is that we can't take care of others or function effectively in everyday transactions when we haven't met our own needs. You can't perform well at work when you are ill or worried about paying your bills. You won't have lasting relationships and feel fulfilled in life if you continue to choose people that hurt you, because your safety and attachment needs will not be met. Plus, you'll never know the feeling of self-esteem. Sometimes we forgo meeting our basic needs in favor of social ones, like rescuers during crises like 9/11 or the devastating 2010 earthquake in Haiti. How many times have you enjoyed talking with someone so much that you put

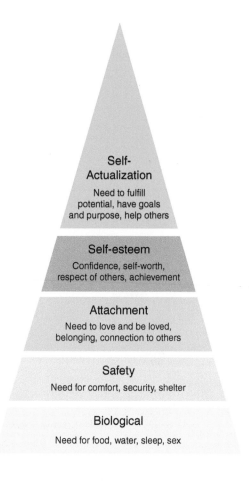

off using the restroom for fear of ending the conversation? Some (Zimbardo, et al, 2006) have questioned this phenomenon. Perhaps we delay gratification because we know we can get the next meal and that we have a place to call home. We feel we have a choice. When we are in a self-actualizing mode of life, we can be fully attuned to growth and change. Thus, we can think and choose more effectively when we don't have to worry about satisfying our basic biological needs. When we are free to focus on individual growth, we are also more able to pay attention to the roles of logic, emotion, and intuition in our daily lives.

Before we move on, consider this quote from one of the greatest minds of our time, Albert Einstein:

I know quite certainly that I, myself, have no special gifts. Curiosity, obsession, and dogged endurance, combined with self-critique, have brought me my ideas.

Logic, Emotion and Intuition: The Crucial Triangle

3

Since we cannot change reality, let us change the eyes with which we see.

—*Nikos Kazantzakis*

As stated earlier, in order to be an effective decision-maker, we must be comfortable with and utilize logic, emotion, and intuition. First off, it's important to know where you stand in this triangle. Are you more comfortable thinking things through before you decide on a course of action? Do you allow emotion to enter into the mix when making decisions? Do you rely more on your emotions or logic when choosing a course of action? Do you take note of your intuitive responses? Do you know what intuition is? More questions to ponder and further self-exploration needed to arrive at a conclusion. Let's discuss each part of the triad in detail.

LOGICAL CONCLUSIONS

A mind all logic is like a knife all blade. It makes the hand bleed that uses it.

—*Rabindranath Tagore*

Are you a reasonable, rational, logical person? What is logic? What does it entail? Why do we assume it is better than feelings in guiding our lives? Logic is a word used frequently in philosophy and critical thinking texts, but no one, it seems, actually defines it. Thanks to Webster's Dictionary (1989), here is the definition of logic:

1. The science which investigates the principles governing correct or reliable inference.

2. A particular method of reasoning or argumentation.

3. The system or principles of reasoning applicable to any branch of knowledge or study.

4. Reason or sound judgment.

As you can see, "reason" and "logic" seem to be interchangeable terms. What is the definition of reason? Glad you asked (Webster's Dictionary, 1989):

The mental powers concerned with forming conclusions, judgments, or inferences. As such, reasoning is the process of forming conclusions, judgments, or inferences from facts or premises.

Logic, or reasoning, has to do with collecting and sifting through evidence (meaning facts) to back up your claims. This does not necessarily include opinion, nor does it preclude it, but you will likely have more confidence in your final decision, and it will typically be viewed as more trustworthy, if you research your subject before choosing a course of action. Logic basically focuses on weighing alternatives utilizing outside data; that is, information that comes from reliable sources outside of your own brain. You seek "expert" advice, review statistical research, and use common sense to make the most practical choice. The use of logic and reasoning are often highly effective when issues involving money or politics are involved. However, trying to use logic alone to decide whether you should get married or have children will usually lead to frustration. When you are involved in major decisions that affect your way of life, like marriage, children, buying a house or a new car, you will want some emotion and intuition to help guide you. For example, the house may be a great financial investment (logic), but you may not really like the layout or its location (emotion). You may have a nagging feeling in the pit of your stomach that makes you feel uncomfortable when you step inside (intuition). It may feel like three competing ideas are pulling you in as many directions, but logic, emotion, and intuition are working together to send you a message. The trouble is, we are taught (especially men) to ignore the latter two in favor of pure logic. We focus on the practical and come up with rational "reasons" why we should buy the house, and deny the discomfort we feel in the process. Sometimes we ignore the practical aspects of a purchase and buy something because we fall in love with it. "Oh honey, I know it's ridiculously expensive and we'll both have to work two jobs to pay the mortgage, but I just love this house!!" This is one of the reasons the United States and other countries got into the financial mess they are in today, along with banking and mortgage lending institutions that played on our emotions, on our feeling that we can and should have it all, right now.

THE VALUE OF EMOTION

Never apologize for showing feelings. When you do so, you apologize for truth.

—*Benjamin Disraeli*

Logic helps us recognize that we are being swayed by emotion. It's what makes us walk away when a salesperson pressures us to buy something we don't really need, or at a price that is too expensive. Logic is neutral; it is not concerned with your or others' feelings. It wants just the facts, like a detective tracking down the suspect and cause of a crime. Once the facts are straight, then emotion can be added to the mix. "Ya know, I didn't see Joe there that night, but he's got a temper and I've always been afraid of him." Emotion fills in the blanks.

It seems that humans—especially adult humans—need permission to experience and express their emotions, as if the presence of feelings is wrong or immoral, ungentlemanly or unladylike. Well, here it is; you have permission to recognize, accept, and express your feelings. We will talk about how to do each of these in healthy ways.

First off, having emotions is your birthright. They are human, natural, and God-given. Emotions help us get adult attention when we are first born. We cannot use words to express our needs so we cry, whine, smile, laugh, pout, and scream. There are many psychological theories and studies regarding how parents should respond when their baby cries (Bell & Ainsworth, 1972; Bowlby, 1969; Gaylin, 1985; Shelov & Remer, 2009). In the past, some theorists argued that we should go to the baby quickly, soothe them with our voices and touch, and address their physical needs. Other researchers believed that it was better to wait a short time before responding, in order to avoid "spoiling" the child. Every effective parent knows the difference between the cry that says "I'm hungry, wet or hurt," which needs immediate attention, vs. the whiny "I'm tired cry" that usually dissipates in a few minutes as baby falls asleep. The bottom line of responding, at least in my educated opinion, has to do with trust. Erik Erikson (1950) in his famous Psychosocial Theory of Personality Development, noted that during the first year of life, adults must respond to baby's cries quickly. If an infant cries and the parent responds by quickly meeting baby's needs, then baby learns to trust that the parents will take care of him. He also learns that crying—his most important form of communication for many months—will be understood and responded to. He learns that he has a connection with others and some control over the world as well. These are good things. He will not become a spoiled brat if we feed him when he is hungry or diaper her when she is wet. Understand that after the first year, the scenario changes in terms of type of response and response time—after trust has already been established and the child becomes increasingly capable of utilizing other forms of communication to obtain what he needs.

Conversely, if Mom and Dad don't respond appropriately or quickly enough to baby's cries, baby learns not to trust that caretakers will meet his needs. He learns that he is not understood and attended to and trust will not develop (Brazelton, 1992; Erikson, 1950; Hunt, 2012). As an example of this, I had a colleague, a licensed psychologist no less, who had his first child around the same time I had mine. As we were describing our new parenting experiences over the phone, he noted that his baby girl was sleeping through the night by the fourth week. Mine did so by the 6th week, which was unusual, so I was curious about how this came about for him and his wife after one month. What he told me made me sick to my stomach. He and his wife discussed that they didn't want to experience the sleep deprivation that most new parents suffer through for the first few months, so they decided that they would not feed their new baby in the middle of the night. I could barely contain my emotions at the thought of this newborn crying herself to sleep for the first week of her life, knowing that when she was placed in her crib in a room away from her parents, and the lights were turned off, that no one would respond to her needs in the middle of the night. I hope she grew up psychologically and emotionally healthy, but I still wonder if she has trust issues to this day, over 16 years later.

What's the point of all this, you ask? The point is that we are born with appropriate, natural, normal emotions, and we are taught early on not to feel or express ourselves. We are taught to control our feelings or they will control us. When a baby cries in a restaurant, take a look at the faces of other diners around you. New parents are typically painfully aware of the visual darts being thrown at them because their infant is "disturbing" others. They desperately attempt to quiet the baby, all the while looking around apologetically. Before you protest, I know what you are going to say. Yes, it is incredibly annoying when you are trying to have dinner in a public place or riding on an airplane en route to your destination and you have to listen to ear-piercing cries. But why are we so annoyed by another's distress? This is due to being taught to keep our feelings to ourselves. Don't dare show your anger to an adult, don't scream when you are frustrated, cry when you are sad, or even jump up and down when you are excited and happy. I have one friend who gets annoyed when anyone gets excited and demonstrates joy during sporting events. Another makes jokes during movies or TV shows when sadness is the emotion being evoked.

We are taught to be uncomfortable with feelings, and thus, uncomfortable with ourselves. We are told that feelings make us weak and that they are worthless in terms of making decisions or recognizing at all. We associate being female with being emotional, as if that is a bad thing. If you are male and you cry once in a while, you are automatically viewed as wimpy or even gay. When we are injured during sports, coaches tell us to "shake it off" and keep going. When toddler boys scrape their knees and cry, they are told to "man up" or "stop crying, " while physically distressed little girls are scooped up, kissed, caressed, and comforted. Didn't your parents ever tell you that if you didn't stop crying they'd really give you something to cry about?

These are all extremely important subtle and not-so-subtle messages about how to behave. Do you know that bottling up, or not expressing, your emotions can eventually kill you? We all deal with stress on a daily basis. "Stress" is a buzz-word that is bandied about often, but what does it actually entail? According to Hans Selye (1976), one of the pioneers of stress research, stress is "the nonspecific response of the body to any demand made upon it" (p. 14). Selye and other researchers soon discovered that the brain was acutely involved in the way we respond to stressors, or things that cause stress, not just for the body, but for our cognitive processes as well.

Selye (1956, 1976) developed a theory regarding phases of stress reactivity, noting a flight-or-fight reaction when faced with a cognitive, emotional, or physical threat or challenge. It's relatively simple for the human to either run or fight when faced with a physical threat to their safety. Then when the threat is over, the person can then relax and return to normal functioning. But what about emotional threats? When you are incredibly sad or angry, running doesn't help dissipate the threat; nor does duking it out with someone. So what do you do with all that emotion? You can talk about it, exercise it off, scream into a pillow, break some old dishes, etc. These are all healthy, but strangely considered unacceptable, ways to take care of emotions. What we do instead is eat and drink too much, sleep too much or too little, use drugs or smoke cigarettes to "relax," or become workaholics. Wonder why roughly 1/3 of America (American Heart Association, 2011), including our children, is obese? We stuff our feelings with food and inactivity and we all know that obesity leads to disease. Even if you are slim, if you continually stuff your emotions, you will become ill. This can mean anything from a cold to cancer. When you are stressed—and who isn't nowadays?—a group of hormones kick in to aid in the fight-or-flight response. One of the most important hormones is cortisol. Cortisol triggers the production of cholesterol which, along with saturated fats in our bodies, creates plaque (like the white goopy stuff on your teeth) that travels to and blocks our arteries, generating the potential for a heart attack or stroke (Rockwell, 2011). If we are frequently emotionally upset, cortisol levels remain high, resulting in more damage to the body and brain, as discussed in chapter 1.

Sometimes we believe that lack of emotional expression indicates that someone is logical, therefore more rational and healthier (physically and emotionally) than others. This is not necessarily the case. Contrary to this, we might believe that someone who shows his/her feelings often lacks logical thought. This is also a myth. Expressing emotion is more a function of social learning rather than belonging to a specific gender, race, or ethnicity. Unless you have a specific brain disorder, everyone is capable of logical thought and appropriate expression of emotions. The differences appear in how we are trained in these areas.

THE IMPORTANCE OF INTUITION

We think conscious thought is somehow better, when in fact,
intuition is soaring flight compared to the plodding of logic.
—*Gavin DeBecker,* The Gift of Fear *(1997, p.28)*

Sometimes it is difficult to distinguish between emotion and intuition. What exactly is intuition? We have heard of "woman's intuition" but men possess this sensitivity too. Intuition is an "immediate perception or comprehension of something—that is, sensing or understanding something without the use of reasoning" (Ruggiero, 2012, p. 22). Intuition protects us to the point of saving our lives, if we honor and listen to it (De Becker, 1997).

Intuition is also referred to as a hunch, an inkling, a suspicion, an instinct, a sixth sense or a gut feeling. I describe intuition as the sensation we feel in our midsection, right around the body's center or belly-button. You might feel a bit uncomfortable and not know why. Sometimes we unconsciously lay a hand over our stomach or cross our arms in front of us. Usually, for me anyway, intuition creeps up when I least expect it. I might be happy to see someone, but all of a sudden, I feel like I'm on a roller-coaster and my stomach just dropped to the floor. I feel uncomfortable, nervous, cautious around the person, and realize that I need to distance myself quickly. I don't ask why, I just respect the sensation and listen. I might figure it all out later, when I am away from the person and feel safe again, but if I don't, that is okay. All I need to know is that I perceived something creepy or not-quite-right about the person. It could have been the words they used, tone of voice, the omission of information during the conversation, eye contact, or other body language. We may never know why we had such a strong reaction to the person or situation but we need to trust it. Just know that you noticed something that somehow felt unsafe to you, whether you can verbalize this or not, and get away from the situation or person as soon as possible. Unfortunately, along with emotions, intuition is typically viewed as unimportant, unreliable, or imaginary, so don't be swayed by someone trying to misrepresent your experience as being "all in your head."

EMBRACING THE CRUCIAL TRIANGLE

> Wisdom is the quality that keeps you from getting into situations where you need it.
>
> —*Doug Larson*

Accepting the crucial triangle is akin to obtaining wisdom. Here's an example of how logic, emotion, and intuition work in conjunction with each other: When the homeless person approaches you in the street asking for money, emotion says, "Oh, poor guy. I want to help." Logic says, "He's fine. He'll find his way." My son and I recently indirectly ran into this situation. We were in a store and a man walked in and told what sounded like a scripted hard-luck story. He was looking for any job because he needed $40 to help his granddaughter, and just for good measure, stated he was a believer of Christ. Let's see: willing to do any job, needs money for kid, good Christian, perfectly spoken and acted. He even blessed all the patrons and employees in the store after he was turned down. Could his story have been real? Possibly. Emotion said to me, "Poor guy." Logic heard the words, watched the facial expression, and pronounced, "Sounds like a scam," and intuition gave me the gift of an uncomfortable feeling in my gut that screamed, "I smell a rat!"

Another story involves a client couple who came to therapy because she felt unsupported by him. She was about to have a complete hysterectomy, a very emotional surgery for any woman, and she needed her husband's love and comfort before and after the surgery. He sat in my office in a straight-backed chair, legs crossed, arms folded tightly across his chest, with no visible changes in facial expression or body language while his wife sobbed that she needed him to soothe her with words and touch because she was so sad and frightened. As I watched this strange lack of outward response from him, I found myself wanting to scream at him to respond. I knew how the wife felt in that moment. I asked if he heard her requests for support and comfort. He did, he told me in a very quiet, monotone voice. I asked what he planned to do to meet her needs. He told her he was there for her, but did not move to sit next to her, smile, or show any emotion. This was not just a one-time-being-uncomfortable-in–therapy response. This was their typical marital interaction. She did tend to be over-reactive, and he was under-reactive. Of course, the less response he showed, the more emotional she would become in order to get his attention. That's what I also felt in the therapy session. I wanted to scream or throw something at him in order to get a response.

Some people are naturally more or less expressive than others. Less expression does not mean that the person has no feelings or no response. Women are always accusing men of being unemotional, and men claim that women can be too emotional. Part of this is personality, the other part is socialization. How much? Six of one and half-a-dozen of the other. This is good information to know about yourself as well. When I was dating, I knew I needed a man who was comfortable with his own and my emotions. One man I dated was smart, funny, and kind, but extremely uncomfortable with feelings. He once said his mother resided in Malibu, on a hill facing the ocean. My curiosity was piqued and after some intensive questioning, I found that his mother did indeed reside in Malibu, on a hill facing the ocean—except that this was the site of her grave. This same man could not appreciate a beautiful flowering bush I once stopped to admire. He yanked me away so quickly when I asked him to come smell a flower that I thought my arm would be pulled out of its socket. If I had continued the relationship, I would have been miserable, as I'm sure he would have been. Too many of us are needy to have someone or some material possession in order to feel good about ourselves. Then we are functioning on pure emotion and make poor decisions. Likewise, you can't do everything "by the book," and choose your mate based on some compatibility quiz in a magazine. Thought, feeling and intuition (in this case, aka chemistry) must be involved to find your soul mate, or at least a really great friend.

Bottom line, in order to be fully functioning, healthy, critical thinkers, we must recognize, accept, and act on all parts of the crucial triangle. We must be able to think clearly, even in times of stress, allow ourselves to fully experience our emotions, and be aware of and tap into our gut reactions in order to make the best decisions. When we leave out or ignore one side of the triangle, the other two sides don't balance. Think of this illustration:

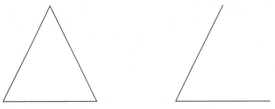

When you have a closed triangle, when you are using all three parts in conjunction with each other, you can be more certain of making appropriate decisions. When the triangle is left open, that is, when one part of the triangle is ignored, it leaves room for one or both of the other two sides to take over and close the gap, or it allows external, irrelevant information to enter and influence your decision making. For example, not listening to your intuition and trying to logically talk yourself out of your feelings of discomfort can lead to serious injury or death. "Gee, this nice young man who appeared out of nowhere wants to help me carry my groceries upstairs to my apartment. I should be nice in return and let him, and besides, if he helps, I could get done faster" This is your brain on logic and emotion, while your stomach is doing backflips and that small but wise voice in your head is saying, "Danger!! Don't do it!" Opening the gap also allows you to be influenced more readily by the opinions of others. You want to buy something because you really like it, regardless of logic trying to remind you of your financial situation, and your friend says, "Why are you buying that one? The more expensive one is better and it only costs a little more!"

This is not to say that you should not seek the advice of others. On the contrary. Just make sure you have allowed all three parts of your psyche to have their say. Write it down if need be. What does each side say to you? You should find a pattern. If you truly can't determine the best course of action after that, then by all means, ask someone you trust for solid advice. Ask someone who will also honor all three parts of the crucial triangle. When you make mistakes, go back and think about how you made the choice. What part did you rely on most? The least? Did you ignore one side completely? Do you use logic more often when making large purchases vs. small ones? Do you buy based on emotion and then feel bad the next day? Do you purchase items to make yourself feel good? Do you stay in bad relationships because you love someone, even though you know and have been told by others that this person is not healthy for you? Why do you stay in a dead-end job when you know you could get employment in a more productive, supportive atmosphere? You get the idea. Start observing how you make decisions large and small in your life, alter your responses, and gain wisdom.

Parental Discipline: The Groundwork for Critical Thinking

4

If you bungle raising your children, I don't think whatever else you do well matters very much.

—*Jacquelyn Kennedy Onassis*

So far we've discussed what it means to be a critical thinker, being responsible for yourself, and how to recognize and include the crucial triangle in your interactions. How and where do you first learn about these important factors that affect your entire lifespan? Our first teachers are our parents. We depend on them for everything during the first few years of our life. They shelter us, provide food and water, clothing, companionship, and structure. They are our first role models, to whom we look to learn how to emotionally respond, think, and behave. Their beliefs and opinions become ours, until we are old enough and educated enough to seek other information and make our own decisions. Parents have, and are given, enormous responsibility to mold their children's character, help them master skills, and navigate the world. It is at once an exhilarating and downright frightening job.

Parenting is a series of lessons and mishaps between adults and children. As we see on the news and in our communities every day, not all parents are good at guiding or mentoring their children. Some are absolutely horrible and never should have had children at all. There are wonderful parents too—caring, compassionate, responsible, mature parents who strive to be appropriate role models, allow and encourage discussion, and have a close relationship with their kids. All parents make mistakes. The most effective parents are the ones who recognize their mistakes and choose a different course of action the next time they encounter a similar discipline issue. Effective parents are also aware of their own issues—including those left over from their childhood, emotional difficulties, and biases—and understand, or try to understand, how these spill over into their present relationships and parenting skills.

Since children don't come into the world with pre-wired knowledge of thoughts, feelings, and actions, parents must teach them about these things. They must talk with them, model the behavior they wish to see, praise acceptable behavior, and punish inappropriate deeds. It all sounds so simple on paper, but in real time, the process can be complicated, confusing, and exhausting for effective parents, let alone those less equipped to deal with the questions, tantrums, and challenges of raising little ones. Parents' own childhood issues and experiences come into play, which is one of the many reasons parents need to understand and deal with their own baggage before having children. Parents need to understand how they respond emotionally, and what they believe about everything, especially how to parent and what kids need from adults. The more past baggage dealt with beforehand, the better the relationship between adult and child later. The problem that arises, though, is that some people think they are good to go as potential parents, without delving into their personal histories for even a second. Some don't care, some don't think they have any issues, and still others believe it is a waste of time to deal with the past. However, the past is not the past. Unless you own it, accept it, learn from it, and move on, the past will continue to crop up, even haunt you, in the present. As an example, I once had a very financially successful, middle-aged male client who failed miserably in his relationships with women. As our therapy sessions progressed, he admitted that his relationship with his mother—a controlling, conniving, castrating you-know-what—had plagued him throughout his life. When I connected that relationship to his failure with women over the years, his reply was something like this: "No, I don't see a connection. My relationship with my mom is in the past and has no effect on the present." It took a while longer for him to see that his unresolved childhood baggage was still being carried on his back, like a Sherpa carrying supplies for hikers climbing up Mt. Everest.

This kind of self-awareness allows us to break free of the past and change our future. Then we can decide what kind of parent we want to be to our kids—what do I want to do like my parents and what do I want to change for the better with my children?

We also need to decide before becoming parents and while we are raising children what we want to teach them about themselves, people around them, and the world. What is our stance on religion, spirituality, education, politics, work, money, alcohol and drugs, sex, family hierarchy and decision-making, entertainment, and personal responsibility? Do we wish to impart a positive view of the world, or one in which negativity and evil abound? Do we want them to follow our views or allow them to develop and discuss their own? How will we discipline them when they misbehave? How do we expect them to interact with others—strangers or loved ones? Do we allow them to be fully responsible for their successes and failures, or are we helping/interfering too much?

There are many more questions in this regard and don't worry, they will come. Parenting is an adventure (how's that for being positive!) as well as a lesson in humility. There are always new things to learn about yourself and your children, as long as you are open to adapting—and helping them adapt—to changing circumstances. I can't say this enough: parents, and all adults, are role models. Kids look to them to figure out how to behave and respond emotionally, other parents (and non-parents) pay attention to what they do and learn from them, positively or negatively, and society both blames and congratulates them for their children's choices. Did I say parenting was an adventure? Sometimes it feels like Man vs. Wild. I understand why some species eat their young . . .

INDUCTIVE PARENTING

Children are apt to live up to what you believe of them.
—*Lady Bird Johnson*

As we struggle with what we want to teach our kids, it is imperative that we understand how to teach certain principles and why this learning is important. Sigmund Freud (1974; Freud & Strachey, 1989) had a theory about this, called **inductive parenting**. Inductive parenting involves setting limits, or boundaries, with kids and disciplining them in such a way so that they understand their own behavior and what effect it has on themselves and others. Freud reasoned that when we know how we behaved and why and how

> **inductive parenting—** Parenting style that involves setting limits with children, including discipline that helps them understand their behavior and effects on themselves and others.

another responded to our words or actions, then we can develop empathy. He observed that empathy is essential for developing healthy relationships with others. Along with the development of empathy, inductive parenting teaches kids how to behave with various people in different situations, and teaches them reasons to keep or alter their behavior. This is the beginning of moral thought, feeling, and behavior, and the development of a conscience. Kids learn how to think critically about who they are, what they are doing, and how they affect others. To a certain extent, it teaches them to conform to societal etiquette and incorporates the Golden Rule. You know, "Do unto others as you would have them do unto you." Treat others the way you want to be treated. Sounds simple, but it is oh so complicated by our wants, needs, and desires. This brings us to another of Freud's theories about the three parts of the personality—the Id, Ego, and Superego.

The three parts of the personality work in conjunction with one another to assist in making rational, healthy, positive choices that further our goals and prevent harm to ourselves or others. The id is the child part of the personality, what I call the "Veruca Salt" of the personality. Remember Veruca from the book (and movies) Charlie and the Chocolate Factory? "Daddy, I want an Oompa Loompa and I want it now!!" The id is selfish, spontaneous, impulsive, immature, and demands instant gratification. The id is what spurs us to buy something we don't really want or need ("impulse buying"), eat and drink too much, drive too fast, and take the gang for taco runs at midnight (even though we're not hungry) after seeing the Taco Bell commercial. The id can be lots of fun, but it can also get us in trouble. As evidenced by Americans' spending habits over the past 15 years or so, our society has been living in the id, buying things we can't afford because we "want it now," impulsively using credit cards for every little purchase, not keeping track of our money or finances, changing significant others as soon as we hit rough times in a relationship, and allowing our children to behave however they please with very little, if any, adult intervention. Living in the id is one of the many reasons parents get angry when a retail clerk or waitperson in a restaurant asks their unruly children to sit down before they get hurt, and then the parents chastise the intervening adult instead of their own children.

Living in the id prevents us from thinking, planning, organizing, and recognizing immediate and future consequences of our behavior. Narcissism, or a sense of entitlement, sets in as we want what we want right now and don't anyone dare get in our way.

According to Freud (1974; Freud & Strachey, 1989), the superego, or our conscience, develops by age 5. Not much time to practice effective parenting skills before your child begins to use his/her skills in the world, but only a beginning to many more years of necessary parental role modeling and communication about relating to others.

The superego is our internal judge or critic. Sometimes it is referred to as the critical parent. You know, that nagging voice you hear in your mind when you should or shouldn't be doing something. "You need to finish your homework before you go to the beach with your friends!" "You shouldn't eat tacos at midnight. You'll get a stomach ache." "I told you that telling that joke would hurt Mark's feelings!" The superego is responsible for feelings such as guilt, shame, embarrassment and pride. Sometimes our internal judge can be positive, "See, you studied hard for that test and got an A! Good for you!" Along with inductive parenting, the superego also assists in the development of **self-conscious emotions**, which include embarrassment, shame, guilt, and pride.

> **self-conscious emotions**—Involve positive and negative feelings about self; aid in evaluation of one's behavior.

The superego is in a constant battle with the id. Whatever the id wants to do, the superego has something to say about it. Think of the trite example of having an angel on one shoulder, the devil on the other. Guess which character falls into which category? Some people have superegos that seem (or are) non-existent, or at least barely noticeable. They don't feel guilty when they have hurt someone's feelings or they have broken the law. They don't care about what other people think, feel, or how their behavior could affect others. Some people were taught not to care. "Son, it's a cold, cruel world out there. You need to look out for number one and to hell with everyone else." There is no empathy, self-awareness, or boundaries, only narcissism.

Others, usually female, were taught so strongly that they are to serve others that the mere act of saying no to someone sends them into all-consuming guilt and depression. This is also the root of co-dependency; in short, taking care of others much more than taking care of you. Most humans are co-dependent and caretaking to a certain extent, otherwise we would not survive. However, those labeled as co-dependent tend to be so afraid of displeasing others that they allow them to run roughshod over their feelings, opinions, and way of life. Think of the housewife/mother who seems to always be doing something for someone else but rarely does anything nice for herself, including getting enough sleep or saying no to outside demands. She is the woman who stays up until after midnight to bake cookies for her daughter's second grade class because buying cookies at the store wouldn't be good enough, and what would people think? She takes on the roles of PTA president and room mother, heads church committees, and rarely has time to make a lunch date or a night out with her husband to just relax. She doesn't get enough sleep, eats her food cold at dinner, and winds up sick every time one of her kids comes home with a stuffy nose. Ask her to turn down yet another request to spearhead a committee or add soccer team mother to her list and it's like you've asked her to give away one of her children.

Neither superego extreme is healthy, so we constantly strive for some middle ground. Some days we feel proud of our accomplishments, other days we feel ashamed or embarrassed by a statement we made that hurt a loved one's feelings. The superego, positively and negatively, keeps us on our toes.

Last, but certainly not least, the ego is stuck in the middle between the exciting, impulsive id, and the restrictive and watchful superego. Which side will win? The ego is always on hand to mediate between the two extremes, which can be quite exhausting. You may have heard the term "ego strength" to describe someone's enviable ability to make tough, sensible decisions in the face of peer pressure. The ego acts (or should act) as our mature adult. The id says "I want!" and the ego says "Let's think about this for a minute." The ego is the part of our personality that is rational, logical, and sometimes boring. It helps us balance our wants vs. our needs, delays gratification—assists us in making long-term commitments instead of quick decisions—and helps us make healthy choices. It asks the id to stop and think before a behavioral choice is made, helps us to feel appropriately embarrassed or ashamed when he do something wrong, proud when we accomplish our goals, and requests that the superego loosen up a bit and let us have some fun.

The turmoil that we can feel when the id and superego are in a battle can lead to anxiety. What should I choose? What if I don't make the right decision? The ego's job is to mediate between the two and decrease anxiety. When the anxiety is too much for the ego to bear, it resorts to **defense mechanisms**, which we use in order to decrease our stress, personal responsibility, or stuff our emotions. Here's a list of the most common

> **defense mechanisms**—Function of ego, which decrease anxiety, stress, or personal responsibility for emotions and behavior.

defense mechanisms, which we all use (yes, you too). Be honest with yourself and figure out which ones you use most often (Freud, 1974; Freud & Strachey,1989; Zimbardo et al. 2006):

1. **Denial**—"I don't have a problem"—claiming that no problem or issue exists.

2. **Repression**—"What problem?"—usually goes hand in hand with denial; "forgetting" that there is or was a problem.

3. **Displacement**—"These slow drivers are making me angry!"—when in fact you are upset with your boss. Occurs in road rage; we take out our feelings on a safer target than the original source of our emotions. The boss yells at us, then we bellow at our spouse, who screams at the kids, who then holler at the dog.

4. **Projection**—"I don't like that woman; she's very aggressive!"—says the female who has been accused of behaving the same way. Whatever we don't like in ourselves we criticize in others.

5. **Rationalization**—"I'm glad I didn't get the job. I don't want to work there anyway."—also known as sour grapes. We make excuses for our failures or poor decisions.

6. **Sublimation**—"I'm going on a 5 mile run to clear my head."—using a socially acceptable way to deal with stress or emotion. Usually through exercise, acting, dance, or artwork.

7. **Reaction Formation**—"Cigarette smoking is bad for you!"—says the new ex-smoker. This happens when we act in opposition of our true feelings or when we have recently made a big change and have "seen the light," especially in religion, politics, or sexual behavior.

8. **Regression**—"I hate you and I'm not talking to you until you apologize!" Under stress, we return to more childlike ways of responding. Think of Lucille Ball in *I Love Lucy* crying when she didn't get her way.

After studying this short list, one can understand why the ego works so hard. The less self-aware someone is, the more likely that person will utilize defense mechanisms and have poor relationships, including the all-important parent/child bond. Parents who don't take responsibility for their lives will typically spawn offspring with the same attitude. This is the new 21st century social disease. More on this in the chapter on moral development, which goes hand in hand with parenting.

In summary, critical thought has its roots in parenting. Open, self-aware, introspective parents with ego strength create kids with high self-esteem, strong morals, and healthy coping and relationship skills.

EMOTIONAL INTELLIGENCE AND COPING SKILLS

If there is anything that we wish to change in the child, we should first examine it and see whether it is not something that could better be changed in ourselves.

—Carl Jung

Okay, so now that you understand more about inductive parenting and how to manage the different parts of our personality, let's turn to some other important factors in critical thinking style. First, let's discuss **emotional intelligence**, also known as EQ. Emotional intelligence includes a number of abilities that help us understand, process, and adapt to emotional information (Goleman, 1995; Salovey & Pizzaro, 2003). Emotional intelligence is separate from IQ, which typically measures cognitive processes and academic success. According to Daniel Goleman (1995, 1998), success in life is greatly influenced by EQ, which is based on self-knowledge and the following abilities:

> **emotional intelligence**—Refers to a number of abilities that help us understand, process, and adapt to emotional information.

- Ability to manage one's emotions
- Ability to motivate oneself
- Ability to handle relationships successfully
- Ability to feel empathy
- Ability to delay gratification

Do these sound like abilities we learn through inductive parenting? Absolutely. Understanding our personalities and that our actions affect others help us to learn self-control. Goleman (1995) noted that the ability to delay gratification was the most important factor in overall success in life. This makes sense when we look at our country's spend vs. save attitude over the last 10–15 years. Those who followed the id and wanted everything now instead of saving money to buy with cash or not buying at all are presently in severe financial straits.

EQ is slightly related to IQ, and is positively associated with self-esteem, empathy, prosocial (helping) behavior, cooperation, leadership skills, and life satisfaction. Those with low or poor EQ skills tend toward dependency, depression, and aggressive behavior (Law, Wong, & Song, 2004; Mavroveli, Petrides, Rieff & Bakker, 2007; Petrides, Furnham, & Mavroveli, 2007).

> **coping skills**—Psychological term for how we deal with stress. Includes ability to recognize, accept, and handle emotions in a socially appropriate manner.

Bottom line, those who have not been taught to recognize, accept, and handle their emotions properly will have poor **coping skills**. "Coping skills" is a psychological term for how we deal with stress. If we have been taught to ignore our feelings when we do have them, as we certainly will each day, they will be overwhelming and uncomfortable. We will more than likely behave in a negative manner that could include overeating, smoking, drug use (including alcohol), yelling at people or employing inappropriate hand gestures to express ourselves, overworking, becoming anxious or depressed, sleeping too little or too much, or withdrawing from others. We all engage in some of these behaviors at various times, but we discussed earlier that over-reacting (yelling and stomping around) or under-reacting (stuffing or ignoring our feelings) lead to feeling physically unwell, even sick. Feeling unwell may include headaches, stomach aches, muscle tension, stiffness or soreness, and fatigue. If these stress signals are also overlooked, we end up with colds, the flu, cancer, heart disease, strokes, and the list goes on. When we don't feel well, we don't think well, and when we don't think well, we don't make healthy decisions either. Thus, everything in your life is negatively affected by the lack of appropriate coping mechanisms, including your parenting skills.

Understanding how you respond to various stressors allows you to plan ahead regarding your behavior. For example, if I know that my day will be incredibly busy and demanding without much down time, I need to bring healthy foods to eat so I can keep up my energy. When I don't or can't plan ahead, I start craving junk food, eat it, then I feel overly full and tired, which doesn't improve my mood and how I treat others. Yuck.

FOUR STYLES OF PARENTING

> A perfect parent is a person with excellent child-rearing theories
> and no actual children
>
> —*Dave Barry*

Parents first utilize inductive parenting when their child begins to walk and talk, and comply with directions. Over the years, there have been many books written about how to parent effectively, from Dr. Spock to Dr. Phil. Check out the self-help section of any bookstore nowadays and try to figure out which book has the best advice—I dare you. Every day on the news and in our neighborhoods we see the wrong way to parent, according to the law and according to our personal beliefs, but what is the "right" way to raise children? Why don't kids come with an instruction manual, warranties, and a 30-day return policy (or a 2, 5, or 15 year return policy . . .)?!

I would venture to guess that almost every pregnant woman in America has read the book *What to Expect When You're Expecting*, by Eisenberg, Murkoff, and Hathaway (1996). This is an incredibly helpful pregnancy Bible that helps expecting parents track their baby's month-to-month development in the womb, as well as Mom's bodily/emotional changes. After the baby is born, the next book in the series is *What to Expect the First Year* (Murkoff, Hathaway, and Eisenberg, 2003). Even though I had parented other people's children in therapy for years before I had my own, I carried, read, and re-read these books like they were God's word. Then a horrible thing happened; my pediatrician strongly suggested that I dump the books and decide how I wanted to raise my child. She wanted to cut off my lifeline, and make me actually THINK about and discuss childrearing with my husband! I'm so grateful that she was brave enough to confront me and glad that I listened. As I stated earlier, parenting is a series of lessons and mishaps between adults and children. If I wanted to be an effective parent, I had to figure out what kind of relationship I wanted with my children, what kind of people I wanted them to be, and what I wanted them to learn. Actually, I discovered that when I asked myself "What do I want to teach my kids in this situation?" that it defined our relationship and their character.

Being mindful of what we want to teach others—children and adults—helps us make better decisions, treat others as we wish to be treated, and set boundaries in regard to how others need to treat us. In that regard, let's discuss three basic styles of parenting that were developed in a series of studies by Diana Baumrind (1971; Baumrind and Black, 1967) and each one's effects on our children. Her findings, and those of others who have added to her work, include three factors that consistently determine what are effective vs. less effective parents. These are acceptance of the child and involvement in his/her life; control of the child; and autonomy granting, which allows the child to be independent and self-reliant (Barber & Olsen, 1997; Gray & Steinberg, 1999; Hart, Newell, & Olsen, 2003). Over the years, I've noticed that whatever category we fit into as parents is typically the intimacy/communication pattern we utilize in other relationships as well. Keep in mind that these are broad categories and people do not always fit neatly into one or another. Sometimes there are shades of a few styles in a parent's repertoire and these characteristics can change over time and with experience.

First is the authoritative child-rearing style, which is the most successful approach. Authoritative parents have high acceptance and involvement, are warm, attentive, and sensitive to the child's needs. They tend to have a close connection and use reasonable demands, consistent discipline, and gradually allow the child to make his/her own decisions depending on age and maturity level. They encourage expression of ideas and emotions and set limits on the child's inappropriate social behavior when necessary. Kids with authoritative parents tend to do well in school, have strong self-esteem, social skills, and self-control (Berk, 2009).

On the other hand, authoritarian parents have low acceptance but high involvement in their kids' lives. These adults tend to be rejecting, cold, even degrading by mocking or putting down their children. They control by using threats, yelling, hitting, withdrawing attention and love, or criticizing. Expression of ideas (especially anything different from the parents' opinions or beliefs) or emotions is discouraged. Children are expected to accept parental authority without question and are punished when they don't. Authoritarian parents have extremely high expectations that are not age-appropriate and they do not grant independence easily or quickly. They attempt to control their children's behavior and decisions and don't allow them to explore their own interests and desires. The parents' needs come first, thus leaving their children anxious, angry, frustrated, and overwhelmed by challenging tasks. Some become hostile, defiant, and aggressive, especially boys. Self-esteem and self-reliance are typically low. Academically, they may do poorly, or strive to do well in order to satisfy their unappeasable parents (Berk, 2009; Hart et al., 2003; Thompson, Hollis, & Richards, 2003).

The third style of parenting is permissive. Permissive parents have high acceptance and low involvement. They are warm and loving, but are either overindulgent or inattentive, exerting little control over their child's behaviors. Too few demands are made on the child and discipline is lacking. Kids are given too much autonomy too soon. They dictate their own TV, bed, and meal times, have poor (if any) manners, and have no household chores. They are impulsive, disobedient, rebellious and overly demanding. They have a sense of entitlement, poor self-control, are dependent on adults or others to do their work, and have little motivation to achieve. Thus, they have poor school achievement and antisocial behavior (Baumrind, 1971).

These are the kids we see acting out in stores, restaurants, and at school, along with parents who defend their angel's inappropriate behavior as "exploration" or "having fun" while they chastise other adults for calling attention to their brat's lack of civility. In fairness, while some parents believe in this approach, others lack confidence in their ability to control their child's behavior (Oyserman, Bybee, Mowbray, & Hart-Johnson, 2005).

Finally, there is the uninvolved parent, who has low acceptance and low involvement. These guardians are emotionally detached, withdrawn, and neglectful. They can be so depressed, drug-addicted, or otherwise stressed that few or no demands are made on the child. They typically don't monitor their child's whereabouts and activities or provide guidance about appropriate choices. Discipline is inconsistent and scant at best. The child typically has too much freedom and while everyday needs may be met, these parents have little energy or mind-set to engage in long-term planning or goals, such as establishing routines and rules about behavior or homework. Not surprisingly, kids of uninvolved parents have many problems, including poor attachment and coping skills, poor school performance, antisocial behavior, and low self-esteem (Baumrind, 1971; Berk, 2009; Aunola, Stattin, & Nurmi, 2000; Kurdek & Fine, 1994).

At this point, perhaps it's a good idea to discover which category your parents (and you, if you are a parent) fall under. This will give you some solid information regarding why you are the way you are. You can change the pattern by being aware of it and making a specific plan to target and modify specific behaviors. This kind of introspection is critical thinking at its finest. Here's a good place to start: What do you want to teach others about you and about the world?

TEACHING EGO STRENGTH

Top cats often begin as underdogs.

—Bernard Meltzer

Now that you know about inductive parenting, Freud's three personality parts, and the basic styles of child-rearing, how do you put this all together to influence and mold another person? It ain't easy folks, but it is doable. First, let's discuss **ego strength**, which was briefly defined in chapter two. Ego strength involves the psychological and emotional stamina we have in defending ourselves from hurt and feeling good about ourselves. Sometimes we refer to this as **resilience**, or the ability to adapt effectively in the face of threats to development (Berk, 2009).

> **ego strength**—Involves the psychological and emotional stamina we have in defending ourselves from hurt while still feeling good about ourselves.

"In Freud's psychoanalytic theory of personality, ego strength is the ability of the ego to effectively deal with the demands of the id, the superego, and reality. Those with little ego strength may feel torn between these competing demands, while those with too much ego strength can become too unyielding and rigid. Ego strength helps us maintain emotional stability and cope with internal and external stress" (Cherry, 2013).

> **resilience**—Ability to adapt effectively in the face of threats to development.

Mosby's Medical Dictionary (2012) gives a more specific set of characteristics. "The traits usually considered important include tolerance of the pain of loss, disappointment, shame, or guilt; forgiveness of those who have caused an injury, with feelings of compassion rather than anger and retaliation; acceptance of substitutes and ability to defer gratification; persistence and perseverance in the pursuit of goals; openness, flexibility, and creativity in learning to adapt; and vitality and power in the activities of life."

It seems in today's "I want it now" id world, along with the inclusion of permissive parents, we are creating kids with poor ego strength. If someone teases us for having what he/she deems a physical defect, we run to the plastic surgeon to fix it in order to be more acceptable to others. If someone makes mistakes that cause an auto accident or other personal (and not so personal) injury, we immediately file a lawsuit. In the past, we had the ego strength to defend and take care of ourselves, continue to experience high self-esteem, and move forward. When I was in grade school, an older boy I didn't know used to tease me about having skin that was darker than his. He was blond and blue-eyed, and very pale. I was Eastern-European-looking with dark brown eyes and hair, and an olive complexion. For some reason, this bothered him enough to call me a nigger. Being in 3rd or 4th grade, I wasn't quite sure what a nigger was, but I knew from his tone of voice that it was not a compliment. After I discussed the situation with my parents, they gave me advice on how to handle this angry, ignorant kid. The next time I saw the boy, I noticed that he had new eyeglasses. Now the playing field was even; we both looked "different." After he once again vocalized his disdain, I said, "Shut-up four eyes!" Happily, he never spoke to me again, I realized I was capable of handling this kind of situation on my own and my ego strength and self-esteem increased.

These days, if an incident such as the above occurs, parents scurry to the school to chastise everyone in administration and threaten to sue the boy and his family. Now I'm not saying that we should ever put up with racist or otherwise hateful behavior, but we need to help our kids handle these situations on their own, stepping in only when the situation turns to constant bullying or threats of physical injury. The main point is that we are not teaching our kids how to deal with conflict, loss, differing opinions or beliefs, or acceptance of self and others. We aren't teaching them to develop a "thick skin," to ignore the occasional foolish remarks of ignorant peers and still feel good about themselves. They don't know how to verbally joust or defend themselves. This also comes from focusing on material items and physical beauty as markers of our worth, vs. character, intelligence, and ability to get along with others. The key to solid ego strength is to develop it in yourself first, and then learn to be an authoritative, emotionally intelligent, empathetic limit-setter. No pressure! And remember, life and learning are a journey, not a destination; now get to work!

Where Have You Gone Character and Integrity?

5

> It is not our abilities that show what we truly are. It is our choices.
> —*Professor Dumbledore*
> *(from the movie* Harry Potter and the Chamber of Secrets, *2002)*

Would you like to hear something sad? Over the years, as I've quizzed by classes on one thing or another, I ask two questions that rarely result in a clear—or any—answer from them. These seem to be relatively simple questions, yet they are stumped and worse, ignorant of the answers. The questions are these: What is character? What is integrity? Sometimes the first question is answered, "Well, like a character in a play." No. "Oh, you mean someone who's a little strange?" No, not *a* character, just character. They wiggle in their seats, looking awfully uncomfortable until I define the first term.

Character is defined by Webster's Dictionary (1989) as "moral or ethical quality," and "qualities of honesty, courage, or the like," and "the aggregate of features and traits that form the apparent individual nature of some person or thing" (p. 247). Okay, so even Webster can't quite put its finger on a clear definition, so here's mine: Character is talking the talk. Ruggiero (2004) states it as "Internalizing ideals of good conduct," also known as doing the right thing.

So if character is about morals, ethics, and doing the right thing, then what is integrity? More quizzical looks from the student audience . . . Integrity is acting on these ideals regardless of the pressure to conform. It is walking the walk. It is doing what you believe to be the right thing to do even if no one is watching. You don't do the right thing to get in good with God, your family, or strangers watching you. You do it because it is part of you and you don't care what others think. This is called **moral self-relevance**. That being said, how many people do you know who truly possess both character and integrity? Do they have a game plan, rules to live by, a moral code to believe in? And do

> **moral self-relevance—** Doing the right thing because it is part of you, without caring about what others may think.

49

they practice what they preach regardless of the situation? More importantly, do you possess character and integrity?

The reason so many young people can't define these terms is because they aren't being taught and trained to possess them. They are taught to want things, but not to work on themselves as people. Think back to the quote by Rabbi Shmuley Boteach (2006) at the beginning of the book: "We are teaching our children how to have and not how to be." In our pursuit of the almighty dollar, Ipad, Iphone, X-box, and luxury vehicle, we have brushed aside the idea of becoming a person of strong character and positive reputation.

MORAL DEVELOPMENT

Character is doing the right thing when no one is watching.

—J.C. Watt

When do character and integrity begin to develop? During the second year of our lives, when we begin to walk, talk, and become a more active part of the world around us. Walking and talking translate into the beginnings of independence—of feeling, thought, and action, which just so happen to be the three components of morality. Morality includes evaluation of good vs. bad, the development of empathy, cooperation, and sharing, and the shaping of character. There are quite a few theories in psychology about how morality develops. We will focus on the two main philosophies espoused by Sigmund Freud (1923/1974) and Lawrence Kohlberg (1981; Kohlberg, Levine, & Hewer, 1983), as well as social learning theory.

Freud

Freud's psychoanalytic theory notes that morality focuses on the adoption (or internalization) of societal norms and rules. It is influenced by the parent's temperament and discipline style, the child's temperament and age, the demands placed on the child, and the child's view of his own and his parent's behavior, emotions, and thoughts (Berk, 2009). It is the parents' job to teach these societal norms and rules and what the child doesn't get from Mom and Dad, he will surely learn from other adults in his world—family, friends, teachers, coaches, preachers, and strangers.

Freud's theory is based on the emotional component of morality, which, according to him, develops almost fully between the ages of 3-6. This is the age span in which the conscience (or superego) and identification with the same sex parent come about. In a nutshell, identification with the same sex parent means that we want to be like and imitate our same sex parent and learn about our own gender identity and social rules for behavior. Thus, little boys want a pretend razor so they can shave with Dad, and little girls want to try on Mom's clothes and make-up.

As stated in the previous chapter, Freud emphasized the use of inductive parenting to help children learn empathy skills, for without empathy, moral thought and behavior would not exist. This is also where a good dose of healthy guilt comes into play. When we have harmed someone or someone's property, we should feel what I call appropriate guilt. We should feel bad and want to make amends; apologize, pay for any damage done, and learn from our mistake. This kind of guilt helps us think before we act and feel empathy for another person. Then we are more likely to treat others the way we wish to be treated. As an aside, inappropriate guilt rears its ugly head when we feel bad for setting limits with others. Your brother asks to borrow your car, and since he totaled your last vehicle in an accident two years ago, you tell him no. He then berates you for being a selfish, controlling sibling and you feel guilty for setting a limit and saying no.

If children grow up understanding how they affect others, positively and negatively, they are more likely to think and act in a way that is **prosocial,** helping others or doing the right thing because it is the right thing to do (Eisenberg, 2003; Eisenberg, Fabes, & Spinrad, 2006). As with anything worthwhile, it takes time and effort on the part of the parents to teach their children how to be prosocial. Herein lies the problem. As we see on the nightly news, in our communities and classrooms, and even in our own homes, many parents are not aware of the importance of this task, don't want to make the effort, or just don't know how. How do you teach a child to be kind, considerate, caring, strong, confident, and self-aware? Be the best damn role model you can be, first and foremost. We can't ask our children to "Do as I say, not as I do," and expect them to make appropriate choices. You don't want your child to smoke cigarettes, drink alcohol to excess, or do drugs? You need to stop smoking, drinking to excess, and using dope. I once had a client who smoked pot with his 21 year old son. The family "rule" was that the kids couldn't smoke pot until they were of full legal age. Well, as this is being written, it is still illegal to possess and smoke marijuana (without medical reason) anywhere in the U.S. I noted the rather twisted flexibility of such a specific family rule, but the father was okay with what he considered a wise decision. The trouble was that he also had a 12 year old son who felt left out of this father-and-older-son time and wanted to at least spend time with them while the other two got high. Of course, Dad said no, but he didn't set aside any father-and-younger-son time. A week or two later into our therapy relationship, the younger son was caught at school with a roach clip; the small silver holder that grasps a marijuana cigarette. Father was outraged that son didn't follow the rules. I countered with the truth that Dad was breaking the law and son was following in his role-modeled footsteps to get his attention. Needless to say, that was our last session. I had no qualms about that; Dad was being contradictory and it bit him in the tushie. He wanted to ignore the law and be a good, moral person too. Sorry, you can't do both. If you break the law once—you get caught speeding—and

> prosocial—Doing the right thing because it is the right thing to do; typically involves helping others.

you learn your lesson, you are still a moral person. If you continually break the law and have the attitude that you can do whatever the hell you want, and you get angry at the cop for discovering your bad behavior, then you are not a moral person. You're not thinking about the right thing to do, you don't care how you might affect others, or you may even deny that your behavior *does* affect anyone else. It reminds me of the guy who was in my traffic school class years ago (yes, even I was caught speeding) who said he never used his turn signals when he drove because it was nobody's damn business where he was going. . . .

Aside from being a positive role model, we need to talk to our kids about what is right and wrong and WHY. Lots of parents leave out the "why" part. The answer: It's the right thing to do. Or if you are more religious, something along these lines, "It's the right thing to do and God wants us to treat each other nicely." Talk about feelings - yours, theirs, others'; talk about behaviors—yours, theirs, and others' and how they make you feel. Teach them to organize and plan what they wish to accomplish before they act. Teach them to think a few steps ahead in regard to how others might react. Teach them that their fun ends when someone else's pain begins. Above all, remind yourself of these attributes first and honestly assess if you are demonstrating how you want your kids to behave.

Another perspective to contemplate is that open, unbiased conversation with adults about various social, political, ethical and religious topics assists in the development of critical thought (Bourne, 2006). Furthermore, reflective conversation with adults teaches children the **pragmatics** of conversation necessary for appropriate communication with others.

> **pragmatics**—Rules for appropriate, effective communication; includes taking turns, eye contact, tone of voice, staying on topic, use of gestures.

It has recently come to light that a large percentage of parents and children don't experience these necessary, in-depth, teachable moment conversations (Bly, 1996; Garner, 2006). They are so busy running from one activity to the next that they never have any kind of family time. Some argue that driving from place to place is their family time. I am talking about time spent together, without riding in automobiles or the interruption of electronic technology, where family members are discussing, face-to-face, the day's events, sharing stories and opinions, asking questions about various topics and learning from each other. That used to be called dinnertime. One study noted that fewer and fewer American families have this time and that kids who don't get this focused togetherness tend to have more emotional, social, and behavioral issues than kids whose families eat dinner together at home on a regular basis (Purdue University Center for Families, 2012). Quite a few of our dear friends are amazed at how close my husband and I are to our kids, and how much we converse with each other. We can talk about anything because we always have. We have had some of our most challenging conversations in the car. There have been questions about why people behave the way they do, queries about sex, gender differences, and existential questions about the authenticity of God. If this happens to you, turn off the radio, don't answer the cell phone, and pull off the road and park in a safe place if you have to think about your answer. Above all, be gentle, honest, and open, and answer the questions. Keep in mind that having no information is always worse than having some information, for both parents and kids. The more you withdraw from fully answering the tough questions, the more they will hesitate to talk to you, and trust you.

Our second major theory of moral development is social learning theory (SLT, for short), which is most closely associated with psychologist Albert Bandura (1977, 1986). Like Freud's theory, SLT focuses on the adoption of societal norms and rules. It is based on the behavioral component of moral development, which is learned through **modeling**—observing and imitating others, and how they are rewarded or punished for their actions. Think: Monkey See, Monkey Do. Pay attention to how you treat others because your kids (or the ones you work with) will treat them the same way.

> modeling—A type of learning involving observing and imitating others, and how they are rewarded or punished for their actions.

Actually, we are all role models, as I stated earlier. Children *and* adults pay attention to others and use social referencing to determine how to respond in unfamiliar situations. When a parent is dealing with an unruly child in a retail store, we watch to see what that parent will do, sometimes out of curiosity and empathy, partly out of wanting to learn what we should/shouldn't do, and occasionally to judge and make ourselves feel superior.

Children are sponges, from day one, and they will emulate how you speak, what you say, how you gesture with your hands, and how you yell when you are angry. They are always paying attention, especially when you think they aren't! Numerous parents have countless stories of commenting about someone else in the presence of their children, only to hear the instant replay later, usually when the subject of the conversation is in the room. Comedian Robin Williams told a wonderful story years ago regarding his then 2 year old son Zach, who heard Robin use the f-word in a phrase while he was driving. Apparently, all the way home and for some time afterward, the boy repeatedly uttered the phrase, humiliating (and humbling) his dad. Furthermore, children, especially younger ones, will speak in the same tone and pitch as you do, accentuating the point that they do listen to and process much more information than they are given credit for.

Besides "doing the right thing," if we want people to emulate our thoughts and behavior, there are other characteristics of positive, moral role models. First, we must be genuinely warm and responsive to others. (Yarrow, Scott, & Waxler, 1973). We must really like dealing with people and demonstrate this. If your feelings are genuine, then you will naturally be friendly and interested in others. Word to the wise: if you don't enjoy chatting with or helping people, please don't be a sales clerk or customer service representative. We must also be competent and have some power over our lives (Bandura, 1977). We must be able to effect positive change for ourselves and others. Last, because people, especially children (Mischel & Liebert, 1966) will naturally tend to choose the most lenient standard of behavior (i.e., the easiest course of action or the path of least resistance), we must be consistent in our words and actions. We need to talk the talk AND walk the walk. Otherwise, we will be taken advantage of and no one will trust what we say. Actions do speak louder than words. This is also the reason kids can play each parent off the other. Johnny asks Mom if he can watch TV. She says no, so Johnny finds Dad mowing the lawn and asks him. Dad says yes. When Johnny comes in and brags to Mom that Dad "said I could," the parental arguing begins. Clever child! He has learned at a very young age that his parents might have different ideas (and Johnny usually leaves out important information in the parent's decision-making process, like whether his homework is finished), and that he can manipulate them to attempt to get what he wants. You might have friends or co-workers who use this method of isolate-and-manipulate as well.

Furthermore, if you do the minimum amount of work necessary to get by on the job, in school, or in relationships, it is likely that your offspring will follow suit. Critical thinkers do more than is expected because they are eager to gain self-awareness, expand their knowledge, get the job done well, and move forward. Those of us who watch the clock while at work and leave exactly at the given end-time each day will not get raises and promotions. Students who look at a course syllabus and question what they need to do to barely pass the class, instead of how much knowledge they can acquire, will sacrifice precious learning experiences. These are the students who decide not to read the required books because they think the lecture notes contain enough information in order for them to pass exams. While this can be true, the books cover what the professor can't during class time, and students will again fail to benefit from further valuable information and quiet reflection. Research continues to show that those who take the path of least resistance in school behave likewise at work (Tracy, 2010). If you want to move up the corporate ladder, socially reference your co-workers, especially the older, successful ones, and imitate their enthusiasm, flexibility, and quest for knowledge.

Kohlberg

Our third and final theory of moral development focuses on learning morality through understanding social rules, changing our reasoning about situations as we mature and gain social experience. Lawrence Kohlberg (1981) emphasized the cognitive component of morality. He believed that the way we reason about a dilemma is ultimately more important than what we actually do, and is most important in determining moral maturity. He developed 3 levels of moral development, each with two stages, in order to classify one's ranking of personal character and integrity. Each level and stage build on the next, while we are aging and actively struggling with various moral dilemmas. He noted that gains in perspective taking (or empathy) lead to gains in moral reasoning and behavior.

Kohlberg's theory painfully demonstrates that it is much easier to think morally than to act morally. Real-life situations are less absolute and objective due to practical considerations, such as our personal safety, legal issues, coping skills, and possible negative effects on our relationships.

It's so easy to watch the news at home on your comfortable couch, bare feet propped up on the coffee table, sipping a hot cup of Joe, horrified at the scene playing out on the television. A video is being shown at a sandwich shop where one person is getting beaten to a pulp by two others simply because he wouldn't let the two cut in line, while 3 other people, including the store clerk, observe without any attempt to call the police or break up the fight. When we witness this kind of behavior, we believe, understandably, that the world has gone mad. We exclaim with self-righteous indignation that people are apathetic, they no longer care for others, they're all selfish and cold. Actually, what they truly are is human. We are in shock and fearful when we are in the presence of such sudden violence. We social reference—we watch how others respond and wait for them to act first. It takes an incredibly strong, self-confident leader-type of person to step in without checking the reactions of others first. Psychology students are all-too-familiar with the tragic story of Kitty Genovese, a New York woman who was stabbed to death outside her apartment complex in 1964 while anywhere from 6 to 38 of her neighbors (the exact number remains unclear) watched and/or listened. The original story claimed that a man attacked her three times, over the course of half an hour, stopping briefly each time as he noted lights turning on in various apartments. The New York Times reported that at least 38 people watched and heard the attacks and not one called the police until Kitty was finally raped and murdered (homicidesquad.com/kitty_genovese).

Television and newspaper reports largely exaggerated the numbers of witnesses and exactly what they saw or heard, blaming the woman's death on "apathy" and the callousness of New Yorkers. It turns out that many of the neighbors in question only heard some brief yelling, but couldn't make out the words, two people did call the police after the first screams, and those that actually looked out the window at the same time only saw a man standing over Ms. Genovese. He ran away and she staggered off the street into a doorway, where the people in her apartment complex could no longer see her and assumed she was beaten up or drunk, but otherwise alive (homicidesquad.com/kitty_genovese). Talk about a lack of critical thinking by the New York Times newspaper staff!

In any event, social psychologists Bibb Latane and John Darley (1968) began research on what was considered to be a bystander apathy problem and discovered that lack of action depended on the number (or perceived number) of bystanders people thought were present in an emergency situation. They noted that the likelihood of intervention decreased as the group increased in size, due to the **bystander effect** and **diffusion of responsibility.** The bystander effect states that people are less likely to provide help when they are in groups than when they are alone. Diffusion of responsibility states why: each group member's obligation to act weakens when they perceive that responsibility is shared by all group members. Practically stated, if others see the situation, we think that maybe they will respond and we won't have to. We conform to what others are doing and look to someone else to lead. Unless the victim gives specific directions to a specific person "You in the blue dress, please call 911 for me," people feel helpless and confused about what to do.

> **bystander effect—** Sociological concept stating that people are less likely to provide help when they are in groups than when they are alone.

> **diffusion of responsibility—**Explains bystander effect; each group member's obligation to act weakens when they perceive that responsibility is shared by all group members.

With that lengthy lead-in aside, let's examine Kohlberg's Stages of Moral Development (Kohlberg, 1981). In the interests of time, space, and clarity, I will scrutinize the three levels, but not go into detail about each specific stage within each level.

Preconventional Level (ages 4-10):

- Morality is externally controlled by others; presence of rules, authorities.
- We behave in order to avoid punishment and do what is best for oneself
- Rules cannot be broken.

Example: A child who sees a driver run a stop sign and thinks that person should get a ticket for breaking the rule

Conventional Level (ages 10-13):

- Beginning internalization (adoption) of social norms
- Understanding that social rules help maintain order
- We behave in order to please others; we need approval for good deeds
- Focus on the Golden Rule (Do unto others as you would have them do unto you)
- Rules should not be broken

Example: A child sees driver run a stop sign and thinks that person should watch out for others and care about what they think.

Postconventional Level (age 13 and older):

- Full internalization of social norms
- Personal interpretation of what is "right" for self and society

- Rules are flexible; emphasis on abstract principles that apply to all, such as justice, equality, human rights
- Development of a personal set of ethics/morals

Example: An adolescent or adult sees a driver run a stop sign and knows it isn't correct, but believes that the driver may have a valid reason for breaking the law.

Kohlberg theorized that not all people reach the postconventional, or highest level of moral thought. He and other researchers (Matsuba, 1998; Wyatt & Carlo, 2002) reported some of the following requirements and influences on moral reasoning:

- The presence of appropriate role models (parents being our first)
- Empathy
- Emotional self-regulation; the ability to recognize and control our feelings in order to complete tasks
- Have an open mind
- Higher education helps
- Practice with conflict resolution (family, peers) and discussion about social issues
- Moral self-relevance: moral behavior is part of you, a purpose and goal in life

Self-Control

As morality and a conscience develop, so too does **self-control.** This is our ability to inhibit an impulse to behave in a way that violates a personal or societal moral standard. We sometimes refer to this as will-power, but it is much more than talking ourselves out of doing something we might regret. Remember, truly moral people possess moral self-relevance, character, and integrity, so very few temptations will cause them internal struggle. However, since we are all human, we all have our vices. Some of us like sweets, some smoke or drink alcohol, others gamble away their paychecks or do drugs. Lots of people (at least in the U.S.) overeat, overwork, and overspend. Still others habitually sabotage their careers, personal freedom and relationships with affairs, spousal and child abuse, and criminal activities.

> **self-control**—Our ability to inhibit an impulse to behave in a way that violates a personal or societal moral standard.

When our parents and others teach us about moral behavior through inductive parenting, modeling, and reasoning, we develop **moral self-regulation,** which more specifically deals with how we monitor and adjust our conduct when temptation is present. Unfortunately, there seems to be a lack of moral self-regulation

> **moral self-regulation**—How we monitor and adjust our conduct when temptation is present.

these days, as evidenced by frequent reports of violence and scandal—and I'm just referring to politicians, celebrities, and sports idols!

MORAL RELATIVISM

> Integrity is choosing your thoughts and actions based on values
> rather than personal gain.
>
> —*Anonymous*

> . . . and character is having these values to begin with.
>
> —*Lisa Weisman-Davlantes*

Mention the following names and their deeds immediately come to mind: Arnold Schwarzenegger, Mark Sanford, Lindsey Lohan, Tiger Woods, AIG, Bernie Madoff. All people who, in some distorted way, believed that the rules didn't apply to them. The attention, publicity, and greed, and in some cases poor parental role models, propelled them into a different plane of existence, called **moral relativism.** Moral relativism is a description of the behavior and mind-set that we often see today, not just in our celebrities, but in our neighbors, our children, and us. Moral relativism includes the idea that whatever we want to do is okay simply because we want to. We think that we deserve special treatment; we don't have to have manners or even think about how our behavior might affect others. We don't care and don't think we have to. And if someone dares to claim that we should take others' feelings or sensitivities into account, we get angry and defensive. How dare that waitress ask my child to stop running in the restaurant! The nerve of her telling my child what to do!

> **moral relativism—**
> Includes the idea that whatever we want to do is okay simply because we want to do it.

This reminds me of a story I read in my local paper a few years ago. A father and his young children were visiting a marine center, similar to Sea World, and they were enjoying the animals in the tide pools. Usually in these quieter areas, one can look at and touch small sea life, and even pick up certain species to get a closer look and then gently place them back in the water. The rules are very clear, both on posted signs and verbal instructions from employees. As the story went, the young children mentioned above began to pick up tiny sea snails and throw them across the tide pool, to the other side. An employee quickly arrived on scene and gently asked the kids to stop, as the sea snails were a sensitive species and hurting them would upset the ecosystem of the tide pool, affecting all the other animals in it. Sadly, the father angrily intervened, telling the employee that the children were just "exploring" the environment.

Stories like this abound. I see them on the news much too frequently, and hear about them from my students, especially those who work in any customer service capacity. Every semester there is a new story, more incredible than previous ones. What is happening here?! Moral relativism is rearing its ugly head, along with a hefty dose of narcissism, which we will discuss in the next chapter.

Cheating in Education

One type of moral relativism has to do with cheating in education (also known in politically correct vernacular as academic dishonesty), from elementary school (Cizek, 1999) all the way up to graduate status. Statistics change every few years but basically, various studies and surveys have reported that 24% - 38% of middle school students have cheated on exams (Evans, & Craig, 1990), 51% - 75% of kids questioned admit to cheating in high school (Viviano, 2012; Reifman, 2012), and roughly 75% - 98% admit to academic dishonesty at some point during college (McCabe, 2001; McCabe, Butterfield, and Trevino (2012); www.educationportal.com). McCabe, Trevino, & Butterfield (2001) reported that cheating has gotten worse since the 1960s and the Josephson Institute of Ethics (2008) noticed an upward trend from 2004-2006. However, the Report Card on the Ethics of American Youth in 2012, also issued by the Josephson Institute, reported a slight decrease in different types of cheating (Viviano, 2012). McCabe, et al (2012) also noticed a slight downward trend, but also note that fewer and fewer students respond to the surveys sent, which could account for the lower numbers. McCabe feels that cheating is still a huge issue, but students decline to discuss it. McCabe et al (2012) also note that many students don't view certain forms of cheating, like plagiarism or collaborating on exams, as academic dishonesty at all.

Let's keep in mind that cheating incorporates many different aspects: looking at and copying someone else's answers during an exam; buying a paper from the internet, a small business, or a friend; having someone else write a paper for you; using someone else's paper from a previous semester; not giving credit for information when writing a scholarly paper; writing exam information on your hands, legs, arms. . . . The list goes on. As technology increases and becomes more (less?) sophisticated, so do the types of cheating that can and do occur. There is more confusion these days about what actually constitutes academic dishonesty. How are students supposed to know the definition of cheating when information is so readily available? The saddest part is that many students believe that it is okay to cheat. They're not *really* cheating by using someone else's paper, or the same paper they wrote for another class last semester; they know the information already, they're just saving time and effort from having to write another essay. They're paying for a term paper via the internet, not stealing it from a roommate, so that's not really cheating, is it? Everybody else is doing it, so it's okay, right? The number of students getting disciplined and/or booted out of colleges every year proves otherwise. Cheating in higher education is an extremely serious offense which not only goes on one's academic record for up to 7 years (depending on the university's policy), but can literally blackball a student from being admitted to another college, at least in the California State University system in California. There may also be civil and legal liabilities as well, such as heavy fines and loss of scholarship money. The loss of your higher education, self-respect, and credibility is not worth a passing grade, so why cheat your way through college or any other arena of life?

> "When people cheat in any arena, they diminish themselves—they threaten their own self-esteem and their relationships with others by undermining the trust they have in their ability to succeed and in their ability to be true."
>
> —*Cheryl Hughes*

Pressure to Perform

This brings us full circle to lack of appropriate parenting, moral development, and hefty doses of egocentrism and moral relativism, as well as the pressure to perform and be "successful," which more and more in our society means monetary and material gains. Pressure to choose the "right" (aka most prestigious) college adds to this concoction as well.

Now before you become angry, shut down, and get defensive and protest that the world has become an extremely competitive place and kids need to have and be the best, I want you to pay attention to how driven you (or your parents or friends) are in regard to what "the best" is. Granted, academic pressure begins in kindergarten, which is the new first grade. Does your child know how to read? Can she write her name? Is he able to use scissors properly? This continual scrutiny would leave any parent feeling anxious and incompetent if their child doesn't measure up. The urgency to perform increases with each passing year. Some school districts begin the higher education discussion in elementary school. It's no wonder that by the time these academic child-robots become preteens, parents are consumed with college admissions, scholarships, and choosing the "correct college."

Some parents push their children to attend prestigious, expensive universities, not so little Johnny and Susie can become the best thinkers and decision makers, but because they (and their parents) can brag that they are attending "the best" college, and that they will make more money because they went to "the best" institution. Parents are scrambling for all kinds of scholarships to these large, prestigious universities as well, and when you ask the children what they will major in, they become quiet, take on a deer-in-the-headlights blank stare and quickly mutter, "I don't know." This is not the indecision of a typical 17 year old, these are kids whose families are so focused on junior getting into the university of Mom and Dad's choice that they've never even considered what career the kid might want to pursue or if their number one choice of school is even appropriate for that pursuit.

Choice of college comes first, choice of career second. They don't think about the kind of student junior is or what he/she wants to do for a living. There is also the stigma still attached to community college (also known as junior college) attendance or gasp (!), a state-funded school (as in Cal State Universities).

My daughter has been questioned about college since she was 11 years old. She has been repeatedly interrogated since then (she is 14 years old at this writing) regarding what institution of higher learning she plans to attend. When the subject is broached, she says she doesn't know. I chime in: "Good Lord, she's only (X) years old! She doesn't even know what she wants to do for a living yet!" Well-meaning friends reply, "Well, it's never too early to think about it." I disagree. There is so much learning to be done and life experience to be had before one can even think about such adult decisions, and there is no race to the college degree finish line. Keep in mind that one study noted that roughly 35% of college freshmen across the U.S. drop out during the first year (Wistrom, 2012). Dr. Daryl Green (2013) reports that one in four freshmen dropout after the first year. Still others are placed on academic probation due to poor course grades. There are numerous reasons why first-time freshmen leave college: need for money, high stress, lack of preparation for the rigors of college, difficulty leaving home or being independent, lack of interest in obtaining a higher education degree, lack of campus support for incoming students, or attending college in order to please parents and/or significant others.

While quitting higher education is not a new phenomenon, we need to find the source of this disconnect between what we think our kids (or we) can do and what they can and actually want to achieve at the moment. In the meantime, we burden them immensely with constant badgering about how to perform in school and the need to join different organizations so it looks good on their resume later on. Then we run them back and forth on a daily basis to so many activities that families lose out on quiet time, conversational and social skills, and truly getting to know each other. Plus, I often wonder how many of these kids want and need some unscheduled time during the week. One of the best sayings I've ever heard is this: Moderation is key.

Last but not least, college is not for everyone and there are different levels of higher education for a reason. We need to start honoring these differences in our children so they can attend the campus that fits their learning and personality styles and their occupational goals. When my 16 year old son is asked about his college plans and he announces that he will go on to a two year community college for education and training in his chosen career (at the moment), the silence can be deafening. Sometimes the question is posed, "Oh, he's not thinking about a 4 year program?" Most of the time the news of his departure from what many believe to be "the best" quickly ends the conversation, as if his choice is not acceptable.

Let's be honest, there has never been any guarantee that college will lead to instant employment upon graduation, so we doubly need to make sure that our kids are choosing careers that yes, allow them to make enough money to live independently AND feel worthwhile to them, not to their parents. In the long run, if our daily work is more fulfilling and prosperous than just glancing at the amount of our yearly salary, we will be less likely to pursue the almighty dollar and what it can buy in order to make us happy. We will have a more profound sense of purpose and happiness in our lives and consequently be better critical thinkers (and financial planners).

Very Casual Sex: Friends With Benefits, Booty Call

Another type of moral relativism surrounds the societal and media attitude toward sex, especially casual sex. You know, friends with benefits (I like to call this FWB), the booty call, or the increasing numbers of teens engaged in oral sex during junior high and high school, because, as one student put it, "You can still have sex and technically be a virgin." Explain that logic to your parents or doctor when you develop a sexually transmitted disease (STD) in your mouth, on your penis, or inside your vagina. Now I know that casual sex has been part of human history since the beginning of time, but it's never been fashionable until now. The 1960s motto, "If it feels good, do it" continues to be the battle cry for younger generations. If two people are friends and want to have sex, but not an emotional, committed relationship, then it's okay, right? If both people know what they are getting into, no one gets hurt. More often than not, however, one or both parties do get hurt because feelings emerge. Feelings that they couldn't have possibly thought would occur because they had no prior experience with FWB.

Women are confused too, unfortunately. They are still trapped between the good girl and the whore when it comes to sex and sexuality (Tannenbaum, 2002). Each successive generation since the 1950s has had an easier time, but in some circles the idea persists that there are women you date (aka "hit it and quit it") and women you marry. To illustrate this point, quite a few years ago an informal survey by members of the newspaper staff at Cal State University, Fullerton, questioned students about the number of sexual partners that seemed comfortable for both men and women before the number became too high. For men it was (ready for this?) 18; for women, 3. Now this isn't to say that no one should have casual sex. That is obviously a personal choice. What concerns me, however, is the attitude that it's all good, everybody's okay. In other words, the lack of empathy and denial of any present and future consequences for self and others frightens me. Remaining a virgin until marriage or until you fall in love makes one a social pariah. If you haven't been in a relationship for a few months or years and you haven't had sex, you are viewed as a freak. How sad that many teens and twenty-somethings have the mentality of "It feels good and I want it now, and that's all that matters."

CORPORATE, POLITICAL, AND RELIGIOUS MISADVENTURES

The essence of immorality is the tendency to make an exception of one's self.

—*Jane Addams*

Yet another form of moral relativism rears its ugly head in business, politics, religion, sports, and entertainment. Gee, where do I begin? There have always been scandals in all these areas, but it seems that the personal lives and information of those with status has become more public with the advent of the internet. In regard to religion and politics, inappropriate behavior by these leaders used to be kept quiet, to avoid further investigation and enormous scandal that could shake up a presidential administration, religion, or individual place of worship. Is it that moral relativism has become more rampant, or are we just hearing more details than we did in the past? Or both? In any event, sexual, financial, and criminal misconduct in all careers and economic statuses are part of the daily news. I thought about listing some recent offenders here but what's the point? They will only be replaced by new names tomorrow.

So why bother to discuss these issues? What makes these influential people different from you and me? Their influence. Their power. Their ability to control resources, and our emotions. We put certain people on pedestals: sports heroes, actors, musicians, singers, religious and spiritual leaders, and elected officials, only to realize that they are human. They make mistakes, they hurt themselves and others, and they succumb to all kinds of stressors and temptations that you and I would never be subject to. But why is it that we so easily forgive some influential people who fall from grace but not others? Why do we grant a second chance (or more) when our favorite sports star is accused of lying about using steroids, but not to our spouses, friends, and children when they make mistakes? Why does John Edwards take a pounding for having an affair when his wife was dying of cancer, but Newt Gingrich doesn't get the same treatment, especially when he not only was having an affair and discussing the details of his divorce with his first wife as she lay in a hospital bed getting treatment for her cancer, but later had another affair on his second (also ill) wife while hypocritically blasting married President Bill Clinton for his involvement with Monica Lewinsky?

For some, if the downfallen idol publicly confesses his sins and weaknesses, all becomes right once again. As I recently saw (12/2011) in a chat room following a Yahoo article on Gingrich's infidelities and subsequent conversion to the Catholic church via his third wife, one respondent claimed that if Newt confessed his sins in church, then he considered him cleansed and was 'okay by me.' This reminds me of the televised, tearful confession of televangelist Jimmy Swaggert in 1988, in his "I Have Sinned" speech after admitting to solicitation of sex from a prostitute. Remarkably, he regained his followers' trust. However, he sinned again with a different prostitute in 1991.

Just in case you want to check, we could also discuss athletes such as Lance Armstrong (and numerous others involved in bicycle racing), Tiger Woods, Barry Bonds, Jose Canseco, Kobe Bryant, OJ Simpson, actor Robert Blake, Senator John Ensign, Governors Mark Sanford, Eliot Spitzer, and Arnold Schwarzenegger, Representatives Mark Foley, and Anthony Weiner. So many others, so little space. Why is it that some people with great power seem to have so little responsibility? Is this a result of poor upbringing? Greed? All-consuming power and ego? Let's face it, those in the public eye tend to love and need the attention. As an instructor, lecturing to 100 plus students at a time, I admit I enjoy the limelight and control. It's even more exciting when my charges laugh at my jokes! I control the timing, pacing, and material content. I choose who speaks in class and for how long. I choose when to move to the next topic, when exams will be, and how assignments will be graded. I am an authority figure with a doctoral degree and a license to do psychotherapy to prove it! I am also a role model for women, the professions of therapy and education, and the field of psychology.

Let me be crystal clear; this is not about judging, it's about expecting powerful leaders to be better than the masses. It's about expecting and demanding that these pedestal-sitters be stronger, wiser, less swayed by temptation, especially when they advertise themselves as having strong moral character. These are people we look up to and want to emulate. During an interview in 1993, basketball star Charles Barkley, in response to his off-the-court exploits proclaimed, "I'm not paid to be a role model. I'm paid to wreak havoc on the basketball court." Just because I dunk a basketball doesn't mean I should raise your kids." Sorry Charles, you were/are a role model. You're correct that your athletic skills do not necessarily translate into being a parent-figure or hero, but that is what you were to millions of kids, and adults, when you played. Whether our society is correct or not in demanding perfection from our role models, it does. Not that Mr. Barkley or any of us should change to please anyone else, but we must be cognizant of the fact that others do look to role models (that is, all of us) to decide how to behave, think, and feel. I am painfully aware of that responsibility as a parent and as an instructor, and experienced it as a therapist. Do I make mistakes? Of course; every day. But the more pressure I feel as a role model, the more I strive for excellence as a person. I realize that I live in a world with others and I have to constantly decide who I want to be and why. Many times I don't care what others think, but I also try my hardest not to do anything that would possibly hurt someone else or give them the impression that poor behavior is okay. That is what critical thinkers ponder and weigh. Mr. Barkley's response fits into the moral relativism category. It can be a way to avoid responsibility for our actions. On the other hand, it is also a reminder that even our most valued role models are humans who are imperfect. As you can see and as can be argued infinitely, there is a fine line between living for yourself and living with others.

The saddest aspect about striving to be someone with character and integrity is that we as a society don't believe when someone actually talks the talk and walks the walk. They are 'too good to be true,' and considered boring and/or worthy of being knocked off their 'goody-two-shoes' pedestal. As such, the Jonas Brothers were the victims of a continual, snarky verbal attack by host Russell Brand during MTV's 2008 Video Music Awards (VMAs) due to their purity rings and virginity vows. This, of course, is nothing new. When I was a pre-teen in the 1970s, I fell head-over-heels in love with Donny and the Osmonds, also a very pious family who amazingly upheld their beliefs in leading a moral, functional life. They were constantly slammed in the media for their "bubble-gum" music, "square" values (i.e., no music or behavior involving sex, alcohol or drug use) and clean-cut appearance. I was mercilessly teased throughout my childhood for choosing fantastic role models, which, even as a child, I knew was sad and wrong. What's not to like about people who are consistent in their words and actions, and care for others as well as themselves? Donny, Marie, and all the Osmonds are still my role models today, and I am proud to say that their example made me a better person as well. Too bad that so many people are threatened by someone with strong character and integrity. I guess it makes them realize what they don't have in themselves, and that is too painful to bear. It's always easier and more comfortable to bring someone down to our level of functioning than to lift ourselves up to theirs.

Narcissism, Sense of Entitlement, and Other Descriptions of Spoiled Brats

The ring always believes that the finger lives for it.
—*Malcolm de Chazal*

Narcissism, egocentrism, being a spoiled brat or having a sense of entitlement, are interchangeable terms for the same personality and social style. I've mentioned narcissism a few times now; let's define it. Narcissism involves an inordinate fascination with oneself; excessive self-love; vanity (http://dictionary.reference.com). The Thomson Gale Encyclopedia of Public Health (2013) defined it as excessive preoccupation with self and lack of empathy for others, adding the following in-depth description:

"Narcissism is the personality trait that features an exaggerated sense of the person's own importance and abilities. People with this trait believe themselves to be uniquely gifted and commonly engage in fantasies of fabulous success, power, or fame. Arrogant and egotistical, narcissists are often snobs, defining themselves by their ability to associate with (or purchase the services of) the "best" people. They expect special treatment and concessions from others. Paradoxically, these individuals are generally insecure and have low self-esteem. They require considerable admiration from others and find it difficult to cope with criticism. Adversity or criticism may cause the narcissistic person to either counterattack in anger or withdraw socially. Because narcissistic individuals cannot cope with setbacks or failure, they often avoid risks and situations in which defeat is a possibility" (Thomson Gale, 2013).

"Another common characteristic of narcissistic individuals is envy and the assumption that others are envious as well. The self-aggrandizement and self-absorption of narcissistic individuals is accompanied by a pronounced lack of interest in and empathy for others. They expect people to be devoted to them but have no impulse to reciprocate, being unable to identify with the feelings of others or anticipate their needs. Narcissistic people often enter into relationships based on what other people can do for them" (Thomson Gale, 2013).

Watch Out! This is my biggest pet peeve, my largest soapbox issue with humanity these days. I've had enough of spoiled brats of all ages, races, genders, and ethnicities. I'm tired of observing their disrespectful, self-righteous, self-centered, whiny behavior in stores, restaurants, during athletic events, and on television. Listen up America, and the rest of the world!! You are not more special than anyone else. You do not deserve to be praised every time you wake up in the morning, make your bed, or breathe. Wanting a new cellular phone does not justify receiving it without any work or money from you. You do not deserve to own a home if you can't afford the mortgage payments. You do not deserve to get a new car just because you turn 16 years old. You do not deserve to be first all (or even most) of the time, and no one wants to hear your phone conversations at the mall, in an elevator, or during a concert. Nobody cares about your minute-to-minute Facebook status report announcing that you are standing in line in the grocery store waiting to pay for a package of toilet paper, a loaf of bread, and a six pack of beer.

Here we go . . . don't say I didn't warn you!

So why am I so passionate (nice euphemism) about the sense of entitlement many seem to have nowadays? It is first and foremost a symptom of poor parenting. Lack of empathy is the key here, which indicates the absence of consistent inductive parenting. Kids aren't taught that their behavior affects others, so they grow up believing that it's alright to do whatever they want and not take responsibility for their actions. If they succeed it's because they are awesome, and if they fail it's because it was someone else's fault. This is moral relativism gone wild. I'm glad to say I am not the only person concerned about and frustrated by this mind-set and behavior. Just a quick glance of the many book titles on the subject will demonstrate the need for attention to this very real problem. Also, check out the list of television shows dedicated to demonstrating and sometimes glorifying egocentric behavior: Toddlers and Tiaras, Sweet Sixteen, Bridezillas, Jersey Shore, and any "reality" show.

COGNITIVE DEVELOPMENT AND THE CONNECTION TO NARCISSISM

You can see the stars and still not see the light.
—*Eagles' song*—"Already Gone"

Cognition is defined as "the inner processes and products of the mind that lead to knowing. It includes all mental activity—attending, remembering, symbolizing, categorizing, planning, reasoning, problem solving, creating, and fantasizing" (Berk, 2006, p.219). **Cognitive development**, or the way these inner processes change and grow over time and with experience takes our entire childhood to establish. This isn't just about academics; it's about people skills as well. By now, you can see where this is going; lack of proper parenting along with the requisite focus on a child's cognitive development lead to increased narcissism.

> **cognitive development**—Includes all mental activity and the way these inner processes change and grow over time and with experience.

In order to develop social skills, we first need to attend to others' feelings, body language, facial expressions, and tone of voice. We need to remember the patterns of behavior and sights for each person we care about and later, each person with whom we interact with socially, at school, church, or work. We can then symbolize what the patterns mean, whether someone is happy, angry, sad, etc. We can then categorize emotions into good/bad, positive/ negative, or easy/difficult. As we become more social and better at paying attention to others, as well as ourselves, we can use reasoning to plan our behaviors so that we avoid hurting someone, purposely try to bring out certain emotions to clear the air, or genuinely want to hurt someone else's feelings. Along the cognitive path we also learn to problem solve by fantasizing about creative solutions and practicing (at least in our own minds) appropriate confrontation skills.

Phew! What a complicated process we must learn and master in order to be fully cognizant, or aware, of who we are and what our effect is on others. As you can probably guess, just being present is not enough. We have to practice, make mistakes, adjust our beliefs, opinions, and behaviors, and learn from those mistakes by practicing more. This is a lifelong process. The good news is that it can develop later in life, but it is infinitely easier when we begin our journey on earth with adults who teach us right from wrong, social skills, and help us by pointing out our mistakes and suggesting ways to fix them.

THE ISMS: EGOCENTRISM AND ETHNOCENTRISM

Human beings are perhaps never more frightening than when they are convinced beyond a doubt that they are right.

—*Laurens van der Post*

Two very important concepts in cognitive and social development are egocentrism and ethnocentrism. **Egocentrism** means being so centered/focused on oneself, one's needs, beliefs, and opinions that we ignore others'. No new or different information is allowed.

> egocentrism—Being so centered/focused on oneself, one's needs, beliefs, and opinions that we ignore others'. No new or different information is allowed.

Egocentric people (Ruggiero, 2012):

- Have limited critical thinking skills
- Have difficulty hearing other viewpoints
- Have little empathy for others
- Act like the world revolves around them and their needs
- Are poor observers and listeners
- Become angry when their opinions or beliefs are challenged
- Don't take responsibility for their actions, especially their failures
- Don't understand when or why they have hurt the feelings of others
- Tend not to evaluate or investigate their opinions or beliefs
- Are really quite insecure

These are people we refer to when the terms narcissism, sense of entitlement, or spoiled brat come to mind. I'm betting you know someone who fits the description. Look long and hard and decide if you fit the description as well, though if you do, you'll just deny it and opine that the author of this book is indeed a charlatan . . .

It is very difficult to be in a relationship with an egocentric person. They are always right, they are smarter than everyone else, and don't listen when you confront them, however gently, about their hurtful statements or behaviors. They are special and expect others to conform to their schedule, lifestyle, and way of thinking. These expectations are typically not verbalized; others are just expected to know what the egocentric person wants without having to ask. As such, many erroneous assumptions are made about others, including their perceived "loyalty" to the egocentric person.

I know someone who fits this profile. He is a warm, generous person, but easily hurt and angered if his friends and family members don't perform to his standards, which usually include unspoken expectations. Years ago he thought nothing of calling one weekend morning to announce that he was having a get-together that day, over 100 miles from where we lived. He was thanked for the invitation, but we already had plans with other friends that day that had been made a few weeks before. The ego's attitude? Cancel your plans. He didn't entertain very often and we were expected to be there when he snapped his fingers. We didn't cancel our plans, of course, and didn't hear the end of it from other friends for a few weeks. When he later changed his religion, the process of do-what-I-do began again, only this time much nastier and uglier. There are countless other examples with him and other people, but that would take up another book. The point is, there is no pleasing an egocentric person unless you do his/her bidding and anticipate his/her needs. You have enough to deal with in your own life. Set some limits with this person (either don't respond or make a quick statement about your decision) and move on. Trying to get him/her to understand your point of view is a waste of time.

Those who are egocentric tend to be ethnocentric as well. **Ethnocentrism** involves excessive focus on one's group (Ruggiero, 2012). Excessive focus includes the beliefs that their group is superior to others and that the motivations of other groups are suspicious.

> **ethnocentrism—** Excessive focus on one's group, including beliefs that one's group is superior to others and that motivations of other groups are suspicious.

Ethnocentric people (Ruggiero, 2012):

- Challenge other groups' views, but not their own
- Tend to oversimplify complex issues, such as those regarding politics, religion, people
- There is no middle ground; beliefs and actions are right or wrong
- Believe negative stereotypes about other groups
- Need to have an "out-group" or scapegoat to blame for individual or world problems, real or imagined

So, put a lot of egocentric people from the same group or belief system in one room and *voila*`! An ethnocentric smorgasbord! The Tea-Party, Occupy groups, far left and far right political offshoots, Fox and CNBC news shows, or any organized religion quickly come to mind. In social sciences like psychology and sociology, this would be defined as **groupthink**. Irving Janis, a research psychologist from Yale University, originally defined the term as, "A mode of thinking that people engage in when they are deeply involved in a cohesive in-group, when the members' strivings for unanimity override their motivation to realistically appraise alternative courses of action" (Janis, 1972, pp. 8-9). Basically, when we are in a group, we tend to conform to the standards of the leader or the majority of the group in order to keep the peace and fit in. We can lose our individuality quickly, so critical thinkers try to be aware of this phenomenon and stay true to themselves, even if they will possibly be rejected by group members.

> **groupthink—**Tendency to conform to the standards of the leader or the majority of the group in order to keep peace and fit in.

As we all have experienced, it can be very difficult to stand alone in our beliefs when faced with a group of our peers. It is akin to the old tale of The Emperor's New Clothes, by Hans Christian Andersen. You remember the story: The emperor desires a new set of clothes and hires a pair of swindlers to create something that they describe as incredibly dashing, original, and debonair, invisible to those who are inferior to the emperor. These con artists convince the emperor of the magnificence of the clothing and that he will be the envy of all. As such, his royal highness decides to "wear" his new clothes to greet his people, who play along and tell him how wonderful he looks, even though the emperor is naked as a jay-bird. One brave little boy finally speaks up to declare, "The emperor isn't wearing anything at all!" Some spectators try to quiet him, but he won't accept the hypocrisy of the situation and continues to speak the truth. In turn, this spurs others to support the little boy. The emperor then learns an important lesson about vanity.

Lovely story, but in real life we don't usually get the support of others in a group, unless they are strong critical thinkers too. More likely, we are banished from the group and, just for good measure, derided for days, weeks, or even years to come.

The same advice applies here as it does to dealing with an egocentric individual. Decide whether you wish to vocalize your thoughts or just walk away, satisfied and thankful that you are more open-minded and tolerant of other people and other points of view.

NARCISSISM IS NORMAL—FOR TODDLERS AND TEENS

When we are infants, the environment is new and ever-changing. If we have loving, appropriate caretakers, the world revolves around us (or at least it seems like it does). When we are hungry, someone feeds us. When our diaper is soiled, it is changed. When we need attention, there is someone present to interact with. This is crucial for our emotional, social, and physical growth during the first two years. The trouble can begin when we are on the path to becoming independent; when we walk, talk, and develop our own viewpoints. Discipline begins when baby starts to walk. He is curious; he sees things from a different perspective—literally—now that he is using his own two feet. After mastering the balancing act of walking without support, he wants to use his hands to explore, to touch, to hold, and to pick up that $50 vase on the coffee table that you got as a wedding gift. This is where the parenting challenge begins, and possibly a personality full of narcissism for junior, if Mom and Dad don't set limits on his behavior. A simple "No" will do for some children. Some need a stronger "No!" Still others might need a quick tap on the hand along with the "No!" before the hand touches the vase. Sometimes "no" needs a brief explanation of the child's behavior and effects on others, as in inductive parenting. Saying "no" does not leave room for negotiation. The child may want an explanation, but this does not mean that they should have the power to eventually wear a parent down enough for the limit to be discarded and a "yes" to take its place.

There has been much debate regarding whether adults should use the word no with young children. There were some researchers and parent groups who were distinctly against using the word "no," for fear of being too negative with their child. In the 1990s classes began to crop up across the country to assist parents in how to set limits (aka say "no") with their kids. Seriously?! Check out your local library or bookstore and you will find enough books on parenting techniques to make your head spin. Over the years, we have evolved from being oppressive and authoritarian with kids, to being too detached, indulgent, or even apprehensive of scolding them. For many, attempting to find the middle ground has resulted in **helicopter parents** and **trophy kids**. Helicopter parents "hover" around their children, constantly planning activities, scrutinizing every bit of schoolwork, and stepping in when their child struggles with a peer or authority figure. Their lives typically revolve around their child's activities and emotions. Young kids are kept physically close, not allowed to get too dirty or be exposed to germs from peers. These parents are also intimately involved in junior's choice of college and career. Protecting our children from emotional and physical harm and attempting to ensure their future success are enviable parenting characteristics. However, the line between creating structure and creating autonomy becomes blurred and results in over-parenting. In fact, helicoptering leads to the development of trophy kids, who exhibit over-inflated egos, great difficulty making their own decisions, and functioning socially (Alsop, 2008). They are hard-working and achievement oriented, but don't excel at leadership and independent problem solving (Alsop, 2008). Many also expect special treatment on the job.

> **helicopter parents—** Term describing parents who "hover" around their children; their lives typically revolve around their child's activities and emotions.

> **trophy kids—**Children of helicopter parents who may exhibit over-inflated egos, great difficulty making their own decisions, and functioning socially.

What is the best way to raise a child? Considering the present, daily, sickening violence and lack of personal accountability in our world, perhaps saying no when they were toddlers would've helped some of these now egocentric, hostile, anxious, or depressed adult children.

If you are interested in your own parenting skills (or those of others), here is a fun quiz to help you determine if you are a helicopter parent: http://www.babyzone.com/mom/motherhood/helicopter-parent_83221

Why all the fuss about parenting styles? When we don't set limits (make rules for behavior) or establish an appropriate structure, we create spoiled brats. These brats rule the home. They demand things and they get them. They want a new video game and the parent buys it, without making junior accomplish something to earn the game. If they want to play a sport year-round parents agree, even if it results in financial difficulty and/or sacrificing family time for vacations. These parents want their babies' self-esteem to be continually high, so they don't want them to be deal with disappointment or failure. They are over-protective of their child's feelings and go to great lengths to make sure they don't experience any negative self-conscious emotions, such as embarrassment, shame, or guilt.

When did this culture of narcissism begin? This seemed to have begun in the "me decade" 1970s (Lasch, 1979/1991) and gained momentum in the 1980s (www.galeschools.com). Programs sprang up in schools all across the country focusing on increasing kids' self-esteem. This was a wonderful idea, especially since study after study continues to demonstrate that girls, especially, suffer from low self-esteem from junior high school onward (Dohnt & Tiggemann, 2006a; Dohnt & Tiggemann, 2006b; Kutob, Senf, Crago, & Shisslak (2010); Tannenbaum, 2002). There are many reasons for this, which we will explore later, but for now suffice it to say that there was a need to help kids feel better about themselves so they could be more successful in all areas.

However, the programs focused more on feelings than accomplishments. It was felt that constant praise would increase self-esteem. It did, alright, but to the point of creating little self-esteem monsters with over-inflated egos (aka spoiled brats) who didn't believe they needed to follow the rules because they were truly special and unique. It turns out that accomplishment is what leads to self-esteem, not constant adoration and praise for doing what is expected of you. Parents and teachers stopped focusing on hard work to earn a reward; now it was given because everyone else had "it" and they didn't want junior to feel left out or be a source of ridicule for not having the latest "thing." True self-esteem leads to ego strength. When we teach kids how to acquire money, possessions, awards, or academic degrees instead of how to be virtuous, respected citizens of the world, we are training them that material goods lead to happiness, status, and prestige. As we all know, the ability to buy something is indeed very powerful. There is a heady feeling we get when we acquire something we really want. It is a sweeter victory when we have worked and earned the chance to obtain the desired object. In the end, though, once we have the object in our possession we quickly get bored with it and move on to the next item on our list. When we don't have to work for something and just receive it when requested, we don't take care of it as well; we don't cherish it as a symbol of our diligence and persistence. If it breaks, Mom and Dad, my spouse, or the government can just buy me a new one, right?

During adolescence, when the individual is making the transition from childhood to adulthood, many demonstrate aspects of narcissism. These traits are related to the adolescent's need to develop his or her sense of self (Piaget, 1999). This is also a normal aspect of development; trying to establish one's independence and place in the world. There's another old therapy dictum espousing that whatever narcissistic traits and behaviors the child demonstrated as a toddler will be repeated in the teenage years. This is not necessarily true, but could be an indicator of things to come if parents don't quiet the ME monster at a young age. Teenage egocentrism is the aspect of family life that every parent dreads. One day your compliant, sweet little girl does what she is told without arguing, the next she is a kettle of rage, arrogance, and eye-rolling every time you open your mouth. It is children's job to **individuate**. As grown adults we continue to do this when we are with our parents, especially when they attempt to give advice on how to raise our children and spend our money. The behavior and feelings are natural. We need our

> individuate—Psychological and physical separation from one's family of origin.

mentors until we can make it on our own; then we leave for greener pastures and the knowledge that we can, indeed, take care of ourselves. This is wonderful, except that some parents and children never get to this point. Some parents and kids can't/won't let go and one recent study concluded that helicoptering may result in depressed and incompetent children (Schiffren, Liss, Miles-McLean, Geary, Erchull, & Tashner, 2013). Children need to learn from mistakes as well as successes. This is one of the ways they practice social and problem-solving skills. If we "fix" every difficulty and rescue them from owning responsibility for errors, we interfere in the "self-determination theory," which states that we all have three basic needs in order to be happy: autonomy, competence, and connection to other people (Schiffren et. al, 2013; Rochman, 2013).

THE PERSONAL FABLE AND THE IMAGINARY AUDIENCE

Teenagers normally engage in two types of egocentric behaviors (Piaget, 1965) during his Formal Operations stage of development, when adolescents are more able to reflect on their own thoughts, especially about themselves and their lives. Piaget believed that a new form of egocentrism emerges during this time: the inability to discriminate between their abstract perspective and that of others (Inhelder and Piaget, 1955/1958; Berk, 2006). In other words, teens have a very hard time seeing the world from another's viewpoint and can seem lacking in empathy as well.

The first of these adolescent egocentric behaviors is called the **imaginary audience**. This is the belief that one is or should be the center of attention or concern (Elkind and Bowen, 1979; Piaget, 1965). Teens dealing with the imaginary audience are self-conscious and afraid of being humiliated, especially in front of their peers.

> imaginary audience— The belief that one is or should be the center of attention or concern.

This is what drives them to scrutinize every aspect of their appearance, especially girls, and become highly sensitive to public criticism or "uncool" parental attention, like waving goodbye when dropped off for school, which, by the way, has to be achieved by driving the "good" car with a well-dressed parent behind the wheel who acts more as a limousine driver than a relative. It feels like everyone is watching the teen every minute and one mistake could lead to his/her downfall among peers. Thus, public criticism regarding their performance in school, social settings, or on the playing field can be especially painful. On particularly difficult, insecure days, girls will empty their closet in an attempt to find the right outfit, or spend a few hours trying to make their hair perfect for the never-ending "show" at school. It's exhausting for both child and parent.

"Because teenagers are sure that others are observing and thinking about them, they develop an inflated opinion of their own importance" (Berk, 2006, p. 248). This is indicative of the second type of egocentric behavior referred to as the **personal fable** (Piaget, 1965). This includes the belief that we are so special and unique that no one could possibly understand our experiences, thoughts, or feelings. Risk-taking behavior could also be present, as teens tend to feel that they are so special that they are invulnerable. "Nothing bad will

> **personal fable**—The belief that we are so special and unique that no one could possibly understand our experiences, thoughts, or feelings.

happen to me!" Think of the adolescent who has just broken up with his/her first crush. Mom and Dad try to comfort their child, stating that they remember how hard it is to lose a first love, when all of a sudden it seems like their child has been overtaken by the Devil himself as he or (usually) she cry out, "You don't understand! No one's ever loved the way I have! I'll never get over this!" This is usually followed by some stinging remarks about how the parents grew up in the age of dinosaurs, before the inventions of personal computers and cell phones and that "things were different back then." In my generation the rant was about growing up in the age of dinosaurs before TV, video games, and microwave ovens were available. Ya gotta laugh, and understand that all this craziness is normal, except when it severely interferes in the teen's ability to make wise choices and/or communicate effectively with parents and peers.

As you can guess from your interactions with adults of all ages, some people never outgrow these aspects of teen cognitive development. Continued parenting plays a huge role in how long these factors remain in play or whether they continue into adulthood. Again, if parents didn't set limits well when kids were little and if they haven't improved their parenting skills since then, the adolescent years will be rife with difficulty for all family members. Plus, kids who are so focused on what everyone else thinks tend to have low self-esteem and an increased possibility of following the crowd in order to fit in (Bell & Bromnick, 2003). When the personal fable pairs up with sensation-seeking, teens can be more likely to engage in drug use, delinquent acts, and risky sexual behavior (Ginsburg, 2007; Greene, Krcmar, Walters, Rubin, Hale, & Hale, 2000). In addition, it seems to me that children who feel good about themselves and have stable family lives have no need to experiment with drugs, alcohol, or early sexual activity.

There is a wise saying in therapy that states: "There are no acting out children without immature parents." 'Immature' in this case refers to adult inability to be adults and set rules for their kids to follow, along with appropriate discipline when the rules are broken. Every child needs structure; they need to know what to expect at home, at school, and in public. They need schedules—not the chaotic running from place to place, but some kind of expectation of what time they will awake in the morning, eat meals, and go to bed at night. They need to know what is expected of them as well. Do we want them to use good manners with others? Do we want them to respect and follow the laws of our city, state, and country? Do we want them to treat others with respect? Do we want them to drink, smoke, or use illegal drugs? Do we want them to lie, cheat, or steal?

The answers to these questions seem pretty obvious, but how many parents (and how many of us) break the rules on a regular basis and either expect our children won't, or that it's okay if they do? How many parents seem clueless about their child's inappropriate behavior at school and actually argue with administrative staff about the unfair treatment of their child? There are too many reports of parents actually contacting their child's boss at work when junior comes home upset! Those in academia know this happens at colleges and universities on a regular basis (re-read the story in chapter 1).

This helicopter parenting commences as early as the second year, when children begin to assert their independence and sometimes continues into our offspring's early adult years. We see children running amok in restaurants and stores while parents are chatting on cell phones or otherwise completely ignoring their child's behavior. When an employee or other customer comments to the child (or parent), the parent lashes out. "Don't talk to my child that way!" My attitude? If you don't discipline him, someone else will, and they won't be as nice about it as you, the parent, would be.

I saw a prime example of this on Dr. Phil's show a few years ago. A mother with three daughters had a second mortgage on the house to the tune of about $40,000. Why? She was trying to please her oldest teenage daughter, who wanted a car. When the kid was 16, Mommy bought her a small SUV. Kid hated it, and Mom returned it for a red Mustang. Daughter promptly trashed the Mustang—totaled it in an accident—and demanded a new one. Mom bought her another one, no surprise there. Two years later, when the little princess was about to go off to college, she stated that the car was old and she needed a better ride. Guess what she asked for? Drumroll please . . . .a Cadillac Escalade—a $50,000 car. When this family arrived at Dr. Phil's show, Mom was seriously considering the idea, while the other two daughters no doubt were thinking, "Hey, if Big Sis gets a Caddy, maybe I can ask for a Porsche!!" Dr. Phil was astonished and asked the college student if she understood the huge sacrifice her mother was trying to make. As Mom put it, "It's hard enough being a teenager. I just want her to be happy." The kid truly did not comprehend that there was a problem. She just knew that she asked for things and she got them. Not one bit of empathy or sympathy for her mother or the family's financial plight. Why should she care? She wasn't taught to. She wasn't raised to earn her own cars by working, she wasn't allowed to fail and deal with the pain of failure. The frightening thing is that there are so many millions of kids and families just like this one, and along with other institutions and individuals, even corporate America is fed up.

CORPORATE AMERICA, AND GEN X AND Y NARCISSISTS

> An inferiority complex would be a blessing if only the right people had it.
>
> —*Alan Reed*

Our offspring are not learning about internal rewards for deeds done. They learn to covet and anticipate prizes/rewards for their performance (or lack of), like trained seals at Sea World. Ask any business owner or older employee and they will have a story to tell about a young, inexperienced, 20-30-something co-worker who expects special treatment at work. These are the recruits that do just enough (if not less) on the job, and who usually don't want or don't think they need to stay past their typical workday time, take on any extra projects, or learn anything new. These people are the front office staff in your doctor's office who don't/won't smile when patients arrive, and sound almost irritated when asked a question or a favor of someone who needs help. They are there to answer phones, input computer data and do some filing. No more, no less. They complain about how boring their job is, and how they can't stand the demands of the patients. The situation is similar with anyone working in retail, restaurants, or a professional workplace. They believe their education and experience in a certain field is all they need to achieve success, then they wonder why they don't get raises, promotions, and bonuses. They will blame everyone for their failure but themselves. "The boss doesn't like me," "She's out to get me," "People just don't appreciate me at work."

I recently had an appointment with my doctor. I filled out my paperwork, gave it directly to the 20-something gal at the front desk and sat down in a chair directly in front of her work area. Almost an hour later, someone from the back came out and asked the gal if I was there. This gal "didn't know." Now, she wasn't very busy, believe me, I noted that the entire time I was waiting to be called in. She was supposed to take my paperwork and have me come in and sit inside the office, but when I gave her my forms, she was busy chatting with a co-worker about something unrelated to work. She wasn't paying attention, and even when she looked my way quite a few times in that hour, she never questioned who I was or why I was waiting so long. I didn't either; I should have spoken up, but really, it's not my job, it's hers. I learned that day to make it my job.

The bottom line here is that she wasn't focused on work, nor did she use any empathy skills in being aware of patients and their possible needs. Is this because she didn't have any compassion? Was she too embarrassed to say anything to me after all that time? Did she think it was not her responsibility to concern herself with me? I don't know. What I do know is that if I owned a business I would never hire her to front it for me.

This workplace narcissism is not exclusive to the younger generations, but corporate America has noticed the vast difference in employee attitudes from 30 years ago to today (Alsop, 2008; Blumenthal, 2012; Buckingham & Buckingham, 2012). While new hires tend to have better technological information, they also expect and demand more in terms of salary, status, and prestige (Alsop, 2012; Blumenthal, 2012). There is nothing wrong with wanting a higher salary and more benefits, but we'd better do the work to prove that we deserve these perks, and just showing up 5 days per week is not enough. Furthermore, expecting a salary on a par with someone who has loyally worked for a company for 20+ years is not appropriate either. It's actually quite arrogant and self-serving.

But this situation doesn't make sense. Surely, many of these new employees played on sports teams, possibly year-round, for a number of years. They understand what it's like to be part of a team, to work together toward a single goal. Do they? With parents' insistence that every semi-athletic kid should be a superstar, complete with regular visits to chiropractors and massage therapists, and youth sports' focus on specialized coaches to train kids to play certain positions on the team, our youth is learning that they are indeed special and that winning and exhibiting individual talent are more important than working as a team. They are regularly told how fabulous and gifted they are, without the requisite constructive criticism about their skills or sportsmanship to balance the praise. They are fine the way they are and don't need to learn anything new, let alone help other, ineffective team members. These are the players who verbally chastise and physically exclude teammates they believe are not performing up to standard. They are ball-hogs who want to score so much that they won't pass to another team member, especially not one who they consider to be weak. The bully and ball-hog's parents openly encourage this behavior. "Take it all the way, son!" "Don't worry about passing Debbie, just score!" This scenario is nothing new, but it now seems to be the norm. I've watched talented sports teams fall apart over the course of a season because of the lack of a cohesive unit. The star players need to help the inexperienced or awkward members, who in turn need to accept the assistance. The coaches need to make sure this happens with respect and compassion.

This applies to the workplace as well. The more experienced, more knowledgeable employees need to train the inexperienced newbies, and the newbies need to accept the assistance and learn how to work as team members. Supervisors monitor the outcome of these unions and provide training when necessary.

Could you imagine a first year baseball player telling a star veteran how to play the game? Or demanding the same salary? Why are young, new employees expecting and sometimes demanding the same treatment as their supervisors? This goes back to self-esteem; teaching junior that he/she is special because he/she got dressed this morning. When we protect our children from failure, disappointment, and hard work, and we give them whatever they wish, we create the sense of entitlement that follows them into school, work, and personal relationships. This inflated sense of self ultimately dooms them to be miserable and confused about how the world treats them. They expect others to let them slide when they make mistakes or fall short of the goal again and again, and they have no empathy for or understanding of others' lifestyles, problems, or deadlines.

Bottom line:

We do a huge disservice to our kids and society by protecting them from life.

Memory: You Must Remember This

Everyone complains of his memory, and no one complains of his judgment.

—*Duc Francois de la Rouchefoucauld*

In a book about critical thinking, why on earth would a chapter on memory be included? What does memory have to do with critical thinking? Memory is the storehouse for everything we know and it provides continuity of life. Memory can be incredibly, painfully detailed, yet very fragile. We can hold information in our brains for a lifetime, yet lose information we just learned if we don't rehearse it for a long enough period of time.

Please note that memorizing something and learning it are completely different animals. Each semester I confuse some students (as is my job . . .) when I state that one can earn an A in a course, yet not learn anything. How can this be? Don't people have to work to memorize facts, dates, theories, and formulas? Yes, but if you just memorize material and don't use the knowledge in your everyday life, then you haven't incorporated that knowledge into your personality and world view. If I take a biology exam and get an A, yet don't remember what I actually learned and I can't use the information to make decisions in my life, then all I've done is memorize a bunch of terms, spit them out on an exam, and promptly dump all that non-useful information into my brain's trash bin. People with photographic or eidetic memories need to be wary of this as well (Encyclopedia of Neuroscience, 2009b; Hunter, 1964). Many of these students I've encountered don't take notes—they don't need to—but they also tend not to read the assigned books and thus do not study and question the material in more depth. They show up to memorize and repeat information on an exam and they earn top grades. They tend to struggle when they need to write a paper and summarize the materials learned while adding their own thoughts and opinions.

There are many different types of memory: visual, auditory, gustatory (taste), olfactory (smell), kinesthetic (touch), and even muscle memory, which allows us to ride a bicycle 20 years after we last used one. These memories are scattered in different parts of our brain, so you may remember an example of one type of memory but not another, due to illness or injury, non-use, lack of emotional connection to the memory, or too much

81

emotional connection to the memory. (Bower, 1981; Codognet, 2012; Encyclopedia of Neuroscience, 2009a; Gilligan & Bower, 1984; Kensinger, 2007; Rimmele, 2012).

There are other factors that affect our memory, such as the intensity of stress, emotion, and discomfort (both psychological and physical). Even though eyewitness testimony makes for great drama on television law and crime shows, research has shown again and again that it is highly subject to error, with about 10,000 wrongful convictions occurring each year in the U.S. alone (Bidrose, 2000; Houston, 2013; Loftus, 1979, 1984).

We also experience **flashbulb memory**, which results in a strong, immediate retention of information involving emotional content. This is certainly connected to traumatic emotional events as well as strong positive occurrences. For example, those of you old enough to have lived through 9-11 would be able to tell another person exactly where you were and what you were doing when you heard the news

> **flashbulb memory—** Type of memory that results in a strong, immediate retention of information involving emotional content.

of the terrorist attacks on the east coast. My mother can tell you exactly what she was doing when she heard from my father that President John F. Kennedy had been shot. We can even remember specific details about what happened and what was said when we won a coveted award, or proposed marriage to our significant other. Whatever had great meaning to you, you will remember. A beloved (by you) celebrity's or athlete's or family member's death, a birth, the list goes on and on. It also helps that we have television and the internet to remind us 24/7 of particular events, complete with pictures, sounds, and gory details.

A further function of memory is something called **state-dependent learning**. This theory states that recall of information is best if learning and recall are done in the same place. This 'place' could be physical, physiological, emotional, or psychological. For example, if students are lectured to all semester in one classroom, then take their final exam in a different room, they are at risk of doing more poorly on the exam due to state-dependent learning (Bower, 1983; Schramke, 1997). Something as simple as tak-

> **state-dependent learning—**Recall of information is best if learning and recall are done in the same physical, physiological, emotional, or psychological "place."

ing an exam in a different room, or even in the same room but a different seat in a different part of the classroom can throw us off. Likewise, I advise my students not to start a new diet, terminate their consumption of caffeine, or stop smoking during the semester. The changes, though positive for one's health, throw off our internal homeostasis, or balance, and we need an adjustment period to regroup. Thus, important aspects of our lives such as concentration, motivation, memory, and sleep patterns are disrupted, which of course lead to difficulties in learning and studying. (Bower, 1983; Schramke, 1997).

As a personal example, you are reacting unconsciously to the idea of state-dependent learning when you arrive late to a class or meeting. Not only is everyone (you think) staring at you, but you quickly realize that someone is sitting in "your" seat and you need to find another one. Notice how uncomfortable you are when this happens. This is not just because you walked in late. Your psychological, emotional, and physical "states" have been disrupted.

Notice how I said "notice?" We don't think much about our memory or effects on it . . . until we lose it. Not until you walk out to the large parking lot where you left your car this morning and now can't seem to remember where you parked it as you're leaving work at 5:00 in the afternoon. Think about how you feel when you can't remember something: a person's name, where you left your keys, what you walked into the kitchen to retrieve. There is an instant feeling of frustration, followed by anxiety, confusion, or even fear. Sometimes we laugh at ourselves; sometimes we get irritated with others for interrupting our thought process, leading to forgetting (anyone with children knows this experience!). In order to connect memory to critical thinking, let's discuss and appreciate the mechanisms and processes of memory.

THREE PROCESSES OF MEMORY

First, there are three processes of memory that we need to be aware of. The first is encoding. **Encoding** helps us change information into a form that can be stored in memory, like typing a paper. This "form" needs to make sense to us, to mean something, in order to move to the next process, which is storage. **Storage** allows us to keep information in memory, like saving a file on your computer. If we can encode and store information appropriately, then we will be able to retrieve the information when necessary. **Retrieval** brings stored material to mind so we can use it when the need arises. So we can type the page (encoding), save the file on our computer (storage), and remember where the file is and what is in it (retrieval) when we need to print the page.

> **encoding**—Changing information into a form that can be stored in memory.

> **storage**—Keeping information in memory.

> **retrieval**—Ability to bring stored material to mind when needed.

At any point in this three step process, our computer could go awry. We may type the information on paper but not really pay attention to it, so we never make it meaningful and thus we never encode it. We may encode the knowledge but not store it in the right file, or only store part of the information. We may even follow through wonderfully on the first two steps and then forget where we put the information. Many things can interfere with these three processes, as we will see later.

THREE MEMORY SYSTEMS

As we acquire and store memories, we need to understand how and where the information is stored and why. We have three memory systems that allow us to sort and categorize our "files". The first of these systems is **sensory memory**. Sensory memory allows us to pay attention to everything we experience with our senses, but only lasts in memory for about 1-2 seconds. This is a good thing. Think about what you experience when you are walking in a fairly busy area, like a school campus, mall, or airport. You see, hear, smell and sometimes touch (hopefully you don't taste . . .) many different people in just a few minutes. If you are paying attention to where you are going and you are not on your cell phone, you will be able to tune into the ticker-tape of information going on in your brain during this time. For example: "Oh, that cologne smells nice;" "That blouse is too bright for her skin tone;" "I wish that man would stop yelling at whoever he's talking to on his cell phone!" By the time you pass by the fourth or fifth person, you won't remember what the nice cologne smelled like, even if you made a mental note to remember it and try to find it in a store. This can be frustrating, but if we took in all that information in such a short amount of time, processed (rehearsed) and stored it, we would have no memory space left for more important things, like where we were headed in the first place. We need that room for the next memory system, **short-term memory (STM)**.

> **sensory memory—** Includes everything we experience with our senses, but only lasts in memory for about 1-2 seconds.

Short term memory is also known as "working memory," because it is busy 24/7. That ticker-tape of information just described is your brain during working memory usage. It's what we are thinking about right now. You are reading this book, but you might also pause every so often in your thoughts and wonder what you will have for lunch today, anticipate a meeting this afternoon at work, or remember a funny story your grandfather told you a few weeks ago. Short term memory incorporates and accommodates sensory as well as long-term memory. However, STM can only hold 7 plus-or-minus 2 items of information at a time for 30 seconds without rehearsal. This is one of the reasons why we have 7-digit phone numbers; they're easier to remember. Years ago, when California (as well as the rest of the nation) was experiencing a dramatic increase in pager and cellular phone use, it was necessary to create more area codes in order to accommodate all the new phone numbers. Thus, the phone companies suggested that the length of phone numbers increase from 7 to 9 digits, so that they wouldn't have to keep generating and rearranging area codes. The public became very vocal, stating that 9 numbers were too many to remember. They were correct. Of course, now it's a moot point as we input

> **short-term memory—** Working memory; holds 7 plus-or-minus 2 items of information at a time for 30 seconds without rehearsal.

the information directly into our phones and memorize very few telephone numbers anymore.

You have noticed that when you are in the middle of memorizing information and you are interrupted, you will lose the information you are trying to encode. That's why we "chunk" information into groups, like items on a grocery list (e.g., peanut butter and jelly) in order to make the information meaningful and thus encoded and stored in memory. You also know from experience that when you are stressed or overloaded, you will also forget information being rehearsed during working memory. This is what happens when you have too many things to keep track of and so you forget why you walked into the kitchen. So, you walk out of the kitchen and walk back in, all the while talking to yourself about what you needed to do or get in the kitchen and hoping the thought will come back to you. College students suffer from overload, especially around mid-terms and finals when they have many demands for projects, papers, and exams. I view the brain as a pitcher that we keep pouring information into. When we are done with certain information, we empty the pitcher, at least a little, like pouring a glass of water. When we continue to pour information into the pitcher without taking any out, it spills over and information is lost.

If we are able to rehearse information for more than 30 seconds and we assign some personal meaning and connection to the material, we can then store the file in **long-term memory (LTM)**. Our LTM has unlimited capacity and is relatively permanent, depending on age, illness, or injury. All of our past knowledge, from how to ride a bike, to remembering a person long ago deceased, to yesterday's dinner are held in different parts of the brain. Because

> long-term memory—
> Has unlimited capacity and is relatively permanent.

short-term memory is so fleeting, it is the first to go when we suffer from diagnoses like dementia and Alzheimer's disease (Bayles, 2003; Borlikova, 2012; Huntley, 2010; Markowitz, 2001; Parra, 2009; Toepper, 2008). LTM bytes are not only scattered across the brain's surface, but also in the deeper recesses of brain tissue. Thus, a disease process has to be extremely advanced before we start forgetting the names and faces of our loved ones (Borlikova, 2012; MacLeod, 1988; Mitchell, 2006). This is also the reason why someone with Alzheimer's may not remember what happened ten minutes ago, but they can tell you, with great detail, a funny story that happened 40 years ago.

This doesn't mean that LTM is infallible. It is only as good as the information originally encoded. John F. Kennedy Jr. was constantly asked if he remembered saluting his father as JFK senior's casket passed by during his funeral procession in 1963. Junior admitted to Larry King in 1995: "I think that what happens is that you see an image so many times that you begin to believe you remember the image, but I am not sure I really do" (www.answers.com/topic/john-f-kennedy-jr#ixzz2MW7VSi8v).

THREE METHODS OF MEASURING MEMORY

Along with the three processes of memory that help us gather, store, and retrieve information, and three ways to categorize and store data, we must be able to measure the kind and number of memories we possess. Thus, we need to test ourselves or be tested in order to interpret how well our memory is functioning. There are three basic ways in which to do this (Zimbardo et. al, 2006). The first has to do with recall. This involves producing information from memory without any retrieval cues, such as on an essay test or during a job interview. You are given a question, and now you must rely solely on your memory, study skills, and experience to answer that question. Some people relish this, some hate it.

Another method of measuring memory involves recognition, in which we have to "recognize" familiar material. This occurs during a multiple-choice exam or when you are driving in a familiar area and rely on 'markers' for directions, such as the bank on the corner, versus having complete written directions. This is also in use when you can't remember the street names but you know where to turn and in which direction. Again, for some, this is easier, for others it is more difficult depending on whether you are a gist or verbatim learner (Gerkens, 2004; Song, 1997).

The third method of measuring memory is typically called relearning. This is akin to the statement, "Learning is easier the second time around." We relearn something when we study it again after not having used our knowledge for a period of time. For example, this is like taking a comprehensive examination in a course. You have already learned and studied the information once, and now, usually for the final exam, you must remember and use it again. You can also think about the time you tried an activity many years after first learning it, such as riding a bicycle. You might think to yourself, "Gosh, I haven't ridden a bike in 10 years! How am I going to do it again?" You begin with hesitation (or in trepidation!), wondering if you will be able to regain your balance, let alone whether you can still swing your leg over the bike to get onto it. You quickly realize that you CAN do it, and it doesn't take long to feel confident and comfortable. This is because you not only have mental memory; you possess muscle memory as well. Relearning really IS easier the second time around!

CAUSES OF FORGETTING

We forget all too soon the things we thought we could never forget.
—*Joan Didion*

Any discussion of memory must include its antithesis, forgetting. As we all know, forgetting information can be frustrating, humiliating, and at times even life-threatening. We forget for a variety of reasons, but the trick to remembering data involves two factors: (1.) Whether or not the subject matter is meaningful to us and (2.) Our level of stress and coping skills.

Hermann Ebbinghaus (1885/1962; Portraits of Pioneers in Psychology, 1991) conducted the first studies on learning and memory and recognized some remarkable insights about how we process information. Ebbinghaus created a large set of nonsense syllables, such as 'zuk', and compared learning of these with memorizing known words, such as 'cat'. He quickly noticed that subjects memorized information more easily when that information was meaningful vs. memorizing nonsense material. He further noted that practicing nonsense material over time led to more effective memorization than practicing in a single session, also described as relearning, which is what we do each time we study the same material. Thus, he discovered that humans memorize information more quickly and retain it longer when that information has meaning to the individual (Ebbinghaus, 1885/1962; Portraits of Pioneers in Psychology, 1991). In other words, if you don't care about the subject matter and can't relate it to your own life, you will have a much harder time remembering the information.

In addition, Ebbinghaus was the first to describe the learning curve, termed **the curve of forgetting** (See graph on page 88). This states that forgetting happens most rapidly right after learning occurs and then slows down over time (Ebbinghaus, 1885/1962; Craighead & Nemeroff, 2001). Again, this speaks to not only the information's meaning to the person, but also the need to study a subject over time, as we lose some information each time we engage in a study session.

> **curve of forgetting—**
> Forgetting happens most rapidly right after learning occurs and then slows down over time.

Lastly, Ebbinghaus (1885/1962) recognized the **serial position effect**, which states that we have a tendency to remember beginning and ending items in a list better than the middle items. This can refer to something as simple as a list of items read or heard, or more complex material, such as an exam covering notes from chapters 1 to 4, but having difficulty remembering information from chapters 2 and 3. I check this regularly to see how my students are doing with their study skills. More often than not, on a 50 question Scantron exam, students tend to do well in the first 5-10 questions and the last 5, but struggle with the items in the middle of the exam. The serial position effect demonstrates that memory depends on a number of factors. Let's explore these.

> **serial position effect—**
> Tendency to remember beginning and ending items in a list better than the middle items.

There are specific causes of forgetting, usually having to do with interference, stress (i.e. emotion), motivation, and priority. Keep Ebbinghaus' theories in mind as you peruse these (Myers, 2002):

Ebbinghaus' Curve of Forgetting

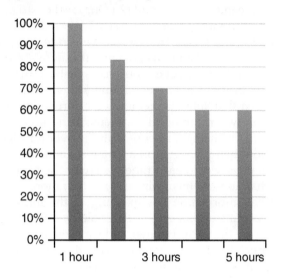

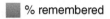 % remembered

Hermann Ebbinghaus:

· Meaningful material
  is remembered
  best/longest.

Curve of forgetting

· Largest amount of
  forgetting occurs
  quickly after study,
  then tapers off.

1. **Encoding Failure**—Information never entered long-term memory. You thought you studied long and hard, but perhaps you memorized a bunch of terms and that never really meant anything to you.

2. **Decay**—"Use it or lose it."

3. **Interference**—Competition between old and new material. Be careful when your old boyfriend and new boyfriend have the same first name. You will have a hard time remembering which "Sam" took you to Disneyland and the one you spent the weekend with . . . . This can also happen when you see that adorable gal at the party and get her phone number. You forgot your phone and you can't find a pen, so now you have to rely solely on your memory skills to memorize that contact number and get it into long term memory. But alas, you have smart-aleck (possibly envious) friends who continue to interrupt your incessant chanting and you fail to encode the number. People with children understand the concept of interference as well. I can't tell you how many times I have forgotten something while walking from the kitchen to my bedroom, due to being interrupted by a request from one of my kids!

4. **Motivated Forgetting—This kind of forgetting happens most often.** This occurs when we purposely forget painful memories, usually prefaced by the statement, "I don't want to talk about it anymore." Many people who have survived trauma and great emotional loss, as well as abuse victims (especially molestation victims) engage in motivated forgetting. The problem is that keeping secrets from yourself

comes back to bite you later in life. This is also referred to as repression and the 'payback' can come in the form of dreams/nightmares, physical illness, a history of failed and/or abusive relationships, or at the most inopportune moment a present experience will bring up past memories and emotions. Just the smell of a cologne or the sight of a certain automobile can bring the painful memories to the surface.

5. **Retrieval Failure**—Inability to remember information. You know you know it and it's on the tip of your tongue (as the saying goes), but you just can't retrieve the name, place, or number from memory. This could be due to decay, interference, or an emotion like anxiety. You met someone interesting at a networking luncheon an hour ago and spent 15 minutes chatting, yet you can't remember that person's name. How about, "You know, that actress . . . oh, what's her name?" I have a high school friend who loves to torture me with, "I saw so-and-so from high school and I can't remember his name." I can't rest until I know, so I stop what I'm doing, drag the yearbooks out, and start naming people, to which she replies "No, not him." Sometimes you win, sometimes you lose.

6. **Prospective Forgetting**—Forgetting to carry out an action. This is mostly influenced by motivation. Let's face it, we have all forgotten about an occasional dental appointment, a lunch date or meeting we really didn't want to attend. Ask yourself these questions: How often do you commit to things that you really don't wish to do? Are you hurting your physical health because you are trying to avoid the doctor's office? Are you avoiding responsibility, confrontation, conflict, or being put on-the-spot?

So how do we avoid memory loss? Practice! For years, teachers and researchers have pushed the same information. Here it is again. You can use these helpful hints not only for memorization and true learning at school, but also at work, for job interviews, and networking situations.

First, many of us have heard of the acronym SQ3R. This means survey, question, and the three r's—read, recite, and review. Skim the material you need to learn (notice how I did not say memorize!), then ask questions. What is this chapter about? What am I supposed to learn from this section of the report? Then go back and read the material, not necessarily all at once, recite out loud the information that is important and why, then continually review the materials in order to encode and truly learn/use the knowledge you studied. Over-learning the material helps too. Read/re-read/review until you are sick of it and you are actually thinking and dreaming about it. Space study over several sessions, as Ebbinghaus (1885/1962) and many others have recommended, and study for an exam or presentation for the last time right before you go to sleep. Remember, the less interference in your studying, the better and faster you will encode the information. If you study in the morning, then go to work, have a doctor's appointment, and finally take the exam or present a project, you are more likely to lose information from memory. Some people do well with a short review session before the exam or presentation, some do not. You must figure out what is best for you and your brain.

DISTRESS, EUSTRESS, WE ALL STRESS

The chief cause of stress is reality.

—Lily Tomlin

Last but certainly not least, we need to recognize and understand the power of emotion on our ability to make clear, rational decisions, as well as re-member important aspects of a person, place, or situation. Let's revisit and expand on the information about stress from chapter three.

Stress has been defined and re-defined many times, most famously by Dr. Hans Selye (1956). To reiterate, he claimed that stress was "the nonspecific response of the body to any demand made upon it" (Selye, 1974, p.14). Walt Schafer (1983p. 24) defined it this way: "A stressor is any demand on mind and body. Stress is arousal of mind and body in response to demands made upon it." Over the years these and many other researchers noted that stress affects both our bodies and our cognitive processes.

Before Selye, Walter Cannon (1932) studied what we call the stress reac-tion, or **fight-or-flight response**. Fight-or-flight comes into play when we are faced with an immedi-ate stressor. You physically and mentally prepare to either fight off the stressor (or attacker) or flee. This response is crucial for our survival, such as when we swerve to avoid an accident (or a squirrel) on the roadway or physically defend ourselves from an at-tacker. When our bodies go into fight-or-flight mode,

> **fight-or-flight response**—Physio-logical response that occurs when we are faced with an imme-diate stressor.

our bodies react the same way physiologically regardless of the type of stressor we experience (Pelletier, 1977; Selye, 1956, 1974). It happens whether we experience distress, "too great or too little arousal which is harmful to body or mind" (Schafer, 1983, p. 26); a negative reaction to a stressor, or eus-tress, "positive stress that contributes to health, satisfaction, and productiv-ity" (Schafer, 1983, p. 25); a positive reaction to a stressor. In other words, whether you have an angry confrontation with a co-worker or you just signed the dotted line on a mortgage loan for your first house, you will ex-perience the fight-or-flight response. The crucial factor is not necessarily what kind of stress we experience, but how we deal with it. Hence, it comes down to how much control we have—or believe we have—over our atti-tude, environment, emotions, and thought processes.

Either way, during any response to stress, Selye (1956, 1974) noted this reaction as a three-phase process, which he called the general adaptation syndrome or GAS. He noted that when we are confronted with a temporary stressor, our fight-or-flight system often works well, but with a repeated or prolonged stressor, our bodies eventually wear out and we become ill. In a nutshell, here are the phases of GAS (Schafer, 1983):

Phase 1—Alarm Reaction. Immediate reaction to a stressor, in which we exhibit the fight-or-flight" response. Can decrease effective functioning of the immune system, in turn making people more susceptible to illness.

Phase 2—Stage of Resistance. As the stressor continues, or as we are continually bombarded with new stressors at the same time and/or before resolving old stressors, we attempt to adapt to or resist the stressors. The body and mind adapt to the stressors and the level of stress hormones (e.g. cortisol) increase. We feel anxious and irritable, forget the smallest details of our everyday lives, and begin to procrastinate on getting our work done. If the stressor is too intense and continues for a long time, the body's "reserve" of energy and immune system functioning begin to break down, leading to the third and final phase.

Phase 3—Stage of Exhaustion. By the time one hits this stage, a stressor has been ongoing for quite some time. The body's (and mind's) resistance to stress is severely reduced either gradually or all at once, almost certainly leading to illness. This illness can range from a mild cold or flu to more serious, life-threatening conditions such as heart disease and cancer.

Sooo . . . .how does this general adaptation syndrome play out in real life? Glad you asked. For example, you are a college student beginning your first semester at the university. You are excited, overwhelmed, nervous, scared, ambivalent, happy—all signs of eustress. For the first few weeks of the semester you are in the alarm phase. You are adapting to college life, scheduling study time, beginning to meet course deadlines. After the first exam, you settle in a bit, getting more comfortable, but at the same time your deadlines for exams, projects, and papers seem to be coming due all at once, so you must rearrange your schedule and time spent on school, making you feel anxious, and "stressed." You can't juggle all these balls at once so you become forgetful and procrastinate until you are constantly under a quickly approaching deadline to finish your work. Congratulations, you are in the resistance phase! As you finally approach the end of the semester, you feel burned out, cynical, maybe even depressed and apathetic. You are more forgetful, tired of meeting deadlines, studying for exams, and just being a student. You might skip class more often than you did earlier in the semester, when you were a bright-eyed and bushy-tailed student starting a new course. You might party more, sleep longer, maybe even through your alarm. You are in the exhaustion phase. You barely get through finals and the day after they are over (or even during the week of finals) you crash. Everyone else is enjoying the winter holidays or summer break but you are in bed with a cold that turns into bronchitis, which then necessitates a trip to the doctor along with a strong dose of antibiotics. Sound like you?

Now, just for good measure and a true serving of reality, throw in family difficulties, conflict between scheduling for work and school, finances, and some personal issues dealing with a significant other. Oh yeah, a great concoction for illness!

If you are reading this and you are not a college student, plug in ever-changing stressors at work, with a spouse or significant other, children, extended family, financial matters, and personal health, just to name a few. With so many balls to juggle, it's a wonder we can remember our own name or get out of bed in the morning! Oh, but that's a stressor too. Remember, too much or too little of a good thing can hurt you. Moderation, delegation, and a good old-fashioned "NO" to new demands on your time and energy are key to success in managing stress. Do you now see the importance of the connection between critical thinking and stress? Going back to chapter one, critical thinkers need to know themselves, be comfortable with logic, emotion, and intuition, and be able to distinguish between relevant vs. irrelevant information when making decisions. When we make a small slight from a stranger the most relevant part of our day, we create our own stress. If you are aware of your thoughts, emotions, biases, and beliefs, you can decrease your stress immensely and improve your overall health by leaps and bounds. Remember this too: "The quality of your life is determined by the quality of your decisions, and the quality of your decisions is determined by the quality of your thoughts (Schick & Vaughn, 2014, p. 13). Breaking down the middle man, the quality of your life is ultimately determined by the quality of your thoughts.

Learning and Decision-Making

We are all educators. What will you teach?

—*Lisa Weisman-Davlantes*

There are many definitions of learning, but here is my favorite: Learning is any relatively durable change in behavior or acquired knowledge that is due to experience (Weiten, 2008). It reflects our adaptation or ability to adjust to the environment. We acquire new behavior or change old behavior as a result of experience. Learning shapes our personal habits, preferences, and emotional responses, and personality traits (Weiten, 2008). We gain knowledge about ourselves and the world using many different modalities: We sit in classrooms and listen to lectures, read books, seek information on the Internet, engage in conversations (or text messaging) with others, observe our own and others' behavior, and use trial-and-error in order to make decisions every day of our lives. You are always learning something, whether you realize it or not. What is crucial as an effective thinker/decision-maker is being aware of what you have learned and how you have learned it. It is infinitely easier to learn something than to "unlearn" it, or change. This is one reason why old habits are hard to break. This can incorporate anything from our attempts to quit smoking to thinking in a more positive fashion. If you are afraid of something, can you learn to be unafraid? Yes, but only through sustained time and effort. Do you pay more attention to negative or positive comments aimed at you? For many people, it is much more difficult to let go of negative comments, especially if they have learned that they are undeserving of praise. We tend to view the negative comments as true, reinforcing earlier learning that we are unworthy of love and acceptance. More about reinforcement later.

You may have heard the saying that one can be the best teacher, doctor, therapist, etc. in the world, but if a student, patient or client is not open to learning, he will not learn. This is always true. How many times have you dismissed a teacher's information in a lecture, or the doctor's or therapist's suggestions on how to improve your life? "That doctor is a quack! He doesn't know what he's talking about!" "The instructor isn't teaching me anything I don't already know." "My boss is clueless about how to run a company!" Statements like these demonstrate that you are not open to learning. You are not willing to listen to someone else's ideas or suggestions. Sometimes this is because they ARE telling us what we already know, or they don't have correct or adequate information, but more often than not, our pride and fear of the unknown interfere with accepting new information. Engagement in honest self-exploration is needed to decide whether to accept new ideas, which may or may not be beneficial to you. Let's just say that if you often feel like authority figures don't meet your standards for learning, you are more than likely closed off. I had a friend who expressed interest in earning a college degree, but he repeatedly stated that he didn't think the professors would have anything valuable to teach him. Subsequently, this person is stuck in a dead-end job, still scraping for enough money each month in order to make ends meet.

At the end of every semester, students are encouraged to complete an online questionnaire regarding their college courses, instructional materials, and of course, the professor's classroom style. Students even have their own website, called www.ratemyprofessors.com, which allows them to report their classroom experiences to future attendees. Ever since I began teaching a critical thinking course, without fail, there is at least one entry per semester that goes something like this: "While I enjoyed Dr. Weisman-Davlantes' teaching style, she really didn't teach me anything I didn't already know. Most of what she talks about is common sense. I really didn't learn very much from her." Wow! I'm impressed. I wish I had known everything there is to know at 18 years of age!

I have been working in the field of psychology since 1985 and teaching since 1995 and I learn something new every semester. While preparing and presenting for each class, the simple task of re-reading books and lecture materials reveals new knowledge that changes my thoughts, feelings, and behaviors. I gain new insights from the psychological principles I teach over and over, as well as from my ongoing interaction with students and the world at large. I am open to the possibility that maybe, just maybe, I don't have all the answers, even after so many years of experience and study. This does not mean that being open to new ideas necessarily leads to greater growth and better decision-making, but it certainly is what opens the door to those possibilities.

Many of us are afraid of the unknown. Being afraid is a human trait that needs to be overcome time and again if we are to grow individually and as a society. Our fear keeps us from seeking or listening to new information, or subject matter that rails against what we believe. We remain ignorant about a topic, then continue to utilize what little we know about it to make decisions about certain people and what we (and they) believe. A lack of information will usually lead to stereotyping. We mentally place others in nice, neat categories ("boxes"), or actually dislike them due to a limited amount of knowledge about them. A simple rule of thumb for avoiding stereotyping or categorization of others is if you don't know about someone or something, ASK! When our children are curious about others, we shush them if we are uncomfortable with the subject matter. "Mommy, why is that man in a wheelchair?" Mommy replies, "I don't know honey, but leave him alone." Why not ask? You might learn something—and give some needed support or attention to the disabled person.

Growing up and being one of a handful of Jewish families in our school district (and in our city), I experienced this lack of knowledge (i.e. ignorance) first-hand. "Oh, you're Jewish? You hate Jesus." "You killed Jesus." "You eat fish with the eyes still in them." "You don't believe in God." "God doesn't hear your prayers." "You don't celebrate Thanksgiving." I am so thrilled when someone is curious and asks about my heritage, instead of just assuming they know about it. How about a more controversial topic, like the origins of homosexuality? I hear the same mantra from those who have little information about the development of sexual orientation: "It's a sin." "They're homosexual because they were abused as kids." "It's a choice." "They shouldn't marry or raise children because they'll ruin the institutions of marriage and family." Why not challenge yourself and find out if these beliefs are true? Look up the information, talk to homosexuals, seek knowledge from both sides of the argument, not just from your viewpoint. There are no definitive scientific answers . . . yet, but many religious people won't take the time to study both sides of the research. They'll tell you that homosexuality goes against God and leave it at that. This is a good way to end the conversation (who's going to question God?), and an excuse to look no further for the truth. Why don't more people explore this or other controversial, uncomfortable topics and get to the truth? The answer is fear. Critical thinking's bottom line is to find out the truth. Truth = fact. Many people are afraid to seek the truth because they know they may have to change their beliefs when they realize that what they have accepted as true their whole lives may not be accurate. If they obtain new information and don't change their beliefs, they will experience **cognitive dissonance**, a psychological term to describe one's mental processes and feelings when information or behavior conflict with long-standing viewpoints. When opinions and actions are inconsistent, when they contradict each other, it leads to psychological and emotional discomfort (i.e. stress) which in turn can result in headaches, stomach aches, and other bodily discomfort until we either change our attitude or behavior.

> cognitive dissonance—When beliefs and behavior contradict each other, it leads to psychological and emotional discomfort. Conflict is reduced by changing thinking to fit behavior.

If we are too uncomfortable and fearful, we can alternatively sink into denial and force ourselves to stop thinking about the conflicting ideas and beliefs altogether. This only works for so long before we are uncomfortable once again, or have chronic discomfort and don't know why. Experiencing distress can lead to attempts to discover the causes of our troubles, so if we don't pay attention to our pain, physical or emotional, our misery and inability to move forward continue.

In psychology, there are three basic forms of learning:

1. Classical Conditioning
2. Operant Conditioning
3. Observational Learning

Let's explore and apply each of these theories briefly, and how they affect and are affected by critical thinking skills. If you would like to study any of these theories in depth, you can read any Introductory Psychology textbook or the works of the researchers discussed.

CLASSICAL CONDITIONING

Classical Conditioning (CC) is most associated with researcher Ivan Pavlov (1849–1936), a Russian physiologist who was awarded a Nobel Prize for his work on the digestive system (Fancher, 1979; Kimble, 1991). His experiments on salivation using dogs as subjects serendipitously led to his lifelong work studying the characteristics and effects of classical conditioning (Zimbardo, et. at, 2006).

Many years of research have shown that CC has a powerful effect on attitudes, emotions, likes/dislikes, and beliefs. Even marketers use it to shape consumer behavior so that we will be more likely to purchase their products. CC begins with a reflex—an involuntary response (R) to a stimulus (S). For example, the dreaded machine at the eye doctor's office that shoots out a quick blast of air into your eye, making you blink. Blowing air into your eye automatically leads to blinking, and you sometimes start to blink even before the event happens. You cannot control whether or not you blink, but you learn to be wary of that machine each time you go to the optometrist. You have been classically conditioned to expect your reaction to the machine.

There are two kinds of reflexes associated with Classical Conditioning:

1. Conditioned (Learned)
2. Unconditioned (Unlearned or Automatic)

Pavlov and his associates originally set out to study the salivation and digestive systems of dogs. They hooked a small tube up to the dog's mouth to catch saliva produced in response to food. As the experiments proceeded, Pavlov noted an interesting occurrence. The dog would begin to salivate before the introduction of food. He would also salivate at the mere sight or footsteps of the assistant who typically fed the animal. Pavlov's study then turned to investigating the dog's salivation (unconditioned response, or UCR) to food (unconditioned stimulus, or UCS). The presence of food led to salivation, shown as follows:

Food (UCS) → Salivation (UCR)

Pavlov then wondered if the dog could learn (be conditioned) to salivate to other things besides food. Could the dog be taught to use a reflex or involuntary action (salivation) to respond to new stimuli? Can something that happens naturally be trained to occur? Pavlov and company then presented a neutral stimulus, such as a bell or tone, before presenting the food. A researcher would ring a bell and bring food to the dog. Then the dog would salivate. Clinically, it looked like this:

Bell → Food → Salivation

After a number of trials, or repeated pairings of the bell and the food, the dog learned to associate the bell with food. He learned that the ringing of the bell signaled that dinner would follow. When the bell pealed, the dog salivated. Then the food was presented. The clinical equation changed to:

Bell → Salivation → Food

Thus, the dog *learned* to salivate when he heard the bell. A reflexive action was now considered a learned response. In clinical terms, salivation became a conditioned response (CR) to a conditioned stimulus (CS), the bell.

Bell (CS) → Salivation (CR)

This is the same learning mechanism that incites fits of happiness from your pet when it hears the can opener, thinking that it signals feeding time.

As the study continued, new questions arose regarding what else could be learned or influenced utilizing the technique of making an involuntary response a conditioned one.If the dog could salivate to a bell, would he also drool in response to a different kind of bell or sound? Pavlov and his colleagues decided to test this hypothesis and found two interesting conditions affected by CC. First, there is **stimulus generalization** (aka generalization). When we generalize a response, it means that we respond the same way to similar stimuli. For example, the dog might salivate to a bell, a doorbell, a beep, etc. The dog's response may not be as strong as to the original stimulus, but

> **stimulus generalization**—Responding the same way to similar stimuli.

it still is applying old reflexes to new, slightly variant situations (Zimbardo, et. al, 2006).

By now you might be asking, "What does this have to do with critical thinking?" Good question! We generalize our responses as well. For example, one of my relatives was bitten by a dog when he was a toddler. He became fearful of that particular dog. As time went on, he learned to be afraid of all dogs. If you are rejected in one relationship after another, you might generalize that pain comes with all intimate relationships. This is the old, "That's it; I'm done with men/women because I can't trust them." Can we prevent generalization from happening? Yes, with early intervention. When my family member was bitten by the dog, someone needed to intervene, to make him comfortable with dogs again. They should have explored why he was bitten in the first place. If you can replace your fear with feelings of control and comfort, anxiety decreases and generalization does not occur. You might continue to be wary of dogs from now on, but you won't avoid them due to an irrational fear. The old saying about falling off a horse and getting right back on applies here . . .

The second style of thought affected by CC is termed **discrimination**. This refers to our ability to distinguish between similar stimuli. Pavlov could have taught the dog to salivate only to one kind of bell, instead of many different sounds. This ability to discriminate is important to our everyday lives

> **discrimination—** Ability to distinguish between similar stimuli.

in subtle ways. Say you're driving a car and you come upon a traffic signal. One of the reasons you know the difference between a red or green stoplight is because of your ability to discriminate between the lights. You learned long before you got behind the wheel that red means stop, green means go, yellow means stop or hurry up. This kind of information is something you take for granted until the environment changes. For example, when you are driving in areas where it snows during the year, stoplights tend to be horizontal instead of vertical. If you are used to a row of vertical lights, horizontal ones will make you take notice and think about what you need to do. This phenomenon is also due to **habituation**, or decrease in the response to a stimulus that occurs after repeated presentation of the same stimulus (Feldman, 2007). When you first get directions to a friend's house, you need to pay close attention to the instructions; make a left at Main, then a right at Lincoln, etc. After being exposed to the same direction of travel over time, you

> **habituation—Decrease** in the response to a stimulus that occurs after repeated presentation of the same stimulus.

will forget the street names and just drive to your destination. Of course, you won't be able to tell anyone else how to get there because most likely you won't remember the street names. How about trying to explain an office procedure to the new hire at work? You've been performing the actions out of habit for so long that you have difficulty verbalizing the necessary steps. You finally give up out of frustration and say, "Just watch what I do."

Getting back to Pavlov and the dog, the experimenters were also curious about terminating the new learned responses. What if they rang the bell and neglected to present the food? Here's what this would look like:

Bell − Food = No Salivation

Again, after a period of trials, the dog's brain will realize that he's wasting all that delicious drool for nothing and stop salivating to the sound of the bell. So, in scientific terms, the conditioned response (CR)—the salivation to the bell—ends. This process is called **extinction**. After extinguishing salivation to the bell, would the dog then remember and respond to the

> **extinction—Termination** of response to a stimulus.

pairing of the bell and food once again? Yes indeedy! This is called **sponta-neous recovery**. After extinguishing a response, it takes fewer pairings of a past-learned stimulus and response pairing to bring back the behavior. For example, say you haven't ridden a bicycle since you were 12 years old and now you are 30. You decide that you want to ride with your kids but think you

> **spontaneous recovery**—Reproducing an extinguished response.

can no longer do so because you haven't ridden in years. You borrow your neighbor's bike, feeling very wobbly and insecure for a short time before you become comfortable once again. You learned how to sit, balance, start and stop the bike when you were a kid and now it's all coming back to you. You have spontaneous recovery of mental memory and muscle memory as well.

How else does CC affect you in real-life? First, every time you turn on the television, check a search engine on the Internet, drive down the highway, or read a magazine, you are exposed to advertising. Advertisers attempt to pair neutral cues (attractive or well-known people, events, and locations) with their products. When beer is being advertised, what kind of people are typically in the commercial? Girls. Very pretty, thin girls. The typical American standard. We all know the message: drink this beer, get the girl. Sex sells. More on advertising and effects on critical thinking later.

Another type of event that involves classical conditioning is an auto accident. Even if you were involved in a fender-bender where no one was injured, and whether you were driving or not, you will remember the site of the accident; well, at least your brain and body will. As you get closer to the scene of the accident, you might begin to feel nervous. You will either reflexively hold your breath briefly or inhale deeply—maybe hold it just a little longer than usual—and then release a quiet sigh as you pass the point of impact. During this short experience and typically unbeknownst to your conscious mind, your body and brain move into a fight-or-flight mode. This is part of the stress response we discussed earlier. During fight-or-flight reactions your blood pressure, heart rate and breathing increase when possible threats to physical or emotional safety are present. Adrenaline, cortisol, and other hormones are released in your body as you prepare to either fight (or verbally confront someone) or run away. When the threat is over, bodily functions return to normal as the danger passes. You might even feel a bit nauseous as the excess hormones are "put away" by the body, to use next time they are needed.

Here's another scenario. You are standing in line to enter the movie theater when you smell the cologne that your ex used to wear. Your first sensation might be panic. "Oh no, I hope that's not him!" Of course, depending on your past relationship, your feelings could vary from panic to anger to embarrassment . . . or all of the above. When you finally get the nerve to turn around and realize it's not him, the fight-or-flight mode ends and you sigh as your physiological functions return to normal.

Taste aversions also involve classical conditioning, but in a much faster way than usual. You snack on some cookies a few hours after dinner. Later that evening, your body decides it doesn't like the cookies and you vomit. Maybe you're sick for a few days, lucky you. Even though you intellectually know that the cookies were most likely not the cause of becoming ill, you will steer clear of those cookies (and maybe cookies

taste aversion— Learning to avoid a certain food if eating it was followed by illness.

in general = generalization) for a long time, if not forever, due to your emotional response to getting sick. Fears and phobias tend to begin in similar ways. You have one bad experience with a bug, heights, water, etc., or you see someone you care about have strong negative reactions to something, and you learn to be afraid too. Finally, the emotional responses and flood of memories we have in regard to songs, the smell or mention of certain foods, people's names, thinking about Christmas, etc. all involve conditioned responses to conditioned stimuli. We learn to respond in certain ways to certain people, places, objects, and events.

OPERANT CONDITIONING

Moving on to the next learning theory, Operant Conditioning was the brainchild of B.F. Skinner (1953), a strict behaviorist who believed our behavior was determined by the environment and always shaped and influenced by others. Skinner (and behaviorists in general) was not interested in studying people's thoughts, feelings, or childhood issues. He focused on here-and-now actions and how they shaped future behavior.

Operant Conditioning (the original "OC"), conditions or shapes voluntary responses. Skinner noted that we behave to either earn a reward or avoid punishment. Clinically, it looks like this:

R → consequence → reinforcement/modification of behavior

Reinforcement, or a reinforcer, is anything that strengthens or increases the probability of a response. It encourages behavior to continue. There are two kinds of reinforcers:

1. Positive reinforcer—A response is followed by a reward; money, praise, good grades, a promotion, etc.
2. Negative reinforcer—A response is followed by the end of discomfort.

Behavior is influenced by the termination or avoidance of a negative or unpleasant condition. For example, you have a headache, take an aspirin, and the headache goes away. The aspirin is a negative reinforcer—it takes away the headache. You will use it again next time you have a headache, so the aspirin increases the probability that you will use it again next time you are in pain. This is also why we use specific brands to feel better. Have you ever been in a room when someone is asking for say, Motrin? One person volunteers Tylenol, another offers Aleve. The requestor might turn down the other medications because they aren't the same as the one that has worked for that person before. Highlighting this issue even further, a few years ago there was an Excedrin commercial on television with the actress turning to the camera and stating, "I use it because it works."

The problem with negative reinforcers is that while they can decrease or end our discomfort for a short time, they can also harm us. We smoke, overeat (or under-eat), seek comfort food, work too many hours, sleep too long, or drink too much, in order to terminate or avoid stress. People who party on the weekends (and sometimes during the week!) are using alcohol, drugs, and even sex to cope with stress. These all become negative reinforcers. They make you feel good for a short period of time and increase the probability that you will use them again. This obviously prevents us from seeking healthier, longer-term solutions to our problems and can lead to addiction and various physical diseases. Chatting on cell phones and texting seem to belong in this circle of reinforcement as well. We get rewarded by friends' quick responses, and we use this technology to take care of our anxiety when we are alone, instead of socializing with strangers.

The next issue of concern regarding OC is punishment. Punishment is the opposite of reinforcement; it lowers the probability of a response. It discourages behavior from occurring.

R → negative consequence

Punishment hurts, emotionally, physically, or both. A negative is added, such as a spank or being yelled at, or a positive is taken away, like a parent's attention or TV. There are advantages and disadvantages of punishment. Some advantages can be that the child is sufficiently embarrassed enough not to repeat the behavior, or quickly realizes that the parent means business and will follow through with whatever consequence is threatened. Also, punishment helps us all deal with natural consequences. When you break the rules, you typically get caught. When you lie or cheat, people don't trust you. When you repeatedly attend meetings at work unprepared, others will avoid working with you on future projects. Some disadvantages to punishment include the following:

1. It may not end negative behavior; it temporarily suppresses it.
2. It doesn't help to develop more appropriate behavior.
3. It can lead to anger, aggression, hostility and resentment.

Punishment works best when it is reasonable based on the offense and when the guilty party has an opportunity to make amends for the wrongdoing committed. For example, when someone gets a DUI, that person should not only be assessed for alcoholism, but ought to be required to complete some community service in order to make amends. Paying restitution to victims is a powerful tool as well. When a child hits a baseball through a neighbor's window, he should work (preferably for the neighbor) to pay back the money spent on repairs. I remember when kids who played with matches were taken down to the fire station to talk with a uniformed firefighter about the dangers of fire. These "old-fashioned" ways of meting out punishment still work well today. Unfortunately, parents today feel the constant strain of being too busy and tend to overprotect their children from feeling bad about themselves. They will quickly pay for any damage done or actually shrug off the incidents as normal childhood activities and let their kids (and themselves) off the hook, emotionally and financially. These kids then grow up to be employees or managers who make excuses for their poor performance or blame others for company failures.

When my son had a temper tantrum in a hardware store years ago, I asked my husband to continue shopping. I quietly scooped my boy up in my arms and carried him, kicking and screaming, out to the car where I promptly put him in his car seat. His punishment was twofold: 1. He left the store and didn't get to manipulate Daddy's time; and 2. He got no attention from me as I sat with my back to him in the car while he cried. There's a saying that a clown will stop performing if he doesn't have an audience; it's the same with screaming children or verbally obnoxious co-workers. The problem is, some kids (and obnoxious co-workers!) can continue screaming for a very long time, and parents can't give in to their desires—not one little bit. Picture the child in the grocery store crying for candy while standing in the checkout line. The mother is tired from lack of sleep and this little one has been in a cranky mood since he woke up at 6:00 this morning. He screams and cries for the candy after his mother denies it, and she is becoming increasingly embarrassed as others in line watch this scene. Her head is throbbing too, and she can't wait to get home so she can take something for the pain. After the third shrill cry for candy, she angrily grabs the package and puts it on the conveyor belt while snarling, "Here! Stop crying!" She's not necessarily an ineffective mother, but she has allowed the child to "win" this one, and just taught him how to scream to get what he wants. This is part of the recipe of making a spoiled brat. Instead of punishing him for his inappropriate behavior—the tantrum- she rewarded his outburst with candy.

OBSERVATIONAL LEARNING

Our final theory of learning belongs greatly to Albert Bandura (1963, 1986). He noted that we learn by watching others and paying attention to the consequences of their behavior. This is referred to as Observational Learning, also known as modeling. This is the origin of the understanding that whether we like it or not, we are all role models, 24/7/365. We watch others—family, friends, colleagues, supervisors, strangers, celebrities—to determine how to respond in social situations. This is called **social referencing**. Those of you

social referencing— Watching others to determine how to respond in social situations.

with older siblings can attest to this. When big sister got in trouble with Mom and Dad, whether you realized it or not, you made a mental note NOT to engage in the same behavior, or at least not to get caught doing it . . .

Bandura and his colleagues did some pioneering work in the 1960s regarding how children are influenced by exposure to aggression, especially TV and movie violence (Bandura, Ross and Ross, 1961) In a study termed the Bobo Doll experiment, researchers hypothesized that children exposed to aggressive adult role models would respond in a similar way. His subjects were 36 boys and 36 girls ranging in age from 3-6 years old. Each group of children was tested alone, either with or without the adult role model in the room. The first group of children observed an adult in the same room with many toys to choose from, hitting a Bobo doll, a large blow-up toy with a sand-filled bottom that bounces back up when hit. The adult used hands, feet, and a mallet to hit the doll in the presence of the child. The second group observed the adult ignoring the Bobo doll and choosing other toys. The third group was exposed to a room full of toys, including Bobo, and no adult role model. One of the most important—and still controversial—outcomes of the study was a strong correlation that kids will model the aggression they see performed by others. Basically, monkey see, monkey do. This study had great implications for further questioning and research regarding violence in the home (Osofsky, 1995; Evans, 2004), negative effects on children in regard to filmed television and movie violence (Bandura, Ross and Ross, 1963; Johnson, Cohen, Smailes, Kasen & Brook, 2002), as well as later studies on the aggressive consequences of musical lyrics (Anderson, Carnagey, & Eubanks, 2003) and video gaming (Anderson, Funk & Griffiths, 2004; Bushman & Anderson, 2002).

We all know that children are sponges. They soak up information quickly and are aware of much more than we give them credit for. We don't pay attention to these details until we spew profanities while driving, only to hear a few minutes later the same words and tone of voice coming from our adorable toddler in the back seat! As we get older and more experienced in the world, we continue to look to others, sometimes to figure out what is appropriate behavior with new people in novel situations, determine a person's or culture's **display rules** (norms that regulate what is deemed to be appropriate expression of emotion), or to judge what we see as inappropriate, even dangerous.

> **display rules**—Social or cultural norms that regulate what is deemed to be appropriate expression of emotion.

CC, OC, AND OL: A MARRIAGE OF NECESSITY

As you have perused this section on the different types of learning, you might have noticed that classical conditioning, operant conditioning, and observational learning tend to interconnect, making it difficult to determine which kind of learning is taking place at a given time. Bandura (1977, 1986) tends to view the three styles as intertwined, believing that classical and operant conditioning can occur inadvertently through observational learning (Weiten, 2008). When I attempt to separate which type of learning is occurring, I focus on the following:

Classical conditioning = the emotional connection
Operant conditioning = the behavior taking place
Observational learning = our cognitive processes

Let's consider this situation as an example:

A six-year old girl is afraid of spiders. How did this fear become established? One day when she was four, she was playing outside when she noticed a small spider. Curious, she decided to touch the spider to see how it felt and what it would do. As her fingers got closer to the specimen, her mother chastised her, exclaiming, "Don't touch that spider! He could bite you!" Being a typical toddler, the child decided to touch the spider anyway, resulting in a spanking from her mother. Later that day, her older sister saw a spider in the bathroom and started to scream. Which type of learning is responsible for her present fear of arachnids? All of the above. A strong emotional reaction from her mother was followed by punishment for the girl's curiosity and lack of fear, followed by observing her sister's negative reaction to another spider.

As you can see, it's nearly impossible to completely separate our emotions from our actions and from our thoughts, but the effective critical thinker understands the value of these processes in goal-setting, planning, and decision-making, and more importantly, that we can and must continue learning and growing throughout our lives.

Part II
Analyzing Critical Thought in the Real World

Higher Education and its Effects on Critical Thinking

> If the purpose for learning is to score well on a test, we've lost sight of the real reason for learning.
>
> —*Jeannie Fulbright*

What is the value of a college education? This is a valid question that is continually being asked due to the increasing costs of a 2 or 4-year commitment, as well as graduate school. Plus, in the last few years the job market has not assisted college graduates in landing employment within their field of study. Let's be clear on one thing before this section continues: There was never any guarantee, for any generation, of a good-paying job in one's area of study immediately after graduation. There are some fields where jobs are plentiful and pay handsomely. However, information about specialties with numerous available positions change rapidly as our technology oriented society demands constant modification and growth.

So, what is the REAL value of higher education if it isn't necessarily monetary reward? The completion of a college or graduate degree should help you refine your social skills, as well as your ability to delay gratification and thus commit to something outside yourself that includes hard work and perseverance. It should assist you in becoming a citizen of the world; one who understands their own and others' cultures, embraces diversity, and learns how to effectively conduct business and communicate with those who are different from us. Higher education should also hone your critical thinking skills. Your beliefs, opinions, thoughts, emotions, and actions should be confronted to the point where you become more open-minded about challenges or problems, and how to resolve these issues as a mature, responsible adult.

Please note that throughout the previous paragraph I used the word "should." Unfortunately, not everyone who graduates college or earns a graduate degree is necessarily a great critical thinker. It takes constant effort, including practice and making lots of mistakes, to change how you think. Many students (and their education-paying parents) focus on getting the grades and getting out. They aren't interested in changing the way they view the world or getting to know themselves. They see college as a means to an end and they want to graduate as quickly as possible. If they do get involved on campus, it may only be to have resume filler. You can have a fantastic resume with all kinds of experience, but if you have poor social skills and can't work well with others, you aren't going to get the job, period (Trunk, 2006). We will talk more about these "soft skills" in chapter 15.

I mentioned earlier in the book that getting an A in a class does not mean that you learned anything. Learning involves making the material meaningful to you and your life, plus being open to changing your perspective to allow new information to be utilized. Learning involves constant adaptation. Memorizing a bunch of definitions or theories and then answering questions correctly on exams does not indicate learning. It shows how well you studied. When you can actually use the information memorized in real life, THAT is evidence of learning. It stays with you; you don't forget about the knowledge 10 minutes after completing the examination. If you want to be considered a great thinker, you should never stop learning. College isn't necessary or important for everyone but learning is. Some of the people in my life that I respect the most are not highly, formally educated, but they are lifelong observers and open to learning about themselves, others, and changing their way of thinking.

Along with the stated benefits of higher education, three other features come into play as well. These are the abilities to question authority and make our own decisions, becoming less judgmental and more objective, and finding a purpose for your life on Earth.

QUESTIONING AUTHORITY

> The important thing is to not stop questioning.
> —*Albert Einstein*

Let me begin this section by stating that questioning authority does not include written or verbal attacks on someone's ideas, character, or beliefs. It doesn't mean attempting to beat down long-standing theories in order to feel superior. It doesn't involve ridiculing or humiliating authority figures in regard to their rules and regulations. Questioning does not mean that you have to or that you are allowed to persuade or bully someone into changing their mind. Questioning authority—whether people or long-standing ideas—simply means to ask questions. What is this about? Why is it considered good or bad? When did this rule or regulation come to be and why? How do I change this? Is this what I believe?

Sometimes my first-year students interpret this questioning attitude as broad permission to act in an arrogant way towards their parents, friends, employers, and yes . . . professors. They believe that they are allowed to challenge anyone, anything, and at any time, and that should be alright because they are practicing appropriate critical thinking skills. They also tend to believe that their questioning should lead to immediate changes in someone else's point of view or personal or professional policies.

As we will discuss in the chapter on communication skills, it's not what you ask (or say), it's how you ask it. Pay attention to how you ask your questions. What emotion are you experiencing and what tone of voice are you using? If you are frustrated, irritated, or angry, your voice might contain a tone of condescending sarcasm. Observe the other person's facial expression and body language, and really listen to their tone of voice in response. You may not intend to be condescending or sarcastic, or think that you are, but the other person's response will tell you otherwise. Don't blame or accuse that person of being defensive before you've truly examined your own underlying motivation, emotion, and verbal delivery.

There can be other difficulties encountered in terms of questioning authority, or just questioning in general. First, no one really enjoys having their beliefs, opinions and behavior scrutinized, so be gentle, especially if you catch someone making a mistake. Treat that person the way you would like to be treated. Second, if you are genuinely coming from a place of confusion or curiosity and your goal is to learn—not chastise, teach, or correct—then your question will more likely be met with the reciprocal goal of teaching or clarifying information.

Another roadblock for many in questioning respectfully may be due to our childhood experience. Did you grow up in a family where it was okay to question your parents or other adults? If so, what were the conversations like? What emotions prevailed? Conversely, you may not have been allowed to question authority, which included anyone older than you. You might have been taught to go with the flow, don't rock the boat. You may now believe that calling attention to someone's mistakes would be considered disrespectful, even when those mistakes could cost you or someone else dearly.

You will have to find or create your own middle ground here, but understand this: There are times when questioning is inappropriate. If you are constantly challenging or correcting your boss or an instructor and interrupting the flow of business meetings or class lectures, then you have some personal issues to work out. The first issue being a bad case of egocentrism. No one likes a know-it-all or attention hog and no one enjoys being publicly humiliated. If you have more than a few questions, meet with the person in private and don't argue about their answers. Know when to question as well as when to be quiet.

I once had a student who didn't like my grading policies. He respectfully asked about the motivation behind my regulations and agreed to disagree. If only he'd left it at that; as the course wore on, he rallied some other students until one day he announced in class that they would like to argue the point. He had all the skills and manipulation of a great attorney, but my classroom was not the place for him to begin his law practice. Let's just say that he and his small group of malcontents got a forceful mini-lecture on learning to deal with policies they disagreed with. Basically, they had a choice. They saw the syllabus the first day of class and could have chosen to drop my course. The way he handled the situation felt like a mutiny. He also tried to control me and our class time by attempting to bully me into submission in front of the larger group. The moral of the story here is that if you don't like the answers you receive to your questions, choose to either live with the situation or move on. It is extremely arrogant to dictate how the boss should run his/her business, how your family or friends should live their lives, or how your professors should conduct their classes.

What I am trying to teach here is how to use questions to help you become a more effective critical thinker. You will also learn more about yourself, others, and the world and make more informed decisions. Not everything you read or hear is accurate, so find out if it is. Do some research on the Internet, in an actual library with books and journals, or speak to experts you respect. When someone makes an outrageous statement, ask where they got the information. When salespeople try to sell you something, especially when that something wasn't on your "to buy" list, ask a multitude of questions. Don't stop questioning until you are completely satisfied or until you fully understand what you are buying or the contract you are signing.

When parents, teachers, doctors, attorneys, religious leaders, and political figures tell you something, walk away and think about what was relayed. Does the information make sense to you? Do you agree with it? What is your intuition, or gut reaction, telling you? Does it feel like something is missing? You don't necessarily have to question the person outright; quietly fact-check on your own. You won't have the time or inclination to question everything, but pick and choose what is most important to you. Do you know someone who always seems to have all the answers? Question and fact-check their pronouncements. When someone starts quoting evidence from articles they read on Yahoo, I question and fact-check. And just because someone has a lot of prestigious credentials doesn't mean they are always correct or even aware of the latest trends in their field. They are human, they are busy, and they make mistakes too.

Furthermore, be prepared to have your own decisions, beliefs, and emotions questioned. Have answers based on logic, fact, and personal experience. Be open to listening to others' concerns and curiosity about your decisions without feeling defensive. Answer as many questions as you feel comfortable with, then end the discussion. If you are feeling uncomfortable when questioned, it could be the way you are approached: the tone of voice of the asker, their perceived underlying motivation for questioning you, or the words used to communicate with you. It could also be insecurity on your part, maybe even fear of being viewed as a failure or somehow weak. You don't have to justify personal decisions such as where you live and what kind of car you drive, and it's not your friends' or relatives' business how you spend your money. However, you do need to answer to your boss, co-workers, teacher, and spouse or significant other when your behavior affects them.

BECOMING MORE CRITICAL BUT LESS JUDGMENTAL

It is the mark of an educated mind to be able to entertain a thought without accepting it.

—*Aristotle*

The words "critical" and "judgmental" immediately connote negative meanings, but becoming a critical thinker implies that one will more closely examine people, events, information, and situations with a discerning eye and ear. In the same vein, being judgmental is not necessarily about being accusatory or disapproving. It simply means that one makes a conclusion or final judgment based on facts. However, when we take a more critical stance in studying ourselves and others, and we truly attempt to understand ourselves and others, then we can become less accusatory and disapproving because we have gathered enough information to utilize our empathy skills. We can give others (and ourselves) the benefit of the doubt in terms of possible reasons for rude, confusing, non-conformist, or inappropriate behavior. When we are being critical of another, we are judging that person's worth. We are focusing on negatives—real or perceived. Women are experts at perpetrating this nastiness on other women (Tannenbaum, 2002). In ten seconds or less, as they notice and pass someone walking down the street or at the mall, some insecure women will mentally pick apart the competition from head to toe. Then the next victim comes into view and the process begins anew.

I once had a student who honestly admitted that she would hang out at the mall with her boyfriend and quietly tear apart the appearance of other females that passed by. She claimed that she did this because she was bored and after all, she was using her critical thinking skills to observe others, right? Formulating disparaging remarks, fault-finding, and rating others in order to feel superior is not a demonstration of effective critical thinking skills. This kind of behavior goes against the very nature of the critical thought process and goals of such.

Higher education should cause enough discomfort to students that they are forced to look inward and pay attention to what and how they think. When you are self-aware and understand that you do indeed make disparaging remarks about others (even if only in your mind), you can then feel a bit embarrassed by this childish response (i.e. experience some emotional pain) and then change it. Continual learning and questioning help us understand why we and others behave as we do, and thus, this understanding can lead to compromise and problem solving as we gain a clearer picture of someone else's priorities, problems, and world view. We eventually learn that we basically want the same things from life. The trick becomes how to give everyone involved a little bit of what they want and enough to make them feel important and heard in the decision-making process. Oh, if only our political leaders could become more critical and less judgmental. . . .

FINDING A PURPOSE

Education is worth little if it teaches only how to make a living rather than how to make a life.

—Mary Hartwood Fatrell

Last but not least, college should assist us in finding a purpose in life. Philosophical questions will be addressed. What is your purpose on Earth? What do you want to accomplish during your life? What kind of person do you want to be, both personally and professionally? What do you believe about yourself, others, and the world? What are your personal values or rules for conducting your life?

These difficult-to-answer questions drive the concrete students crazy. These are the students I discussed earlier who want to complete their classes, graduate, get a job, and start making money. They aren't interested in self-reflection. They have no use for thinking for thinking's sake, and especially not about their inner psychological and—gasp!—emotional mechanisms. However, if you don't reflect on the above questions (and many more), you miss out on the most important aspect of this equation: You! How will you get up every weekday morning, make your way to work, and do meaningful work if you have no clear purpose for doing so? Paying your bills won't be enough of a reason for working those long hours. We always hear that we should love what we do. How do you know what you will love doing if you don't think about it? How will you truly be happy having a career that your parents suggested when you don't even like the work? How will you do a great job if you could care less about how you spend your valuable time?

Finding your purpose helps energize you every day. You look forward to new challenges in your career and while you may not jump out of bed singing Disney songs every morning (along with the requisite adorable animals to help you get dressed and make your breakfast), you will feel like you are making a difference in the world. It doesn't matter what you do or whether you directly aid others; if you enjoy your work and believe that you are in the right profession, you will feel like you are making a difference. Isn't that why you educate yourself, whether that is through formal schooling, training, or reading? You want to be knowledgeable. You want to be intelligent, resourceful, and important in the scheme of things. You also get to leave a constructive legacy when you pass on. Who knows? Maybe you'll even help the next generation discover their purpose on Earth.

If you don't know where or how to begin finding your purpose, here are some suggestions: (1) Self-reflection, journal writing, observing and writing down what you like and don't like. What moves you? What are you passionate about? (2) There are many free aptitude tests on the Internet that will help you become aware of your interests, skills, and talents. (3) Seek the support of a good therapist or minister. (4) Ask some loved ones for feedback. (5) Locate a book on the subject, such as Pastor Rick Warren's *The Purpose-Driven Life* (2002). Though Pastor Warren's book is geared toward Christians, you don't have to be a Christian, or even a religious person, in order to reap the benefits of the book's insightful, profound personal questions. Another awesome reader is *What Color is Your Parachute?* by Richard Bolles (1971). Google some other book titles as well. There are many. Keep in mind that finding your purpose in life is a journey. Our life's purpose changes as we learn, enjoy new experiences, age, and shift our priorities. Further, as discussed in an earlier chapter, the purpose must be yours, not your parents', friends' or culture's. What line of work (and this includes "domestic engineer") will make you happy?

I know that my purpose is to help others, but I am constantly questioning God and myself about where I should be (in a philosophical sense, not based on location), and what should I be doing. Sometimes I ask what is needed from me. I am receptive to the answers. In fact, after this book is finally published, I will be questioning what I need to do next. This helps me remain alert to all possibilities and opportunities, even if new prospects and challenges are drastically different from what I am currently experiencing and comfortable with. I therefore have more control over my life as I utilize all the tools at my disposal in order to make the best informed decision about what is right for me. I question authority (my own and God's), gather enough information about the choices presented in order to arrive at a solid judgment, and use logic, emotion, and intuition to regulate my ongoing purpose-driven life.

How Technology Helps/Hinders our Thinking and Social Skills ■ *10*

> Technology . . . is a queer thing. It brings great gifts with one hand, and it stabs you in the back with the other.
>
> —*C.P. Snow*

When I was growing up in the 1970s, television, radio, and print (actual paper) media were the avenues for dissemination of information. Many television stations would go off the air around midnight, displaying a test pattern or a set of vertical rainbow colored bars until they resumed programming in the morning. Television was free in those days, and there were limited channel choices. Then the dawn of cable, pay-TV, arose. Their hours were limited too, as people attempted to adjust to this new medium, wherein they not only had to subscribe to watch, but had a larger variety of program choices.

At the same time, the first video games came on the market. These hooked up to the television and we used joysticks and other controllers to play simple (and I mean graphically as well as intellectually) games. With each new manufacturer, the video games became increasingly complex (graphically and intellectually), expensive, and fun. The advent of the personal computer was also a major contributor to the media boom. Now one could play games on that instead of hogging up the television. One person could watch TV, the other could play video games on the computer! Of course, with the advent of the personal computer came the Internet and the rest is, well, history.

It is amazing, especially from my experiences as a kid, to be able to access any information any time I want. I can download music and buy clothes online. I don't have to wait until stores open the next day. I can own and watch my favorite T.V. shows and movies at a moment's notice, and enjoy the amazing graphics of today's video games with my kids. We can now send and receive information over telephones that fit in our pockets, and use mini-computers to keep up with emails and work while we wait to be seen by a doctor.

However, some feel that our present-day, 24/7/365 information system is both a blessing and a curse. I feel this way too at times. It seems like all this media bombardment owns us. Some argue that being connected enables us to reach out, feel closer to others, and make more informed decisions (Coady, 2011; Fokkema & Knipscheer, 2007). Others believe that there is a decline in social skills as well as the ability and desire to think for ourselves (Goldman, 2008; Pula, 2011).

If you are in your teens or early twenties at the present time, you may be tired of hearing all of this talk about the decline of civilization. You don't know any other way of interacting, but I do, and so do your parents and grandparents. Even though you might be bored with hearing about "the good old days," bear with me. There are lessons to be learned and one day you will have children of your own to teach and nurture.

Let's begin with this: When we rely mainly on electronic forms of communication, we miss opportunities to learn about the social cues and pragmatics of communication mentioned earlier: body language signals, eye contact, facial expressions, tone of voice—ours and those of others, taking turns speaking, and resisting the urge to interrupt. As we all know too well, emails and text messages cannot convey humor, emotion, and sarcasm as well as face-to-face interaction. We need to see the person's face and hear their voice in order to distinguish these subtle speech enhancers.

I do know that some of my students are frustrated by the fact that I won't let them use technology to take notes during lectures. I want them paying attention to and listening to me, not focusing on a keyboard and laptop screen. Some have complained that they type faster than they write, and others have even insinuated that I am a "dinosaur" and need to progress with the technological age. I tell them that when every student using technology in the classroom is actually using that equipment to take notes versus watching movies, checking email and Facebook pages, I will again allow laptops and tablets in the classroom. Besides, I can still argue that studies have shown increased brain development, cognitive skills, and a stronger connection to the material being learned when we actually write on paper, versus type on a keyboard (Berninger, Abbott, Augsburger, & Garcia, 2009; Bounds, 2010).

In an effort not to praise or damn the cyber-space age we live in, I ask my readers to view both sides of the coin. This is one crucial area where critical thinking skills really assist us in daily living; being aware of our use of technology and how that affects ourselves and others.

SOCIAL NETWORKING AND YOUTUBE

Let's begin with websites like MySpace, Facebook, Twitter, and YouTube. By the time this tome hits the bookstore there will no doubt be countless other Internet ways to develop and maintain our social contacts. As with other modern issues, I view the presence of these sites as a blessing and a curse. They definitely feed into a growing national and international narcissistic attitude of "Look at me!" We can now "check in" with everyone while we are out shopping, eating, or attending various events. Everyone can be their own producer, director, and star of their very own video, and we can have "followers" who receive every tidbit of information we share in cyber-space. We feel incredibly special and important in the process—geez, who wouldn't when you make a simple statement on Facebook or Twitter and within minutes, 20 people have commented on your status?!

On the flip side, it really is wonderful to be able to connect with family and friends at a moment's notice. We can strengthen relationships this way, especially when we reside far apart from one another. We can download pictures and videos and others can listen to our voices. My kids will know how their toddler voices sounded. I never got to hear my own. We can have discussions with others and practice appropriate communication skills, as well as expose ourselves to the very different viewpoints and experiences of those we care about.

These are the black-and-white aspects of social networking. There is also an ugly dark side to all this chatter and ego stroking. Bullying others, cyber-stalking, the need to share everything with everybody, the neediness that leads us to collect "friends" we don't even know, in a futile effort to feel more special and important than anyone else. The pictures and comments posted in haste that never, ever go away and can negatively affect relation-ships, college admission, and job opportunities. How about the enormous amount of time spent on checking your account, checking in with others, and checking out of other areas of your life?

Many of us are drawn to this type of communication, like moths to a flame. We log on to our computers in order to check our emails or bank ac-counts, and then get sucked into checking up on everyone on Facebook. All of a sudden, an hour (or more) has passed and you not only forgot what else you needed to accomplish that day, you don't care. I am expecting the Di-agnostic and Statistical Manual (aka DSM, therapists' diagnosis manual) to create a mental health diagnosis of social networking disorder, or something along those lines. I know it's being discussed.

Sites like Facebook can be especially perilous for adolescents. These kids are smack dab in the middle of the personal fable and the imaginary audi-ence—the most egocentric time of their lives—and then we allow them to advertise how wonderful they are on Facebook, begetting further ego-centrism! For some, this includes collecting as many "friends" as possible, stretching the truth (i.e. lying) about their abilities and talents, or using this website as a way to humiliate and bully others in order to increase their own self-worth.

Further, since many of our cell phones now come with video capability, we can make brief films about our lives or opinions and become instant celebrities on YouTube. Artist Andy Warhol was brilliant when he propheti-cally remarked in 1968 that "In the future everybody will be world famous for fifteen minutes" (http://www.brainyquote.com/quotes/authors/a/andy_warhol.html; Warhol, & Colacello, 1980).

Why is there such a strong need for many people to be noticed, loved, to be a celebrity? I understand teenagers wanting to fit in, be cool, popular, admired. Their adolescent struggle is to seek and settle on a comfortable identity. What's really sad is that many adults feel the need to relive this teenage time too. What are we missing at home that leads us to seek attention at such a high cost of our privacy and, at times, our dignity? Hmmm, this is a good time to re-read the chapter on parenting.

CELL PHONES—TALKING, TEXTING, AND SEXTING, OMG!

A few years ago during a lecture, I began my typical rant about cell phone use in public, especially when we are in the middle of paying for goods and services. I fervently declared how I despise watching someone chatter away on their cell phone when the clerk is trying to finish that person's transaction and proceed to the next patiently waiting customer. The chatterer continues their conversation, oblivious to the salesclerk or the growing line of annoyance behind him or her. The employee usually has to repeat questions or statements because the phone talker isn't listening. In the meantime, everyone within the immediate area is subjected to this person's very loud conversation about so-and-so's medical condition, child, etc. When it is finally my turn to pay for my items, I usually make a joke about the phone offender, because I know the salesperson can't.

At the conclusion of my mini diatribe, a student quietly stated that he had no idea that that kind of behavior would be considered rude. That comment just about knocked me off my feet. I suddenly realized that younger generations might not think the same way I did. After all, they grew up witnessing this kind of behavior as normal. However, I recognized that many of the phone offenders I come across are middle-aged. They didn't grow up thinking that their public phone behavior was okay, so what was their excuse? Was it because my generation of parents grew up during the 1970s and 80s, the "Me" generation? Probably. Was it also because this kind of technology is so new and exciting that we just don't think about what we are doing? Possibly. Maybe there was a bit of narcissism mixed in too. Clueless, spoiled-brat kids come from narcissistic, permissive parents.

As with social networking and YouTube, other forms of technology give us an outlet to feel important and special. When a phone chimes everyone looks. When we started with pagers, these were typically used by people who needed to be contacted at a moment's notice, like doctors, attorneys, or therapists. When a pager beeped in a public place, people noticed and maybe "knew" that the owner of the pager was a very important person. When I carried a pager and was on-call, when that little black box vibrated or beeped, I would occasionally get comments like, "Oh gosh, someone must need you." When I returned after my phone call, sometimes a conversation would begin about what I did for a living, with the inquirer in awe of my occupation.

Ironically, I hated that pager. I didn't (and still don't) like being tethered to someone or something 24/7. When I got my first cell phone from work I hated that too. I was afraid of what I (and many others) now see happening: Smart phones are making us socially dumb. We rely extensively on these expensive little computers to communicate, entertain ourselves, and otherwise tune out the world. It saddens me to see an entire family sitting down for a meal in a restaurant, only to see them immediately whip out individual cell phones and communicate with everyone except the people sitting with them at the table. Pay attention to what people do the next time they have to wait in line for more than a few minutes. Here come the cell phones! We don't talk to strangers anymore, we don't use the downtime to think about our lives or recent decisions we've made or even how we physically or emotionally feel in that moment. We distract ourselves with mindless video games and think we're missing something if we don't check our email every 10 minutes. We have become uncomfortable with periods of silence between each other and in our own minds.

I've got news for all of us: we're not that important. When Wellesley High School teacher David McCullough presented his graduation speech in 2012, he expressed what thousands of instructors at all levels of education were feeling: that graduates weren't as special as they were told or as they thought. His goal was to remind students about loftier goals and experiences outside of themselves. He ended the speech by stating " . . . the great and curious truth of the human experiences is that selflessness is the best thing you can do for yourself. The sweetest joys of life, then, come only with the recognition that you're not special. Because everyone is" (www.myfox-boston.com).

Mr. McCullough's speech generated mixed reviews. Some were horrified that the students were told they weren't special; some were amused, and still others cheered. It was a wake-up call about self-absorption and it is relevant for all age groups.

Let me repeat it: We're not that important. We don't need to tell others about our lives every minute of the day, and they don't care where you are at 2:30 in the afternoon or about what you ate for lunch. You don't need to incessantly talk on your phone at the restaurant table. How do you think your lunch partner feels about being constantly interrupted? Do you think they'll want to share another meal with you? The next time you see a fight breaking out between two people, please use your phone to call 911 before you start taking pictures/video. I always feel sorry for the victims of beatings when I see a bunch of kids surrounding them and no one helps; the spectators all have their phone cameras clicking. Call on your empathy skills and understand how frightening it would be to look up at the crowd while you are being pummeled and realize that no one is going to help you. We watch people getting seriously injured for the sake of a picture . . . and maybe our 15 minutes of fame!

Try not to have a long conversation on the phone while you are out shopping or otherwise running errands. Keep in mind that we speak louder when on the phone, so everyone within a few feet can hear your business. You might like that or not care, but it is annoying to everyone else who don't care to listen to your personal problems. Plus, being on the phone slows you down. You have to talk and think about why you are in a particular store, so you are more likely to stop short in the middle of an aisle or linger too long getting something off a shelf while others need to wait for or move around you. Being fully cognizant of your surroundings keeps you physically safe too. How many times have you been talking or texting and crossing a busy street at the same time? Countless times I have watched in horror as I come upon a pedestrian whose head is down, texting, while crossing a street or parking lot. I fight the urge to honk my horn just so they'll look up and notice the vehicles around them.

And don't get me started on the teenage trend of sexting! That seems to have quieted down during the last few years, but with the advent of cell phone cameras, thousands of girls somehow felt the need to take nude or half-naked pictures of themselves and send these to their "friends," who of course sent them to other friends. Sending or possessing these pictures of underage kids is punishable by law, so teens are being educated about curtailing this activity. Again, this goes back to how we feel about ourselves. Sexting seems to be due to a number of reasons, from typical teenage egocentrism ("Look at me!!") to the need for attention and acceptance, to peer pressure, and a desire to "hook up" (Lohmann, 2011). Unfortunately, there are plenty of female role models to demonstrate how to dress and act in sexual ways in order to get men's attention; however, not all of these role models are celebrities. Some of them share a home with these teens.

I'm not just complaining and advising because it feels good; I have strong feelings about cell phone use because it diminishes our ability to think critically—to make rational informed decisions, utilize empathy skills, and treat others with respect. I understand that the lure of instant information and connection are intoxicating. I know that the ring of the phone brings a certain amount of panic, "Answer the phone!!" but we have the ability to turn off the contraption when we are spending time in the presence of actual humans. Why don't we know about and follow this kind of common sense? Why do we feel indignant when others ask us to turn the phone off? It's gotten so bad that doctor's offices now have signs requesting that cell phones be turned off in the waiting room. How pathetic!

Here's a challenge for you: turn your cell phone off, yes OFF, for a whole day. If you can't handle an entire day, try a few hours. For good measure, turn off your computer too. Turn all the technology off and tune into life—your own and others'. I love our yearly camping trips for many reasons, but especially because we stay in areas that have no cell phone or internet service. We are then forced to converse with each other, play games, hike, or bike together, read a book, and contemplate life and our beautiful surroundings in silence. You know, the elements of life that are really important . . .

> "To make the right choices in life, you have to get in touch with your soul. To do this, you need to experience solitude, which most people are afraid of, because in the silence you hear the truth and know the solutions."
> —*Deepak Chopra*

GAMING

On to another aspect of technology that can be a blessing and a curse. The gaming industry has exploded since the 1990s. Like the controversies surrounding violence and blatant sexuality on television as well as in music, the social and emotional effects of these video games have been scrutinized. Even with ratings in place for video games, kids are exposed to adult intensities of content either when they visit the homes of others or their parents buy these games. Sometimes games are purchased without consumers really knowing exactly what kinds of violence or sexuality are portrayed. Then there is the peer pressure exerted on both kids and parents alike to have the latest games, like those in the Halo, Call of Duty, or World of Warcraft series. How much violence is excessive? How much sexuality or gender stereotyping are too much? How do you control for these factors?

There have been many studies for and against video game usage. Video games can assist with and improve hand-eye coordination, learning about and accepting structure in the form of rules, development of logical thought, problem solving, observational skills, multitasking and rewards for a job well done (McGonigal, 2011; Roach, 2003; Shaevitz, 2012). Our gaming systems now include activities in which one can exercise, compete with the computer or other players while physically and/or verbally engaged, act as stress release, or train our brains to remember things more efficiently. Studies also show that prosocial video games lead to an increase in prosocial behavior (Gentile et. al, 2009; Greitemeyer & Osswald, 2010/2011). On the other hand, some studies have also shown that a steady diet of video gaming (along with other "sit time" activities) can lead to obesity and other health problems (Kelly, 2012), and a higher propensity to act violently (Bushman & Anderson, 2002; Gentile & Anderson, 2003).

There have been plenty of studies over the years, basically beginning with Bandura's research (1962), that have shown that we are indeed affected by watching and listening to violence. Some studies have focused on the diminished emotional responsiveness that occurs with over-exposure (Engelhardt, 2011; Fraser, 2012). Other studies have noted how we behave more aggressively after exposure (Bushman & Anderson, 2002; Gentile & Anderson, 2003). However, not everyone who is subjected to live or filmed brutality becomes violent or murderous. There are many more factors involved in our choice of behavior.

With so much conflicting information, what's a concerned parent or non-parent to do? You know by now that knowledge and moderation seem to be the key factors in making decisions about what is best for yourself and/or your kids. Let's return to the requirements and goals of critical thinking. Let's discuss this in terms of being a parent and wondering about the violence and sexuality depicted in video games. If you don't have your own children at this time, think about your own gaming habits and personality. Here are some CT goals to keep in mind include: What do you want to teach? Are you utilizing logic, emotion, and intuition to examine the situation? Are you questioning the research you're reading about video games? Are you seeking answers? Are you looking at all sides of the argument, or just your own?

In this case, the first CT rule of thumb is to know thy offspring. Is your child very sensitive to viewing violence on television or hearing you and your spouse argue? Is your child very social? Does he/she have good friends and do they keep in contact with each other? Does your child have a fascination with violence, or wanting to watch more and more programs involving aggressive and/or graphic sexual behavior? Does he/she enjoy programs and music not involving violence or sexuality? How does he treat animals? Younger, smaller kids? Women? How do you deal with the topics of violence and sexuality? How do you and/or your child deal with stress or difficult feelings like anger and disappointment?

Second, how much dialogue do you engage in regarding what you or your kids view on the nightly news, movies, or in television shows? Are you discussing how and why people behave the way they do? Are you talking about and teaching yourself and your kids how to handle stress appropriately?

Third, how much aggression or violence is going on inside your own home? Are you modeling constructive communication (especially during conflict) which respects all involved, or is there name-calling, hitting, people leaving the house, "the silent treatment," or degrading comments made about one gender or the other?

In terms of critical thinking, are you fully aware of what is going on within yourself, your home, and your child? Are you willing to observe the good, the bad, and the ugly? Can you take responsibility for the atmosphere in your head or your home and change for the better?

Be prepared to realize that the kid who is already verbally or physically aggressive, treats animals or smaller kids poorly or even cruelly, and seems to have little respect for authority should probably not be exposed to violent programming or video games. It's very difficult to see your child (or yourself) this way, but it is crucial to making the best decision in terms of exposure to graphic violence or sexuality in any form of media.

What about those little kids in restaurants whose parents come armed with not only snacks and sippy cups, but tablets and video games as well? It's like the VCR or DVD was to my kids' generation. As much as I hated the show *Barney*, my kids loved it, and sitting them in front of a video on the T.V. in my bedroom while I took an uninterrupted, unhurried shower was a godsend!

Having instant child entertainment while dining can be great for parents, who can actually eat and finish a meal before junior becomes bored, fidgety, or has an all-out tantrum. However, I wonder if these kids are actually learning to be patient and behave properly while in public or if they just go along with the program because they are being stimulated every second. Does this constant stimulation have the same potentially mind-numbing effects seen in their older siblings or their parents? Does this teach kids to critically and thoughtfully attend to others and their surroundings? Time and research will tell.

TECHNOLOGY AND ANONYMITY

One of the other concerns I have about the use of technology is the sense of anonymity it affords us. We believe that because we aren't using our real names or other identifying information that others will not be able to locate us. We take comfort in the fact that we can say whatever we want to whomever we want, with no negative consequences. We couldn't be more wrong. We treat people differently depending on whether we are communicating in person, on the phone, or over the Internet. This is one of the reasons I tell students that if they wouldn't say something to me in person, don't write it in an email. Due to the inability to observe facial expressions and hear someone's tone of voice, the proper translation of sarcasm, jokes, and emotions is absent in email communications. We can do great harm to our personal or professional reputation if we lack the ability and insight to deal with this type of correspondence correctly.

Furthermore, some people post incredibly harsh, cruel statements in blogs and "comments" sections of articles on search engines such as Yahoo and Google. I had to force myself to retreat from these sections—reading and responding—because it was just too painful or scary to witness anymore. I was constantly questioning if people were really so clueless, so invested in stereotypes or believing information that was totally untrue. I saw rampant racism and hatred, and lots of rage. Do people actually feel and believe this way, or are some making blatantly hateful statements "just because?" And if these people were making these statements "just because," what must their lives and emotional functioning be like?!

These behaviors and responses seem to be symptoms of a larger phenomenon that has been occurring for years. We have become disconnected from each other and the world. We have drive-thru restaurants, coffee shops, and banks. We handle personal and business transactions through machines instead of humans. We no longer rely on and know the guy at the service station who pumps our gas or checks our oil. I bet some people have never gone far enough inside a bank to actually speak to a teller because they use ATM machines to conduct their business. This is how we are losing our social skills. We don't need to practice manners, small talk, or conflict management with strangers because we don't see them. We can even darken our car windows enough so that we can see others but they can't see us (even though this is illegal in many places).

I love the city of San Luis Obispo, California, for many reasons, but especially because it refuses to modernize the town by allowing drive-through businesses. If you want to purchase something or conduct business, you have to leave your vehicle, go inside, and actually speak to a human being! I've been to the city many times and it's amusing when I run across someone new to the town that is frustrated by the "inconvenience" of having to park the car and talk to someone in person in order to get what they want.

To reiterate, when we use our cell phones and tablets as tools to avoid interacting with others, we can tend to view ourselves and our personal business as much more important than they are, and more significantly, we lose countless opportunities to network, practice social skills, make a new friend, teach, and maybe even learn something new.

IS ANYBODY OUT THERE? DOES ANYBODY CARE?

As you can see, just like guns, junk food, cell phone use, and prescription medications, to only name a few aspects of our lives that constantly get blamed for all human woes, technology isn't necessarily the problem. We are the choosers. Really, pretty much everything we do or eat has possible positive and negative consequences. This includes using technology in its many forms. The key to managing all this new information is to control its presence in your life. As in other areas of our lives, we need to find a balance. Video games can be great, but there can be a point where they are harmful. Guns don't fire themselves. Having a cookie or two can taste wonderful and make you feel good, but eating a whole bag in one sitting will not be good for you. Having a quick cell phone exchange while shopping can be helpful, but know when to hang up and tune into what you are doing and the effects your behavior has on others. Prescription medications are helpful when used appropriately and for the conditions they were designed for.

Each of us has to decide what our limits are, but we have to do so realistically. We have to take responsibility for our choices and the consequences of those choices. We do have to care about others' sensibilities when we join them in public places. Those of you arguing about this just remember: you choose the way you think, feel, and behave. Others will respond to you in kind. If you are respectful, you will earn respect. If you are considerate of others, they will more than likely be considerate of you. If you utilize technology in moderation and wisely, you will be rewarded with control of your life in addition to very powerful tools to make your life more enjoyable. When you feel anxious about not "checking in," know that you may be feeling inadequate, unappreciated, or lonely. If you are spending entire days or weekends playing video games, perhaps you are depressed or have some social anxiety that prevents you from feeling comfortable interacting face to face. Know thyself and ask for assistance.

Bipartisan Politics and Critical Thinking ... a Very Brief Chapter!

11

> Victory has a thousand fathers, but defeat is an orphan.
> —*John F. Kennedy*

In very few areas of our lives is the above quote truer than in politics. Everyone will claim responsibility for a win, but very few of us will acknowledge our defeat or failure. Now before you get excited or nervous, dear reader, I am not going to take sides. You know by now, as a developing CT'er, that any time we choose sides, our thinking and decisions become either/or, black or white. Politics is no exception. Try telling your die-hard Democratic Uncle Joe that you voted for both Republican and Democratic candidates during the last election, then watch the burst of emotional fireworks!

Religion and politics, two topics and belief systems that tend to include either/or beliefs, tend to push rational people over the emotional edge. In fact, otherwise focused, inquisitive, open-minded, effective thinkers can lose their utilitarian cognitive skills in a millisecond when religion or politics is placed on the table. The old adage of "Never discuss politics or religion" can be helpful and prevent serious family conflict, but not discussing our similar and divergent viewpoints prevents us from learning, educating, questioning ourselves, others, and ideas, and growing as individuals.

Politicians are typically highly educated, savvy, and persuasive, which makes it more astonishing when they make extremely questionable statements or decisions. We demand and expect them to be wiser than "the common man," and for good reason. They are elected in order to represent their constituents' best interests, not their own, but they are human and they want to keep their power and job like the rest of us do. They are leaders, who are also role models. We tend to place our role models on very high, narrow pedestals and then we are shocked when they fall from grace. However, those role models, by the very nature of the term, should be stronger, wiser, and psychologically healthier than those they lead. They should have character and integrity. They shouldn't succumb to the temptations of lust or greed or the abuses of money and power. They should be people we strive to be like, not people we ridicule for their poor personal and professional decisions.

DONKEYS VS ELEPHANTS

> Political promises are much like marriage vows. They are made
> at the beginning of the relationship between candidate and voter,
> but are quickly forgotten.
>
> —*Dick Gregory*

Sometimes I really wish the United States, in particular, and the rest of the democratic and semi-democratic world in general would discourage a two-party system. There are more than two sides to a story or solution to a problem. Why can't we just be people with different ways of viewing issues? Why are we forced to choose one ideology over another? In recent years, the nastiness between "Democraps" and "Repubtards" has grown uglier. I'm tired of hearing the stale refrain that Democrats are "bleeding heart liberals" and Republicans are "right-wing, nut-job, evangelical Christians." Though at times it does feel like some fit these stereotypes, many on both sides of the aisle do not, thank goodness, land in these rigid categories.

In courses regarding critical thinking, we are taught that one can like their own idea or group as well as another's. This is ideal, since each person or group focuses on different priorities. Once we understand each set of priorities, it follows that we can then compromise and everyone gets a little bit of what they want. No one person or group's priorities are better or worse than another's. Simple in theory, complicated when human egos become involved.

As evidenced by what is reported on the nightly news, our legislators seem to consistently throw the principles of critical thinking out the window in order to "win." If they, heaven forbid, agree with a member of another political party, they are viewed as traitors. How can these men and women ever resolve the major issues facing our country when this absolutist mindset exists? It's the Hatfield and McCoy feud played out every day, only this time between adults wearing business attire and using the media as their weapon of choice. We can do better.

PLAYING THE POLITICAL GAME

> It would be a great reform in politics if wisdom could be made to
> spread as easily and as rapidly as folly.
>
> —*Winston Churchill*

Here's an idea for a new game: One player says something off-the-cuff that seems completely outrageous and non-factual, and the other player gets to use the media to make the first player look like a complete fool. Sadly, with the political nastiness in effect, especially since President Obama was first elected, some of our elected officials don't need much assistance in looking foolish. I understand that politics is a very stressful occupation where members are spontaneously asked incredibly difficult questions, but there are highly educated leaders at all levels of experience that seem to have little knowledge of our country's constitution and history. Okay, they're politicians, not historians, but politics involves focus on many issues, least of all our federal and state laws, which happen to be based on the principles espoused in not insignificant documents like the Constitution, the Bill of Rights, and the Declaration of Independence. It's sad enough that a good number of citizens in our population don't know basic U. S. history, but these leaders claim a love of country and demonstrate their ongoing patriotism by wearing American flag pins on their lapels! If these people love their country so much, shouldn't they be required to know the basics about it?

Along the same lines, if said leaders are to serve on government committees focusing on health, education, and finances, shouldn't they possess basic knowledge of human biology, learning and the structure of academia, and business management? I would think that in order to do a job properly, and serve on a committee appropriately, one should have a passion for the topic being studied and discussed, plus a strong working knowledge of the principles of that topic.

One particularly irritating case of lack of basic information came from Congressman Todd Akin from Missouri, who in September 2012 commented in regard to rape:

> "First of all, from what I understand from doctors (pregnancy from rape) is really rare. If it's a legitimate rape, the female body has ways to try to shut that whole thing down."

> "Let's assume that maybe that didn't work, or something. I think there should be some punishment, but the punishment ought to be on the rapist and not attacking the child" (Phillips, 2012).

Because rape tends to be under-reported, we can only estimate the number of pregnancies that occur due to rape (RAINN, 2009) but in the end, whether rape leads to pregnancy rarely or often, it is no excuse to have inaccurate information on women's basic biology, and then attempt to make laws or regulations based on this inaccurate information. Furthermore, Akin has a record of other condescending political and factually incorrect statements, especially in regard to women. Recall his comment about his 2012 election opponent, Senator Claire McCaskill, claiming she was not being "ladylike" when she verbally reprimanded him due to his remarks on rape. Oh, by the way, ex-Representative Akin was a member of the House Committee on Science, Space, and Technology. Granted, this committee doesn't focus on human biology, but wouldn't you think someone interested in space, aeronautics, energy, and the environment would be somewhat savvy about medical science as well. Just saying . . .

The fact that politicians make statements that aren't quite appropriate or factually accurate is nothing new. However, they (and the rest of us) could take some advice from Mark Twain (1835–1910), who stated, "It is better to keep your mouth closed and let people think you are a fool than to open it and remove all doubt" (www.americanliterature.com/quotes).

TALKING HEADS: TECHNOLOGY, TELEVISION, AND TUNING OUT

> The most important truths are likely to be those which society at that time least wants to hear.
>
> —W.H. Auden

Speaking of the media, news agencies and their representatives can and do help and hinder the political process and the sense of absolutism inherent in that process. Recently, with the terrible tragedy in Newtown, CT, there was much sorely needed discussion about gun violence in this country. The executive vice president and CEO of the National Rifle Association (NRA), Wayne LaPierre, held a brief press conference on December 21, 2012, one week after the tragic events at Sandy Hook Elementary School in Newtown, CT. As a disclaimer, I want to be clear that I am not a member of the NRA. I am including a description of Mr. LaPierre's comments because I want to examine our critical thinking skills. Yes, "our," not his. One very difficult part of CT, and the bottom line of CT, is finding the truth, no matter from whom or where it comes. Sometimes we can despise or vilify a group (as has typically been the case with the NRA) or individual, but that doesn't mean that we should dismiss everything that group or individual discusses or believes. In order to listen with an open mind like this, we must recognize and set aside our strong emotions in the moment and humbly realize that maybe, just maybe, a person or group does have something reasonable to say.

In the case of the NRA and Mr. LaPierre, if we peruse the transcript of his speech, we have to admit, whether we like it or not, that he had some very insightful things to say about violence in the United States. For years, we have focused on guns vs. no guns, assault rifles and large ammo magazines to banning both, at the expense of other issues that play a huge part in the perpetration of violence against fellow human beings. He mentioned the significant factors of mental illness, violent video games, Hollywood movies, and other forms of entertainment that we are all too aware of (www.nra.org). Now I didn't agree with all of Mr. LaPierre's proposed solutions, like creating a national listing of those diagnosed with mental illness, but he asked us to pay attention to the many, complicated factors involved long before someone pulls the trigger. I would add self-awareness, stress management/coping skills, parenting, and proper training in dealing with/securing weaponry to that list. He noted that the media would probably attack him, his speech, and the NRA immediately after he left the podium, and sadly, he was correct. Many in the media returned to the tried and true vilification of the NRA and its members. They focused solely on what Mr. LaPierre said about not wanting to place further restrictions on the purchase of assault rifles or large ammunition magazines. They fed into the decades-long stereotype that the NRA's main focus is guns, guns, and more guns. However, the NRA has lent itself to such ongoing criticism and even ridicule, as their lobbying is so powerful that they have been very successful over the years at persuading elected officials to vote in favor of NRA principles involving less and less control of the purchase and use of guns.

Furthermore, immediately after the Sandy Hook massacre, the media began to speculate about the role of guns in these mass killings, comparing the Connecticut events to those recently reported in other areas of the country: the theater shooting in Aurora, CO, the mall shooting in Clackamas, OR. No problem there, right? But when the connections are made over and over again in the absence of other information on parenting, mental illness, and our violent media-infused culture, people begin to believe that guns are the only issue that should be addressed. There is a name for what transpires when we believe what we hear the most often; this is called the **availability error** (Schick & Vaughn, 2014). Joseph Goebbels, the notorious Nazi war criminal also understood this. To paraphrase: "If you tell a lie big enough and keep repeating it, people will eventually come to believe it." Also, he stated that: "The most brilliant propagandist technique will yield no success unless one fundamental principle is borne in mind constantly - it must confine itself to a few points and repeat them over and over." These principles are inherent in the availability error. This "rule of thumb" can also explain why many people believe that it is safer to travel by car than by airplane. We hear and see, over and over, the disastrous results of an airline crash, but we aren't alerted to the hundreds of auto accidents and deaths that occur on our global roads every day. If we did, we wouldn't step outside the house, let alone drive our cars!

> **availability error**—We believe what we hear the most often.

As critical thinkers we are susceptible to this narrow, emotionally-based thinking too, so we especially have to stay focused and aware of the process. We need to be the voice of reason when others begin to assume that what they see and hear is what the world has become. Understand that people and situations are more complicated than we realize, and historically, the most beneficial answers lie in the gray area, or middle ground.

We allow other "talking heads" to permeate our lives. I know people who feed themselves a steady stream of Fox News, CNN, CNBC, MSNBC, ad-nauseum, and begin to quote what these "experts" are telling them, without once using the Internet (or their own brains) to check on the validity of the daily monologues and rants they are fed.

Start asking questions—lots of them. Who are these "experts?" What makes them more adept at discussing political, religious, moral, financial, and economic issues? Why do you need/want to listen to them? Are you looking for someone to argue with so you can feel better about your beliefs or are you hoping to find agreement with your views? Are you willing to change the channel (God forbid!) and watch a panel of "experts" who have views unlike yours? If so, are you able to listen without criticizing their views or preferences? Are you able to question and criticize the views and preferences of those that agree with you too? I think you know which qualities belong to the best critical thinkers here.

Here's a radical thought: turn off the TV, get off the Internet, and think for yourself. Some people are very threatened when you do think for yourself, but do it anyway. We'll discuss these issues at greater length later.

FAMILY FEUDS

Every time you open your mouth you let men look into your mind.

—Bruce Barton

Think back . . . how many times have you dreaded attending certain family gatherings because so-and-so was going to be present and this person has an annoying habit of starting arguments with anyone about anything? This past Thanksgiving-time, 2012, post presidential election, I ate breakfast while listening to a television station report on a list of things we probably shouldn't discuss during the holidays. One wise entry was "Don't assume that everyone voted the same way." I prayed that certain friends and family members would take this advice to heart. There's just something about discussing politics and religion that brings out ugliness in people. I believe that most of the ugliness involves the absolutist belief system that underlies both ideologies. You are supposed to believe one way or another. You are either right or wrong, and if you aren't with us, you're against us.

Sadly, every family seems to have one person who enjoys lighting an emotional fire regarding these ideologies when he/she has an audience. It certainly makes for miserable get-togethers, especially around holiday time when we need and want some peace and enjoyment in our lives.

Here's my piece of advice: Don't be that relative that everyone dreads seeing and remember: if you can't say something nice, don't say anything at all. If you find it impossible to have a reasonable, intellectual conversation about any possibly controversial issue (be it religion, politics, sports, or what dessert you will choose after dinner), find something else to talk about. If you can't be truly open to another's beliefs and opinions without criticizing or attacking, be quiet. Pay attention to what you say and how it is received. Explore your need to control, win, and bully others. Yes, that's right, bully. You need to win at all costs so you will attempt to humiliate anyone who disagrees with you. You aren't always right, and they aren't always wrong. Not everyone will think like you, behave like you, or share your beliefs. Deal with it, get some professional help if necessary, and re-read the chapter on narcissism.

To those of you who have to put up with these negative, bullying windbags, try to use your critical thinking skills. Be assertive and state that you do not wish to discuss sensitive issues with this person at this time. If you feel the need to educate, keep it brief. One or two sentences regarding information and people being much more complicated than we realize should help (at least it will benefit you). You can always agree to disagree and walk away. Try not to educate too deeply and bring up lots of factual information that you can look up on your phone right in front of the buffoon. I know, it's tempting, but you'll either make the bullying worse or humiliate him, making your future relationship, and everyone present, uncomfortable. People who need to win will not listen to rational discourse, at least not in the middle of a highly-charged emotional situation.

Once in a while, however, sarcasm and humor can help ease tension or call attention to another's outrageous statements. Someone I know once made a comment, after searching for a restaurant in his community, that there were "no good restaurants for white people" in his city. I HAD to jump on that ridiculous statement so I asked the obvious question: "What do white people eat?" When a Republican relative sputtered that President Obama and all those "bleeding heart liberals" were turning the USA into a socialist country, I reminded him that he was living on his socialist benefits: Medicare and Social Security. The Democrat who screams about tax breaks and other "perks" for large corporations needs to remember that she works for one of these companies and those tax breaks help her keep her job and "perks" (aka benefits).

Again, this isn't about taking sides, it's about looking at both sides and realizing, whether we like it or not, that both sides have positive and negative philosophies and ideas to offer. Maybe one day our politicians will realize this too and concern themselves more with the condition of our country than the magnificence of their career. A pipe dream, but a very possible one.

CAN'T WE ALL JUST GET ALONG?

The problem of power is how to achieve its responsible use rather than its irresponsible and indulgent use—of how to get men of power to live for the public rather than off the public.
—*"I Remember, I Believe,"* The Pursuit of Justice *(1964),*
Robert Kennedy

According to Ruggiero (2008), ideas are seldom of equal quality; some are great, some are awful, many have positive and negative qualities. In order to solve problems, all those who work together to decide the best course of action must be humble and willing to compromise. We build on each other's ideas, even in politics, which hopefully strengthen the original concept proposed. Take a look at the beginning discussion about requirements and goals of critical thinking and then decide how many of these characteristics are actually in play when hired officials attempt to resolve issues. I know, it's the nature of the beast, but it doesn't have to be that way. We can do better than bickering, name-calling, mud-slinging, and finger-pointing. I have a daydream of attending a day of Congressional meetings and the whole time I am disciplining the members, like 5 year olds. "Now just a minute Senator #1. Please let Senator #2 finish what he was saying." "Senator #3, please stop spreading rumors about Senator #4." "Representative #7, there isn't enough (money) to go around so you must share with the constituents of Representative #8."

Okay, while we may not be able to affect the behavior of a bunch of manipulative children disguised as adults, apart from utilizing our voting rights, we CAN learn to get along with each other in our daily lives. Some of us do this quite well already, while others struggle to do so their whole lives. As with everything else in this game of life, growth is a journey, not a destination. The only people done growing are dead people, yet we seem to encounter many "walking dead" who have given up, don't think they need to change, or just don't know how to change.

Something else to keep in mind is that, unlike television sitcoms where serious problems are resolved in 30 minutes or less, people don't change quickly. There is a hierarchy of change. Alcoholism researchers Prochaska, DiClemente, and Norcross (1992) created a five-stage model of change to help health providers understand and treat addicted clients. The model is based on their observations of how people struggled with changing behaviors such as smoking, overeating and problem drinking.

The six stages of the model are:

- precontemplation
- contemplation
- determination
- action
- maintenance
- termination

What Prochaska et. al (1992) also noticed is that people can become "stuck" at the same level for years. How many times have you thought about making a change in your life (like losing weight) but you never planned and carried out the steps necessary to effect that change? Maybe you briefly modified your behavior but didn't have the determination to follow through for a long period of time or understand how to maintain the changes.

When you attempt to change someone else, which is never a good idea, you will find that even if you have the facts and can support them with lots of evidence, there will always be those who refuse to listen or believe. I once had a client family that was constantly no-showing or late-cancelling both group and individual sessions in regard to their severely emotionally disturbed 7 year old. Each time they were absent, I was required by the county mental health agency to record this on a form kept in the family's file. Before I knew it, this family had been absent for a total of 13 out of 26 total appointments made, and we saw clients weekly. I approached my supervisor about his problem, and we both realized that this family, despite their severe and pressing issues, just wasn't ready for intensive therapy. At the beginning of the next session in which the family actually presented, I gently confronted them about their poor track record. The first thing the father did was deny the problem. "That isn't true," he said. I showed him the record I had been keeping, thinking that this would be incontrovertible proof of their absences. The client perused the page and then noted that I had been absent twice. True, but I had been ill and called ahead to cancel. He continued to focus on my absences and how the recorded dates of their missed appointments couldn't possibly be true. He didn't want to see the truth, and couldn't, because he had built himself up to be a great parent in his own mind. His fear of failure, pride, and stubbornness interfered with his ability to take responsibility for his son's lack of psychological improvement over time. Of course, then he went on to blame the treatment program and the entire field of clinical psychology.

As you can see, even clear evidence will not convince some of the truth and they will not change. Remember, we only change when we are in pain. I was hoping to lovingly inflict some psychological pain in order to get this family to commit to healing, but learning something new, even if you know your life would or could be better, can be a frightening thing. Change means having to let go of part of oneself. A part that may not be very functional, but it is predictable and affords us some, albeit dysfunctional, control.

This lack/fear of change is especially obstinate when we hold onto absolutist ideals, as in regard to our political beliefs. We have been "right" (or so we think) for so long that the possibility of seeing ourselves any differently can throw us straight into depression and despair. So, when you are in the presence of a strong-willed individual who won't listen to facts or reason, be kind. They are scared of feeling powerless. Don't ever put up with abusive language and taunts from them, but utilize your empathy skills and try not to take their stinging comments personally. Again, agree to disagree, and then find someone with whom you can discuss politics at length without resorting to childish accusations and name-calling.

In conclusion, keep an open mind, question everyone and everything, be the change you wish to see in the world, and practice listening to the divergent ideas of others. In my family, one of our favorite sayings is "Solutions, not excuses." Let's stop blaming one party or the other for our country's woes. We need to stop glorifying one side while disparaging the other. Be brave enough to see the middle-ground or gray areas where answers are not very clear and concise.

Religion and Critical Thought

12

> To know a person's religion we need not listen to his profession of faith but must find his brand of intolerance.
>
> —*Eric Hoffer*

As my husband insightfully commented, "We all choose the tribe we belong to." For some, religion is a wonderful way to connect with God and others. It is a source of comfort, predictability, and community with kindred spirits. It is a guide to living honorably, respecting self and others, and it gives us a sense of purpose.

For others religion is a relief from having to be fully responsible for our thoughts and actions. If we screw up, we can atone and ask forgiveness, say some prayers, perform some good deeds, and we are back in good standing with God and our spiritual community. As we have seen all too often in history, religion can also be an excuse for bad behavior, such as war and destruction, sexual and physical abuse of our children and spouses, and cold-blooded murder. Religion is also used to manipulate by inducing guilt and ensuring conformity.

"Religious morality is also used to justify political reasoning and supremacy. In the U.S., the First Amendment draws a clear separation between church and state, between religion and politics. Yet every presidential candidate is judged by his or her religious beliefs."

"Prospective Republican candidates use their Christian beliefs as a form of qualification and go to great lengths to show that a good Christian is a Republican, thereby implying that Democrats are not" (Shapiro & Shapiro, 2011).

Some say that they have no religion or that they are not very religious. In response, here is a passage to ponder:

" . . . everyone has a religion . . . We all have some sort of beliefs about the cause, nature, and purpose of the universe. Our religion is simply our map, our paradigm, our beliefs that answer the difficult existential questions . . . Even atheists are religious people because they too have answers to these questions" (Hunter, 1998, p. 93).

Any time the subject of religion is broached, anxiety seems to ensue. We might welcome a discussion on such a topic, but have concerns that it will turn into an argument. Conversely, we might not want to discuss the subject for various reasons. No one enjoys being criticized or questioned, and that is what we are afraid of when we discuss our most personal beliefs, especially if these beliefs haven't been explored deeply by us.

Why can't we have an intelligent, respectful conversation about something so pervasive in our culture? Why can't we listen to and learn from each other, instead of quarreling over whose belief is right and/or attempting to use passages from our holy books to persuade others that they are wrong? Why is there such a strong need to label ourselves and others?

DON'T ASK, DON'T THINK

> Too often we enjoy the comfort of opinion without the discomfort of thought.
>
> —*John F. Kennedy*

For the record, I am not an expert on religion or religious beliefs. I am simply an observer attempting to utilize critical thinking skills in order to understand why humans think, believe and behave the way they do. Just like every other topic in this book, your observations may not match mine. This is perfectly natural. However, because of the emotions any discussion of religion entails, I ask that you read with a very open mind and notice when your own feelings become involved. Write these down and explore them as you read this chapter. Don't just dismiss what is stated because it is different than what you believe or what you were taught to believe. If you can use your empathy skills to see another's viewpoint, even if you don't agree with it, then you are wisely employing critical thinking skills. You will learn about yourself along the way and have a better understanding of others. You will earn respect and this will result in happier relationships as well.

Years ago, a very religious friend gave me her beautiful coffee table book about Native American culture. I perused the tome and couldn't believe she wanted to pass it on. She stated that it had been a gift and that she felt uncomfortable with it because it didn't match her religious beliefs. She also felt that it would be a bad influence on her children. Another friend, in the same vein, would not allow her children to watch programs about other cultures when those programs involved the culture's spiritual beliefs, again, as they were different from her own and she didn't want that information to possibly persuade her children to believe otherwise. Still another friend announced that she couldn't have a close relationship with me and my family because we did not share the same religious beliefs and we could possibly be a negative influence on her and her family. To add insult to injury, she admitted that her religious leader recommended this type of separation to all his congregants.

I truly do not understand this kind of fearful mentality. I was raised in a home where nothing was taboo. We could (and still do) talk about everything. We were free to explore the beliefs of other cultures and religions and ask questions. There was never any concern that we would be negatively influenced by possessing knowledge. My husband and I have carried on this tradition with our children. They are becoming well-rounded critical thinkers and tolerant of those who are different. My friends were and are a very diverse group of people who are also open to new ideas. We have great mealtime conversations about many topics and always learn something new about each other.

There seems, in some people, to be a fear of religious or spiritual exploration. Let's face it, if you grew up and attended religious services on a regular basis, you were taught to believe one set of rules, one way of thinking, and one way of living. You were also taught, either deliberately or indirectly, that other belief systems weren't quite correct, or even altogether wrong. Hence, you only learned about your particular belief and organization and remained fairly uninformed about other religious faiths. For many, there was also inherent in this process a sense of don't ask, don't think. You were expected and taught to accept what was in the holy texts and teachings and to allow someone more experienced and wise to interpret these for you.

This works until you get a job after many years of religion-based primary and/or secondary education or you attend a secular school. You become desegregated and spend time with others who are the same age, yet they can be very different from you. When you are introduced to their customs and beliefs, as well as those studied in textbooks, it can be a bit of a culture shock. The first time I was called a "dirty Jew" was when I was six years old, in first grade. An argument with a peer disintegrated into religious name-calling. I was also accused of killing Jesus. At six years old. Even then, I was angry and appalled that this kid knew nothing of my family's belief system, and I knew he was repeating what he had been told by adults. I naively figured this ignorance and hatred would end as I got older but of course, it didn't. It just wasn't as blatant. A don't ask, don't think mentality damages our ability to think for ourselves and to relate to others. We don't question, seek further knowledge, or pay attention to our gut feelings when making decisions. We are programmed to listen and follow directions. We label ourselves and others as "good" or "bad." We either have the answers or we don't. For some, questioning God, His works, or His representatives (e.g. clergy) is viewed as blasphemous, walking a path straight to hell and eternal damnation. This is not a message wherein its strength diminishes with time or age. I suppose if I learned this early on I wouldn't inquire either. Furthermore, as many parents have painfully discovered, weekly religious instruction and/or sending their kid to a private religious school or college doesn't guarantee that their offspring will adhere to the faith they were born into. Many will question and some will convert to a different religion or abandon the concept altogether. It is a good lesson in realizing that we can't force someone to believe a certain way. Faith has to be in one's heart in order to be sustained.

Another idea to think about is what Kirby and Goodpaster (2007) claim: that most Christians (and I would add those of other faiths as well) "have not objectively investigated alternative religions or looked extensively into the history of their own religion" (p. 17). This investigation would include recognition of contradictory statements and alterations of stories in sacred writings and books, and the fact that religious doctrine has been modified by less-than-holy individuals and groups for purposes other than religious enlightenment. Fear or lack of knowledge of the necessity of educating oneself in regard to religion in general and one's own faith in particular, prevents us from finding and accepting the truth.

When relating to others, the "don't ask, don't think" mentality can be self-injurious in that we cannot grasp another's experience because we only have the filter of our own lives and traditions to rely on. For example, a co-worker of my husband asked him if we celebrate Thanksgiving, since I was raised Jewish. He replied that Thanksgiving is a national holiday, not a religious one, so yes, we do celebrate. Puzzled, she then asked him, "Well if your wife celebrates Thanksgiving, how come she doesn't celebrate Christmas?" I wasn't sure whether to laugh or cry. I guess ignorance really is bliss for some people, but they aren't critical thinkers. I continue to be questioned about certain stereotypes or beliefs, but at least people are asking! If they ask, then I can fulfill my duty as a critical thinker and educate them.

Don't ask, don't think also leads to stereotyping, prejudice, and hatred. Reflect on the reaction you get when you tell someone your religious (or atheistic) preference. You are automatically put into a cognitive box. You can see the expression on the other person's face or hear it in their voice. "Oh, you're (fill in the blank)." Whether this statement is said with delight or barely disguised derision, you know you're sunk. Before you say another word, your conversation partner has already formulated a description of you, your life, everything you believe because you are part of "that group," and a decision is hastily reached about whether or not you'll be friends. I get this all the time whenever I tell someone that I am a therapist, let alone that I was raised Jewish! Oy, a Jewish therapist?! Forgettaboutit! It's funny and sad at the same time.

Critical thinking asks us to assume that no solitary person sets the standard for an entire group. Every person is an individual and their religion (or absence of it), just like their race or ethnicity, does not automatically provide information about whom they are. Move past the stereotypes and get to know them as people, not as members of a specific group. Educate yourself on your religion and theirs, and ask questions.

Please notice as you finish reading this section that I have used the descriptive word "some." There are some people who are taught not to question, and some others who are taught to seek their own knowledge and/or interpret holy books with little assistance or with the support of study groups within their faith. Let's just say that the more you utilize your own thoughts, feelings, and intuition to process information and seek the truth, the better critical thinker you will be.

CAFETERIA RELIGION

Man prefers to believe what he prefers to be true.
—*Francis Bacon*

Some, if not many, of us pick and choose what we want to believe. We staunchly follow and defend some of the rules of our religion and completely ignore other principles. This has been likened to eating in a cafeteria; moving our food tray along the counter and choosing what we like and passing on what we don't like. Hence, **cafeteria religion**. If we are truly honest with ourselves, many of us have to admit that we engage in this process of picking and choosing which parts of our religious doctrine we want to believe and follow. We are human; we want some control over our lives. We don't like being dictated to: what to eat, what to wear, what to believe. Others have explored various belief systems and decided to incorporate ideas from those systems into their own "religion," so to speak. Some principles from Christianity might make sense to you, along with some ideas from Judaism, Islam, and maybe Buddhism as well. This personal view of religion fits our own perception and experience of how the world and people operate.

> **cafeteria religion—** Picking and choosing which parts of our religious doctrine we want to believe and follow.

Cafeteria religion is typically used as a derogatory description of one's philosophy, while others view it as a way to incorporate what feels right to them. It is utilized by those who feel that there are many paths to God, not one correct passageway. For me, the difference is in our awareness of our beliefs, why, and how we follow them.

Let me give you an example. I had a client years ago who presented with moderate depression and anxiety. She was a single woman having an affair with a married man. That would have been enough stress to establish her symptoms, but there was another major factor at work. She claimed to be a devout Catholic. When questioned, she noted her lifelong devotion to the Church, going to Mass every Sunday, being involved in pious activities, and faithfully reading the Bible.

As a therapist, my job was to gently confront clients' contradictory behaviors in order to help them become more aware of their choices, how these choices lead to emotional distress, and how to make healthier decisions in order to stay true to one's self and avoid unnecessary crisis and stress. Of course, I questioned how she could be a devoutly religious person, yet not follow the rules of her belief system. I am fully aware that this is the age-old struggle of humans and temptation, but her contradictory belief vs. behavior was causing her great emotional discomfort. She couldn't continue to ignore the cognitive dissonance and subsequent guilt. Here's what it comes down to: if you talk the talk, you'd better walk the walk. If you're all talk and no action, you will not be trusted or respected. This will be true at work, in your personal life, and in your religious works and worship.

The point here, the one I hammer home to my students every semester, is this: if you are going to believe in something, make sure it is your belief. Explore it, question it, look at alternatives, and decide that the belief does indeed make sense for your life. An atheist student once said that his father asked him to study all religions, Western and Eastern, before deciding on atheism. The student stated that he did so, and still believed, even more strongly, that God did not exist, at least not in terms of a religious version of Him. A wise father and astute son. We are taught our religious beliefs by parents and others early on. We go along with the program and don't question it until we are much older (if at all) and have the cognitive capacity to grasp religious principles on our own. When we just accept our parents' beliefs and traditions without question or exploration we can be comfortable, but not necessarily knowledgeable. If you don't feel religious or spiritual passion in your heart and soul, you will be more likely to stray from your stated beliefs, because they really weren't yours to begin with.

Your principles, if you truly own them, will stand up to questioning and scrutiny, making your faith even stronger. New information may add to your beliefs, allowing them to become richer, deeper, and more personal over time. Different ideas may also force you to decide if what you say you believe is really what you accept as true. This is painful. Do you talk the talk and walk the walk in regard to your declared convictions? If not, time for some soul-searching. This is the scary part for many people. If I question the religion (or lack of religion) I grew up with, others will take offense, maybe to the point of ending their relationship with me. I might find out that I don't agree with the holy principles being espoused, and then what? What if I change religions? What if I decide not to follow any one religion at all?

This is why those friends I mentioned earlier couldn't have a closer relationship with me, though they were unable to state it due to their own lack of self-awareness or because they didn't want to hurt my feelings. Our differences might make them question their own beliefs. They might be confused about how my husband and I (and our kids) can live a functional, happy life and behave morally when we don't espouse specific religious beliefs. This will force them to feel uncomfortable and question the value of religion, or scare them into believing that the Devil is at work in their friend. Thus, it is easier to remain with their "own kind" and not have to deal with or acknowledge differences in others. Besides, they can quote some perceived holy book passages that warn them to stay away from those that might wish to negatively influence them or who might do so unknowingly. They can then claim that they have proof that they are righteous in their beliefs and behavior.

You can't truly know where you stand until you question. God gave you a marvelous, complex brain and the ability to explore it. Think about what you say when you pray. Are you just reciting words that you've spoken for years, or do you really listen and understand what you are saying and asking for? Once, in a Catholic Church service with my husband and his family, the congregation said the Lord's Prayer in unison. I began to notice that many around us were quickly mumbling the words without sentiment. I turned to my husband, who was doing the same thing, and nudged him. "What are you saying?" I asked. "Do you know what you're saying?" He shushed me and promptly forgot the rest of the prayer. I'm sure some of us drift off when we pray at home too, me included. This is normal behavior, but as a critical thinker, strive to focus on how often you say something without really paying attention, like asking "How are you?" when we really don't have the time or inclination to hear how someone is feeling. The bottom line is to be fully present and engaged in what we are thinking, believing, and doing. This is critical thought at its highest level, and yes, you can be devoutly religious and be a critical thinker. Read on to learn how.

At the very least, learn about cultures and beliefs that are different from yours. Whether you like it or not, throughout your life you will be exposed to many kinds of people with various attitudes and ideas about a multitude of topics, including religion. If you know some basic information, you won't end up looking foolish in conversation, you will be more tolerant and accepting of others and you will have more empathy towards them.

This reminds me of the sports teams my children played on for many years. When it came to pizza parties, the team parent ordering the food would invariably be unaware of the Muslim player who did not eat pork products. When the pizzas arrived covered in pepperoni or sausage, the player and parents would feel offended, and the team parent would be mortified. There are two issues going on here. One, if you are different from the mainstream, speak up and educate others. The player's parents never stated their preferences, assuming others would know. Two, pay attention to those you work with or service in some way. The team parent was not purposely hurtful; she just didn't have background information on those different from her. She assumed that everyone had the same preferences as she did. "Assume" is the key word here. Remember, assuming causes us to feel like we know about someone or something when we really don't. If I think I have the answer, I won't feel the need to ask for clarification. What ensue are stereotyping, misunderstanding, anger, resentment, and possibly humiliation.

To reiterate, the best thing you can do you are unclear about someone's beliefs and customs is to ask! How wonderful it feels when someone truly wants to learn about our way of life! What a great way to get to know someone and maybe make a new friend at school, on the soccer field, or build an innovative connection at work.

Here's a nice segue into the next section:

"When we were with the Dalai Lama at his residence in India, we asked him what we could do to help humankind to awaken to caring and kindness. He said how people of different religions should come together in peace and respect and talk openly, honoring each other's differences and similarities. This is a great example of religion and spirituality coming together" (Shapiro & Shapiro, 2011).

RELIGIOUS VS. SPIRITUAL

Nothing is so firmly believed as what we least know.

—*Michel de Montaigne*

Moving into another line of thinking, let's discuss the difference between categorizing oneself as religious and describing oneself as spiritual. They aren't one and the same and exhibiting one aspect does not necessarily mean that you experience the other. By definition and according to the Merriam-Webster dictionary (2013), religious means:

1: relating to or manifesting faithful devotion to an acknowledged ultimate reality or deity

2: of, relating to, or devoted to religious beliefs or observances

3*a*: scrupulously and conscientiously faithful

  b: FERVENT, ZEALOUS

(www.merriam-webster.com).

and spiritual means:

1: of, relating to, consisting of, or affecting the spirit :

2*a*: of or relating to sacred matters

  b: ecclesiastical rather than lay or temporal

3: concerned with religious values

4: related or joined in spirit

5*a*: of or relating to supernatural beings or phenomena

  b: of, relating to, or involving spiritualism :

(www.miriam-webster.com).

One can be abide by religious (aka moral) values, such as The Ten Commandments, or believe in the existence and influence of God, but not adhere to a particular religion. On the flip side, one can conform to the tenets and ceremonies of a particular religion but not really experience a close, personal connection to God. Here is an interesting explanation of the two, from Shapiro & Shapiro (2011):

"Essentially, religion is designed to be our spiritual source of comfort and advice, a structure to provide moral guidelines, a caring community and help for those in need. And in many ways it is. But religion is also the cause of violence, wars, discrimination, bigotry, pain and suffering, all of which are a long way from kindness, compassion, comfort and spiritual reassurance.

At the same time, spirituality is a loaded word, often misunderstood, as its practices include meditation, contemplation and direct communication with universal consciousness. Pope John Paul condemned meditation and yoga as immoral, deluding and even sinful. Yet spirituality is simply the discovery of our authentic self without any trim-mings or labels, which gives us a rich source of values and a deeper meaning to life, whatever our religion.

In the seeking of such meaning, religion and spirituality come together. Spirituality highlights qualities such as caring, kindness, compassion, tolerance, service and community, and, in its truest sense, so does reli-gion. But where religion is defined by its tradition and teachings, spir-ituality is defined by what is real in our own experience, arising from an inner search within ourselves, the finding of our own truth.

Where religion tends to breed separation—my religion vs. your re-ligion, my God is the only real God, my ethics are better than yours, etc.—spirituality sees all people as equal. We are not an "ism" or a label, we are spiritual beings whose purpose is to awaken to our true nature."

Linda Brown Holt (2006) discussed another way to approach the assumed dichotomy:

"Ideally, spirituality emanates from religion, religion creates a safe, encouraging environment in which spirituality emerges and grows. Religion is form: tradition, doctrine, rites and rituals. Spirituality is content: communion with the divine, seeing the holy in all creatures and objects. In reality, this is not always the case. Religion gone bad results in the triumph of form over content resulting in rituals without meaning and the exaltation of dogma. Spirituality at its worst is mind-less drivel, the egotism of the individual believer, even madness."

"One may be a spiritual person, living in communion with God, nature and one's fellow beings, *without* the structures and formulae of orga-nized religion. On the other hand, organized religion is not the ogre some freethinkers would have us believe. Many of the most sublime outpourings of love and faith have occurred within the sanctuary and teachings of church, mosque, zendo and ashram. Where spirit is con-cerned, the forms cherished by the many *may*, but do not necessarily have to, lead to a life of spiritual fulfillment."

As you can see, the differences between religious and spiritual can be viewed as an either/or relationship as well. Even when sources discuss the similarities and differences, it's easy to see which side of the fence these researchers and bloggers sit on. So if religion tends to separate, and spiritu-ality tends to connect, how can one be both religious and spiritual? I guess this could bring us back to cafeteria religion or demonstrate how one can be fully engaged in religious doctrine and truly feel an emotional connection to all of God's people, creatures, and creations. I suspect this unification is what we experience when we proclaim that someone is the embodiment of the Holy Spirit. There is unwavering faith and non-judgmental love. This person can discuss their own beliefs, listen to those of others, and remain attached to those who believe differently. I am honored to have such a friend. We discuss each other's views and lifestyle; she has invited me and I have participated in her church's social activities without once feeling pressured to join, convert, or otherwise change who I am. She truly exemplifies the mindset of critical thinking.

RELIGION AND SCIENCE: A TENTATIVE RELATIONSHIP

> Science without religion is lame. Religion without science is blind.
>
> —*Albert Einstein*

There is probably no other subject that I tiptoe around more than a discussion regarding religion and science. I want to educate, but not offend. I want to enlighten, but also prevent feelings of disrespect. For the record, I don't believe that there has to be such a wide chasm between the two philosophies. I find the combination of Creationism and Evolution to be most reasonable. This philosophy is also known as theistic evolution. I know, this is like cafeteria religion; I should call this cafeteria philosophy. However, I don't accept that one idea or doctrine is the correct one. I see too much gray in the world, too many questions are unanswered and when they are, they encompass remarkably complex explanations. This is where science comes in. We adore science when it solves everyday problems, like how many cups of flour we need in order to bake a cake, or like medical cures and treatments for headaches, cancer, and other illnesses. We are thrilled that we can carry a telephone in our pockets and have instant access to anything, anyone, anywhere, at any time of day. We treat our technologically advanced cars, computers, and televisions better than we treat each other, and we are truly blessed by the number of creature comforts available to make our lives easier and more fun.

However, mention the existence of dinosaurs, briefly chat about the possibility that man descended from apes, or that global warming is occurring and then "science" becomes a pariah. A young woman pursuing a college degree told me that she chose a private religious institution because she didn't "want evolution crammed down my throat." I questioned why she believed that would be the case in a secular university and she said, "Because that's what they do." Interesting that she had that attitude, yet no one in her immediate family had any college experience. After I assured her that is NOT what happens at a secular college, she still was not convinced. She had already been programmed to believe that a secular education would somehow damage her thought process and lead to changing her religious belief. Every theory studied in college is treated as just that: a theory. A theory is a well-thought out idea, not necessarily a doctrine of truth. Some professors are more passionate about these theories than others, but there is no mandate that students must believe and agree with everything the books and instructors say. We strive for critical thought—thinking for oneself while exploring the ideas of others. We want college graduates who have enough background information about different cultures, topics, and beliefs to make their own decisions.

There is also a nasty stereotype that college professors are atheistic democrats who discourage collegial discussion both in and outside the classroom. Again, some fit the stereotype, but many more do not. I know instructors from many positions on the religious and political spectrums.

On the contrary, I have heard from students over the years that their religious education was lacking in exactly this area. One gal in particular admitted that she attended a high school in which discussion about the Democratic party or Democratic candidates was basically not allowed. She stated that students were told that Democrats were "atheistic baby-killers" and that they were the enemy. The student went on to say that even though she disagreed with this vile description, there was no opportunity for debate. Quite frankly, any teacher or professor who discourages open discussion and opposing opinions shouldn't be teaching.

By the way, you don't have to believe that man descended from apes in order to understand and believe in the existence of evolution. Even Charles Darwin, who had a religious background, was extremely skeptical, but still open-minded enough to consider a possibility other than what he had been originally taught. You really can't call yourself a critical thinker at the same time that you denounce any part of evolution as a viable theory. Evolution is a process of change, plain and simple. You have certainly been a recipient of evolution (or a victim, depending on your attitude about aging!) as you have grown from a child to an adult. Certain animal species have become extinct due to changes in hunting by man, weather, and other environmental conditions. And why do you think doctors are always cautious about prescribing antibiotics? Bacterial germs become resistant if we continually use the same medicines to destroy them. They mutate into new forms, or super-bugs, that are extremely resistant to destruction (West, 2013).

Here we are, back to science as being helpful. At the extreme ends, there are scientists who disavow anything having to do with religion and there are religious citizens who will not allow any medical intervention even if their child is dying. Let's not focus on these groups, but on those more or less inclined to study different points of view. Keep in mind that higher education—or the lack of it—does not determine the presence or absence of critical thinking skills.

A particularly offensive example comes to mind at this point. In 2009, actor and devout evangelical Christian Kirk Cameron was indignant about the influence of Charles Darwin's book, <u>Origin of Species</u>. On its 150th year of publication, and under the guise of concern that those entering college were "stripped of their religious beliefs", Kirk and Ray Comfort added a preface to roughly 50,000 thousand copies of the book, in order to present a "balanced" view of religion vs. evolution (http://www.huffingtonpost. com/2009/09/22/kirk-camerons-origin-of-s_n_294349.html). He then had representatives of his faith go to "the top 50" college campuses across the country, including CSU Fullerton, to give these books to students for free. I couldn't wait to get a copy and read the preface. I naively hoped that it would indeed present a balanced viewpoint, but I knew better. Besides being all about contradicting Darwin's theory—though he did give credit to Darwin for being skeptical of his own ideas—it was an exercise in religious guilt and pressure to conform to "the one true way to believe." I wondered how Kirk and his disciples got away with adding the preface to the book and I discovered that, like many early classics, it was never copyrighted; thus, it is public material and can be manipulated in any way.

What was specifically provocative about this whole situation is the way it was presented. Students were told that the book was a new version, but weren't told what the preface was really about. This made it simple for the book to be handed out without discussion or opposition. Many of my students took the book unknowingly and then were furious at the desecration of Darwin's work. Kirk took a lot of flak for his involvement and he tiptoed away with his tail between his legs.

Hopefully, what Mr. Cameron and his associates learned is that if you want to truly educate someone, being sneaky and underhanded isn't the way to go. If you want someone to see your point of view or convert to your way of thinking, tricking them or using guilt as your reinforcer only leaves people angry and even less likely to listen to you next time. What a great way to lose credibility with the audience you are trying to capture.

The idea of combining science and religion also brings up many concerns: fear of the unknown, fear we may change our minds; fear of repercussions from others and God if we rely mainly on science to discover the ways of the world. Those who have been taught black/white, good vs. evil, God vs. Devil might believe things such as people become severely physically ill because they let the Devil into their lives. Mental illness might be viewed as an inner "demon" that needs exorcising. Natural disasters are due to God's anger with man for all kinds of transgressions, and these disasters are signs that the world is truly ending. Going back to the chapter on politics, this is why leaders like Todd Akin make irrational, non-factual comments about basic biology. It is why we hear religious leaders, like Pat Robertson, continually make inappropriate and ill-timed comments about hurricane Katrina being due to God's wrath about the issue of abortion in John Roberts' Supreme Court nomination (Friedman, 2011), over the devastating earthquake in Haiti in 2010 being attributed to a pact made with the devil almost two hundred years before (Fletcher, 2011), and his agreement with Jerry Falwell regarding the causes of the events of 911:

"Just two days after the Sept. 11 attacks in 2001, Robertson welcomed the Rev. Jerry Falwell onto his show to discuss the cause of the tragedy. Falwell's list of guilty parties included "the pagans and the abortionists and the feminists and the gays and the lesbians who are actively trying to make that an alternative lifestyle," not to mention the ACLU and People for the American Way for good measure. Robertson's response to Falwell's venom? "I totally concur" (Romero, 2011).

My personal favorite example of the power of manipulation in religion came from preacher Oral Roberts, whose fundraising techniques tended to be controversial. In January 1987, during a fundraising drive, Roberts announced to a television audience that unless he raised $8 million by that March, God would 'call him home.' Some parishioners feared that he was referring to suicide, as his plea for money was extremely emotional and tearful. He ended up raising $9.1 million (James, 1989; Ostling, 1987).

In conclusion, whatever you choose to believe about religion or science, keep in mind that there is positive and negative on both sides of the fence. Speaking of that fence, let's remember that it has been constructed by man. You decide whether that barricade is necessary or not.

The pure and simple truth is rarely pure and never simple.
—*Oscar Wilde*

Mass Media, Advertising, and the Lack of Critical Thought

■ *13*

> Advertising is based on happiness. We make the lie, we invent want.
>
> *Don Draper, Season 1, "Smoke Gets in Your Eyes"*

Good ole' Don Draper, the advertising executive on the television show Mad Men, got it right. I am constantly amazed and saddened by how we (me included) get swept up in whatever is being told or sold in the media. Everything is fair game, from selling cereal and deodorant, to what she should/shouldn't eat, to intimate relationship "rules," to how we should feel about our bodies. Notice the presence of the word "should." You "should" buy this for your family. You "should" wear this kind of make-up in order to look your best (and attract a mate). You "should" buy this car if you want to be the envy of your friends. This kind of guilt-trip sickens me, especially when I catch myself getting caught up in it during times of low self-esteem or self-doubt. What really infuriates me is the selling aimed at children and the subsequent denial of advertisers when confronted with their obvious psychological and emotional manipulation. I despise being lied to or being treated like I am an idiot.

PERSUASIVE TECHNIQUES—"HEY MOM!"

> Every time we buy something we deepen our emotional deprivation and hence our need to buy something.
>
> *—Philip Slater*

Kids are big spenders

- Teens in the United States spent $189.7 in 2006 and this was expected to increase to $208.7 billion by 2011 (www.statisticbrain.com).

- 80% of girls identified shopping as one of their "hobbies and activities" (www.statisticbrain.com).
- Tween (8-12 years old) buying power was estimated at more than $260 billion in 2008, including their own cash and their parents' (www.marketingsherpa.com).
- Tweens spend 82% of their money on video games, music, movies, books, videos/DVDs, and online virtual worlds (www.marketingsherpa.com).
- 83% of teens own a cell phone and 18% of younger kids own a cell phone (www.youthbeat.com/data-snapshots).
- Youth are more likely to spend their own money on food and beverage than any other type of product or service (www.youthbeat.com/data-snapshots).
- 86% of boys regularly play video games, compared to 57% of girls (www.youthbeat.com/data-snapshots).

It's well-known that advertisers have target audiences. They perform and utilize extensive research on viewers' age, income, educational level, race, and gender. They also recognize that ". . . the earlier a child learns about a brand, the more likely they will be to buy it later (or beg their parents to buy it). And children under 7 can't tell the difference between advertising and entertainment" (Knorr, 2010). Advertisers reach children (and adults) in numerous ways: Through ring tones, ads connected to games, internet sites, phone apps, and of course, television programming.

"Brands sell images to kids as much as they sell products. Companies are smart about making brands seem so cool that every kid will want the products."

". . . advertisers have adapted to children's media, using sneaky methods that don't look like ads. Product placement, online promotions, viral videos, cell-phone updates—even Twitter and Facebook are all reaching kids directly. And with location-based apps like Foursquare, marketers can determine exactly where your kid hangs out and shops to target ads based on your kid's location."

"Ads come to our kids disguised as "free" cell phone ring tones, surveys, and pass-along games and quizzes that capture email addresses when kids respond or forward the pass-alongs to one another. (This is called viral marketing.) And every time a kid puts on a T-shirt or a hoodie with someone's brand on it, he becomes a walking ad for that company." (Knorr, 2010)

When you watch the Super Bowl, to who are the commercials directed? Let's face it; most of the people watching sporting events on television and in particular, the Super Bowl, are men. Beer, junk food, cars, tires, and tools will be hawked, usually including the presence of a hot babe or two. More than likely, you're not going to see a commercial for Kotex or a home cleaning product during the game.

Yes, advertising still resides in the dark ages of male and female stereotypes, but it works. During Super Bowl XLV in 2011, "an estimated 111 million viewers (i.e., consumers) watched the game" (Bickle, 2012). According to the Associated Press, the average Super Bowl advertisement costs $3.5–$4 million per 30 second spot (Bickle, 2012). BIGinsight^{TM} , a consumer information portal provided by a company named Prosper Business Development, asked fans' opinions about Super Bowl commercials. 7.3% stated that commercials influence him/her to search online for more information; 8.4% state that the commercials influence him/her to buy products from the advertisers. 16.9% become more aware of the advertiser's brand (Bickle, 2012). The percentages may seem low, but let's say that 8.4% of 111 million people bought your product within a few days of seeing it advertised on TV. That's over 9 million new customers acquired due to one 3 hour football game. Not too shabby!

Commercials and print ads work because they speak to target audiences' interests, strengths, and weaknesses. Create a fear or need based on these interests, strengths, and weaknesses, and voila! You have a customer for life. So, why not start 'em young? Targeting products to children and teens is nothing new, but it seems like the messages are becoming more blatant, or maybe I am just more sensitive to them since I have my own children. I'm guessing that both reasons are true.

"This generation of children is marketed to as never before. Kids are being marketed to through brand licensing, through product placement, marketing in schools, through stealth marketing, through viral marketing. There's DVDs, there's video games, there's the internet, there are iPods, there are cell phones. There are so many more ways of reaching children so that there is a brand in front of a child's face every moment of every day" (Susan Linn, The Commercialization of Children, documentary, 2008).

Almost every parent will have a story about their child watching a kid's program on TV and suddenly becoming extremely excited, almost hysterical, when certain commercials were aired. In my house, one of the can't-live-without-it products was the chocolate fountain. My kids could be reading or otherwise engaged in something else while the TV blared on and they would immediately come alive when the chocolate fountain commercial came on. "MOM, MOM!! We have to get a chocolate fountain! PLEAAAAAASE! " I instantly hated that commercial and the company that made the contraption. The kids became little advertising experts, attempting to manipulate my emotions too. "Mom, you would love it! We know how much you love chocolate!" Needless to say, reason (my reason) won out and we never purchased the thing. Again, if your child is watching the Disney Channel, Nickelodeon, or any of the other numerous kiddie-programming stations, the obvious target audience will be children, so product-hawkers will advertise items that will interest your child. There might even be ads of interest to mommies too, since they are still more likely to stay home with their children during the week than daddies do. Thus, for advertisers to say that the Frosted Flakes commercial isn't really geared towards children is ridiculous and condescending. Some adults do eat the cereal, but most of us are aware that the sweet taste is meant for children, and the commercials show children eating the cereal more often than they show adults doing so, if at all.

Have you also noticed all the "systems" that are popping up in advertising? You aren't just buying some supplies to clean your car; you are purchasing an auto washing SYSTEM. You need some face wash, eye cream and moisturizer? Invest in a skin care SYSTEM. You don't have word processing software for your computer; you are the proud owner of an operating SYSTEM. It seems that including the word system to the name of any product is synonymous with costly merchandise.

And don't you intensely dislike telemarketers and in-person salespeople who read from a script or have specific, patronizing ways of speaking to you? Sales tactics like using someone's first name over and over really annoy me. Playing to stereotypical male or female sensibilities is insulting. Think car salesman. Don't assume that my gender means that I want a safe, practical vehicle to haul kids and groceries, like a mini-van. Don't be shocked when I request a red car and ask about tire size or horsepower. Just a few years ago a friend in my age group went to look at a vehicle and the salesman actually told her that he would let her test-drive the car when she brought her husband in. Needless to say, he lost that deal. Some ideas and some people don't change, at least quickly.

SENSATIONALISM VS. NEWS

> Whether or not you love television, you've got to admit that it certainly loves itself.
>
> —*Mignon McLaughlin*

I've come to realize as an almost-native Southern Californian (my family emigrated from Washington D.C. when I was three months old) that when it rains here, it's a big deal. How do I know that? The local news stations preface their weather reports using the title "Storm Watch." Whether we are expecting less than ½ an inch of rain or thunderstorms and hail, we are put on alert through "Storm Watch." No wonder residents of other states make fun of us! When I think of a storm that needs watching, I picture an impending tornado, hurricane, or severe downpour that dumps a couple of inches of rain in just a few hours, causing flooding and other chaos.

I suppose that since my state doesn't experience a lot of severe weather conditions, the news reporters need to build the stories into something much bigger than they actually are. Perhaps they're bored reporting only on murders, robberies, and snarled traffic. Sensationalizing news stories is an ancient game, designed to attract and sustain the audience's attention. Nowadays, it also helps a television station's/news program's ratings. What it does for the rest of us is cause anxiety. It's a bit like the story of the boy who cried wolf. Making a big deal out of small incidents too many times leads to the audience becoming skeptical; this in turn leads to apathy and lack of trust. Then, when there really is something urgent to report on, people will more likely tune out, possibly creating a dangerous or even life-threatening situation.

This is different from warning people of, say, an impending hurricane. When I was younger, I heard about people having hurricane parties as a storm approached. These people wouldn't listen to the authorities, who strongly urged evacuation or gave mandatory orders to leave the area. Residents refused to leave their homes and belongings, believing that the authorities were not to be trusted. This is called denial. In recent years, as reports of serious injuries and death emerged due to this denial, as well as more deadly and destructive storms, hurricane parties were no longer cool (Armario, 2009).

This seems like a matter of common sense to me. When emergency personnel tell you to evacuate an area, they are not sensationalizing a problem. They are trying to save lives and get people out of specific areas so they can do their job and not worry about the residents' safety while trying to respond to a crisis involving roads, buildings, etc.

We also see this kind of behavior during California's fire season. People are interviewed on the news declaring that they will stay with their homes, even if firefighters and other emergency responders tell them to evacuate. In 2008 when we had a fire raging very close to our home, a neighbor ranted that he didn't trust firefighters to do their job. They were only interested in saving certain properties, he screeched, and if necessary he would stay and hose down his home. He would even fight them off if he had to.

We started to pack up that night, just in case, while the rest of our neighbors chuckled at us and went to sleep. I'm glad we did; it made us acutely aware of what was truly important. Our family's lives are more important than our belongings. We remembered past reports of people who stayed in their homes until the last minute, and then died trying to evacuate. We watched the news and the path of the fire all night, knowing we might have to make a decision without being alerted by emergency personnel, who would be pretty busy trying to save our neighborhood. Luckily, our homes were spared. We were glad that we took control of our lives and prepared for the worst instead of putting our collective heads in the sand. We utilized logic, emotion, and intuition in being mindful of the situation.

This is what we all have to do when we listen to or read any media accounts of events. How many times do you amuse yourself by reading the headlines of celebrity magazines while waiting in line at the grocery store? Talk about sensationalism! We have to be able to distinguish between real hazards and situations that are exaggerated. We have to trust ourselves and emergency personnel, understand the way the earth functions and renews itself, and learn how to deal with possible negative or dangerous situations. So many of us focus on only part of this equation. I notice that the "dealing with negative or dangerous situations" part tends to be lacking. If we have an earthquake, reporters' interview subjects tend to be either doomsday preppers ("Watch out, the end of the world is upon us") or deniers ("Hey, it's California, we're used to this!"). Of course, what makes things worse is the continual looping of information. Newscasts repeatedly show the same pictures of devastation over and over, for hours on end. Sometimes this is necessary in order for facts about tragic events to sink in, like during the events of 911. People also become aware of breaking news at various times, so news stations need to repeat basic information. However, when we continue to sit in front of the television or computer screen and expose ourselves to this incessant loop, the availability error takes over and we might feel like the world is indeed coming to an end.

After the 6.7 earthquake in Northridge, CA in 1994, I got caught up in this loop and it affected my psychological functioning for weeks. We lived over 60 miles away from the epicenter and had a very strong shaking, and throughout the next few days we experienced mild aftershocks. A few of the local television stations, I believe in an effort to prepare the public for aftershocks, kept a picture of the Richter Scale in the bottom corner of the screen during their daily programming. Quite frankly, trying to watch a sitcom with this picture continually in view scared the hell out of me! I kept glancing at the bottom of the screen, waiting for the needle to move up and down, signaling that an aftershock was in motion. Even worse, when the needle did move, the shaking would start a few seconds afterword. Those 2-3 seconds may not seem like much, but it was just enough time to build up a fight or flight response. It got to the point where, for a few weeks, I'd be walking through the house at various times, pause, and touch something or look at the light fixtures because I perceived that the ground was shaking.

So how much news is too much? That depends on you. My perception is that if the knowledge transfers you from a state of preparation to a condition of paranoia and anxiety, it's time to step away from the media coverage. This way, you can continue to use your critical thinking skills—logic, emotion, and intuition, in order to make the most sensible decisions possible about the world's state of affairs or your own.

BEING POLITICALLY CORRECT AND OTHER EUPHEMISMS

Now, I know among the politically correct, you're not supposed
to use facts that are uncomfortable.

—Newt Gingrich

In his books, insightful comedian George Carlin (2001, 2004) included
wonderful sections scattered throughout on **euphe-
misms**. A euphemism is "The act or an example of
substituting a mild, indirect, or vague term for one
considered harsh, blunt, or offensive" (http://
www.thefreedictionary.com/euphemism). Using a
euphemism helps us to accept a phrase or description more easily, or soften the blow of a difficult or

> **euphemism**—Substi-
> tuting a mild, indirect,
> or vague term for one
> considered harsh,
> blunt, or offensive.

emotionally painful situation. For example, instead of saying that someone
has died, we gently state that he or she passed away. A used car is a pre-
owned vehicle, making it more palatable to purchase one, instead of saying that someone else ate their lunch in it, blew their nose in it, and drove
it first. Euphemisms have also made their way into job descriptions and
statuses. Stewards and stewardesses have become flight attendants. Jani-
tors have become custodians, and housewives are now referred to as domestic engineers. These new titles ensure a feeling of greater respect for
certain employment positions, but they can also make situations or merchandise seem more significant, prestigious, or necessary than they actually are.

When euphemisms are used in regard to differences among people, we
say that we are using politically correct (PC) language. Stating that someone
is African-American vs. Black is a politically correct euphemism, to a point.
Some African-Americans are White (sorry . . . "Caucasian"). I also notice, especially in business and politics, that "politically correct" sometimes means
not directly revealing our prejudiced attitudes. Here's where character and
integrity come into play. Don't claim that you genuinely care about the concerns of homosexual domestic partnerships and then make disparaging remarks about gays and lesbians when you think the microphones are turned
off. Listen to yourself as you respectfully address a person who belongs to
a minority, and then make an ethnic joke about them when they leave the
room. Don't address your administrative assistant (i.e. secretary) as an equal
part of your work team, and then speak to or about him or her in a condescending manner after the meeting is over.

Using euphemisms, including being politically correct, can lead us to
imagine that we are being socially appropriate and thus, we will have no
need for further self-reflection about our true feelings. We can fool ourselves
into believing that we are excellent critical thinkers because we employ the
proper terminology. Remember, whatever you have in your heart is what

you see in the world, so all the politically correct language in the universe won't convince you or anyone else that you truly talk the talk and walk the walk.

MESSAGES ABOUT MEN, WOMEN, AND RELATIONSHIPS

> There is nothing wrong with the world.
> What's wrong is our way of looking at it.
> —*Henry Miller*

As mentioned in regard to advertising, stereotypes about men, women, and relationships are rampant in TV shows, music and music videos, movies, magazines, and video games. As modern as we believe we have become, various media outlets continue to feed into specific gender identities and roles that are really outdated in everyday life. It's confusing to watch TV shows whose main 30 minute focus is finding a sex partner for the evening, then be taught by parents and religion that we should stay chaste until marriage (or at least until Mr. or Ms. Right comes along). We try to teach young women to be independent, not to rely on a man to feel whole, yet women are constantly being portrayed as victims in need of male assistance, or worse, clueless sex objects whose only worth is in regard to their ability to please men (Kimmel, 2009; Tannenbaum, 2002). Conversely, we attempt to educate young men about respecting women, yet the emphasis on voluptuous female super-model bodies (with their subsequent lack of intelligence), and finding hit-it-and-quit-it girls permeate every form of media. Furthermore, men in TV shows or movies are portrayed as inept child caretakers and house cleaners, whose only focus in life is sports, drinking or sex (or all three).

If our family relationships reflect more egalitarian roles, we still have to explain to our children—and model—respectful communication and behavior. What do we want to teach our children about men and women? We also have to set some limits on media exposure.

I had a single-mom student a few years back who bragged about her high-paying job as a cocktail waitress in a males-only club. As part of her contract, she was required to weigh 120 pounds or less. Any more than that and she could be fired. She also described her "uniform," basically a lingerie-type corset, as so body-hugging that she couldn't bend down to pick something up if dropped on the floor. She also noted that each cocktail waitress was shadowed by her own bodyguard, in case the male customers got grabby. In addition, she was also proud that her seven year old son was "becoming a man" (her words). He demanded and received whatever he wanted, and he was allowed to play extremely violent video games such as Grand Theft Auto, which has a mature rating, meaning adult level. She would also happily relate incredibly disrespectful examples of his communication with her and his female teachers. She honestly couldn't understand why he was always in trouble at school. Once, she reported that he told a younger male cousin to "stop crying like a bitch and play the game." Mom didn't want him to be negatively affected by all the females in his life (and the lack of appropriate male role models) and hence, possibly be sensitive instead of macho. He reminded me of the kids in the movie *Talladega Nights*, with Will Ferrell. The movie parents were proud that they were raising their sons to be men who wouldn't put up with garbage from anyone, except that the children were allowed adult privileges and status, turning them into extremely disrespectful offspring. Alas, between my student's job allowing her to be exploited (and controlled) by men, and the messages she was communicating to her son about women and relationships in general, I feared that she was raising a future bully and abuser, not a healthy, loving man.

That's the other bone of contention, amazingly, with some of my female students. They strongly believe that if they choose to play the sexual game, then they are not being exploited. They experience the illusion of control. Another student related her experience as a bartender in a mostly-male club. She noted that she knew exactly what to say and how to show off her body in order to gain larger tips from male customers. She asked what I thought of her choice of occupation. I told her she was worth more than that. A heated discussion among other students ensued, with proclamations about sexual freedom and that men have been manipulating women for centuries. Just because something has been happening for a long time doesn't make it right (or psychologically healthy), and just because you have power equal to someone else's, it doesn't mean you have to use that power in the same way. Find and use your personal power based on your intellect, not your looks. I'd rather get what I want because of solid logic than how much cleavage I expose.

There are many complicated reasons and arguments in regard to this kind of sexually manipulative game playing, but for me, the bottom line is that these women are being taught that exposing their bodies is cute and fun and that playing a role in order to win men's attention is not sexual; they are just expressing themselves. I suppose when they have role models such as the Bratz dolls, and stores like Victoria's Secret selling shorts with writing across the derriere as well as Abercrombie and Fitch hawking thong underwear for tweens, they would naturally not understand that there is a difference between "cute" and "sexy" (Durham, 2008).

In contrast, the young men I have taught over the past ten years or so tend not to want the sex kitten girlfriend. They continually report that they want a friend and lifelong companion, and while they, like women, have certain physical preferences, they aren't all about breasts and tight tummies. Sadly, some of my female students tend not to believe them. They are certain that the fantasies generated by the media are truer than reality.

In addition to gender and sex, I must mention the amount of violence portrayed or implied in today's movies, music/music videos, and video games. As a parent, at times I too have turned a blind eye and a deaf ear to the war-themed video games and harsh music filled with anger and curse words. A relative celebrated her 16th birthday with a party, complete with a disc jockey, music videos, and dancing. I am pretty open-minded and I don't embarrass easily, but I couldn't believe what I was seeing and hearing in the videos and music. So many songs about sex and videos filled with erotically, barely clothed women who were portrayed as sex objects. One video in particular was about "Birthday sex. Got to get me some birthday sex." I wondered what her parents were thinking, especially as the night wore on and the adolescents began to bump and grind on the dance floor.

When we continually focus on the differences between men and women, and relationship rules and gender role "norms" exist, anyone outside these made-up boundaries can begin to feel odd, outcast, or even disconnected from others. As critical thinkers, we need to view people as individuals, not subsets of males and females, wives and husbands, bosses and secretaries. These categories lead to stereotyping and assumptions of how people are "supposed" to be. Thus, we miss out on rewarding relationships because of our preconceived categories and ideas of what are normal or typical behaviors and attitudes.

THE DECLINE OF SELF-ESTEEM AND THE RISE OF COSMETIC SURGERY

Taking joy in living is a woman's best cosmetic.
—*Rosalind Russell*

Manufacturers, magazines, and advertising agencies only make the male/female stereotypes worse. Scan through any women's magazine and you will see page after page of advertisements and articles regarding how to look "better." We waste money on these periodicals seeking reassurance about ourselves (is my wardrobe up-to-date? Do I need to build more muscle?) along with some tips on beauty, sex, and relationships. What we also receive are many subtle and not-so-subtle messages that we aren't good enough. Get rid of those facial lines or you'll look too old! Shave that hair off your chest because women don't like it! Use these products in order to feel beautiful, handsome, sexy, or desirable. We forget that the images in these publications are Photo-shopped and air-brushed, thinking we too can and should have skin, hair, teeth, and bodies as perfect as the models do. In an effort to educate people about photography and computer imaging practices, super-model Cindy Crawford remarked in 1993 that "Even I don't look like Cindy Crawford in the morning" (People magazine, 1/11/93).

For the adolescent crowd, social standing is the focus. Teens are trying to find themselves and fit into social groups comprised of their peers. What better way to influence their budding personas than to not-so-subtilely tell them how they should look, dress, and act in order to measure up and even obtain a boy/girlfriend? These messages are especially insidious for adolescent girls, who are taught early on that their worth is determined by their physical attractiveness, not their intelligence (Berk, 2009; Durham, 2008; Tannenbaum, 2002).

This brings to mind another example of media influence on young women. My daughter, 13 years old at the time, wanted to subscribe to the magazines *Seventeen* and *Teen Vogue*. I used to read *Seventeen* as a teenager and I loved it. It was and still seems age-appropriate in terms of fashion, feeling good about oneself, and even one's budding sexuality. *Teen Vogue*, on the other hand, was filled with advertisements for upscale clothing, accessories, and make-up brands. I cancelled the subscription after we received the first issue.

As I thumbed through this rag, I was sickened by the blatant and sophisticated selling tactics. Some of the ads were highly sexualized, with seductive poses and facial expressions on both the men and women. They were "branding" at the teenage level: a certain look, the self as sexual, and creating a very expensive taste for the finer things in life. There was page after page of perfume sample inserts from the likes of Dior, Burberry, Coach, and Givenchy. Seriously?? I started to wonder how many parents (read: mothers) were really buying their teenage daughters eau de toilette (cologne) or eau de parfum spray (perfume) at prices ranging from roughly $50—over $100 per a one to two ounce bottle. There were ads for Coach purses, Tiffany jewelry, and Gucci sunglasses. How many young girls, in the prime time of their lives for creating an identity, and with their self-esteem usually at its lowest point since birth (Berk, 2009; Tannenbaum, 2002) covet these high end fashion products in an effort to be cool and be viewed as pretty and popular?

Along with the need for high end merchandise and beauty products that is created, girls are continually bombarded with messages in ads and articles about what to wear, which make-up and nail polish to use, and how to exercise to get their bodies in thin "bikini shape" for the summer. The emphasis is on thin bodies, glowing skin and hair, and the perfect outfit. O—M—G! No wonder eating disorders such as anorexia, bulimia, and overeating/obesity exist. Add an unhealthy dose of peer pressure (obvious or indirect) and possible messages from mom or dad at home ("Don't eat that, it'll go right to your hips!"), and now we have a highly toxic mix of low self-esteem, even self-hatred, and the need to fix whatever we perceive (or what others perceive) is wrong with us.

I recently read an article about a 14 year old girl who was mercilessly teased about her large nose and ears over many years (Golodryga & Singh, 2012). This kid had such low self-esteem that her mother contacted the *Little*

Baby Face Foundation in New York, which provides free surgery for kids with facial deformities. Dr. Thomas Romo, president of the foundation, heard of the girl's plight and offered to perform $40,000 worth of plastic surgery for free to help her feel better about herself. When questioned about the message this might convey to other kids bullied because of their appearance, Dr. Romo stated "She wasn't picked to have surgery because she was bullied. She was picked for her surgery because of her deformities." This young lady didn't have a cleft palate; she had large ears. What a horrible message that was sent! If people tease you for any kind of physical difference, they are "deformities" and need to be fixed. Don't assert yourself; don't point out one of their physical weaknesses as a comeback. Gee, that wouldn't be nice to hurt someone else's feelings! It wouldn't be polite to call attention to someone's rude behavior! And if they don't like your nose, ears, chin, breasts, or butt, they must be correct; you do look weird. Call the doctor, get some Botox, or have some potentially risky or damaging "cosmetic" surgery and feel better about yourself. This girl's own mother likened the surgery to ". . . having teeth that required braces" (Golodryga & Singh, 2012). Not quite, Mom. Cosmetic surgery is about vanity; braces are about oral health.

Of course, boys are affected too. They suffer from eating and body image disorders as well, though at a lesser incidence than girls (Berk, 2013), and as they get older they are seeking the services of cosmetic surgeons as well (Kimmel, 2009; Tannenbaum, 2002).

Further, it is no secret that parents have a huge influence on their children's self-esteem and body image. Studies have shown that when parents focus on their own body image, such as weight, eating, focus on being handsome or beautiful, kids are likely to emulate these behaviors. When it comes to mothers and daughters, if Mom diets and worries about her weight, her daughters will too (Tannenbaum, 2002).

Some of my female students share my concerns, and some ask, "If the procedures are available and they make you feel better about yourself, then why not do it?" First, just because something is available doesn't mean it's good for you. Think junk food, cigarettes, alcohol, illegal drugs. Yes, I put cosmetic surgery in the same category because all these examples help us deal with anxiety and help us feel more comfortable, albeit for a short time.

Second, we are talking about surgery here. Someone is cutting open your body and you are given anesthesia, either general or "twilight sleep." Obviously, you run the risk of infection, medical/human error, or even death. There are plenty of stories about those who went in for "simple" procedures, even liposuction, and either were severely injured or died during or after their surgery. Third, as stated above, you will feel better about yourself, or at least the part of your body you fixed, but that doesn't guarantee that your self-esteem will stay elevated for a long period of time. Many people who choose one surgery return for others (Durham, 2008; Tannenbaum, 2002). For some, surgery becomes an addiction.

Fourth, doing the surgery once also doesn't guarantee lifelong results. Once you start Botoxing, you have to continue. If you have breast augmentation, as you get older and gravity takes over you will have to replace the implants. Last, but certainly not least, cosmetic procedures do not magically eradicate your negative feelings of self-worth, childhood abuse issues, or history of failed relationships. There are still internal issues that need to be examined and healed. Notice I didn't say "fixed." This is the word I use for unnecessary surgical/medical procedures. You are getting your nose fixed or erasing laugh lines. When you have internal (i.e. emotional) impairment, you are wounded and need to heal.

Furthermore, all that agonizing while standing in front of the bathroom mirror either aggravates narcissism or creates it. You aren't going to be able to sustain any kind of healthy relationship if your main focus is your appearance instead of your character. Every time you go to a restaurant, you'll worry and talk about calories. When you go to the beach, you'll be too embarrassed about the size of your chest (men and women) to take your shirt off. This will also be a topic of conversation between you and your beach buddy, who will quickly tire of your insecurity and run off to have fun while you continue to wrestle with your internal demons.

With so much social pressure and so many negative messages weighing on us, it's a small wonder that some people have issues with body image! The ever-present focus on physical appearance can lead to depression, anxiety, and eating disorders, which brings us to the key factor in avoiding these situations: self-esteem. When we like and accept ourselves, inside and out, we have no need to purchase anything or overhaul our bodies in order to feel better. Furthermore, when we are empathetic, focused on assisting others, respect and take care of ourselves, and follow a path that is right for us, we don't spend a lot of time worrying about how to be more attractive; we already are appealing. Remarkably, if people would spend half the money disbursed for cosmetic procedures on some psychotherapy, not only would they be able to heal, they would have a permanent "fix" - a lifelong ability to feel good about themselves, regardless of their physical appearance or what others think.

Change what you more safely can, like your weight or hair color. Get away from the mirror and focus on others. I guarantee that once you take control of your life, you won't be so concerned about your physical appearance because you'll have more important tasks to attend to—like caring for, educating, or serving others.

NUMBERS DON'T LIE . . . UNLESS YOU INCREASE YOUR SUBJECT POOL

Clear thinking requires courage rather than intelligence.
—*Thomas Szasz*

When I was in graduate school, I learned of a very interesting, yet sad, phenomenon. Students who were completing master's theses or doctoral dissertations were purposely manipulating research data in order to match their hypothesis. For example, let's say that my hypothesis states that there are a larger percentage of people who have experienced car accidents due to texting while driving, than those people driving without texting on their cell phones. Since I would begin by believing that texting while driving does indeed lead to more accidents, I would want my numbers to match my hypothesis. If I questioned 100 subjects about their texting-while-driving use and found that my data was not statistically significant (that is, within a 5%–10% margin of error), I could either end the study and state that my hypothesis was not correct, OR I could add more subjects to the study in hopes that the numbers in favor of my hypothesis would rise, and thus, the hypothesis would be more or more likely to be correct.

This doesn't exactly sound intellectually honest, does it? Now I know that sometimes it is a matter of numbers, like on election night when newscasters and political watchdogs predict who will win based on 1% of the vote tallied. Later, as was so painfully discovered on election night 2000 between George W. Bush and Al Gore, we realized that the pundits spoke too soon. Sometimes we have to add or subtract (or wait for more information!) in order to get a clearer, more realistic picture of a situation. Drug companies attempt to maintain this balance in finding the safest lowest and highest dosages of medications. They may not be able to get a medication approved through the Food and Drug Administration (FDA) at a certain dosage, due to reports of too many side effects. However, lower the dosage a few milligrams and the drug can still be effective without so many possible side effects. Thus, it can now be deemed safe for public consumption. However, read on to educate yourself about other insidious effects that can happen when we manipulate numbers to our advantage:

"The FDA announced last week that the 300mg generic version of Wellbutrin XL manufactured by Impax Laboratories and marketed by Teva Pharmaceuticals was being recalled because it did not work. And this wasn't just a problem with one batch—this is a problem that has been going on with this particular drug for four or five years, and the FDA did everything it could to ignore it."

"The FDA apparently approved this drug—and others like it—without testing it. The FDA just assumed if one dosage strength the drug companies submitted for approval works, then the other higher dosages work fine also. With this generic, American consumers became the FDA's guinea pigs to see if the FDA's assumption was right. It wasn't" (Maris, 2012)

Here's another example:

"In order for pharmaceutical companies to earn a profit, they must develop drugs that are potent enough to patent and can be approved by the FDA. To gain FDA approval, these drugs must demonstrate an acceptable safety profile. However, the safe dose of potent drugs can vary considerably among individuals. What is safe for some people can be a lethal overdose for others. Yet doctors and drug companies usually recommend the same dose for everyone, even though lower doses of many prescription drugs can achieve the same beneficial effects, while dramatically reducing side effect risk and the cost of the medications."

"Consider the cholesterol-lowering drug Zocor, for example. The recommended starting dose is 20 mg, which has been shown to lower LDL cholesterol by an average of 38%. Scientific studies show, however, that 5 to 10 mg of Zocor works almost as well as 20 mg. This lower dose could reduce the risk of side effects by as much as fourfold."

"If your LDL-cholesterol level is 130 (mg/dL) and your objective is to reduce it to under 100, just 5 mg a day of Zocor should accomplish this. Yet, the typical starting dose of Zocor is 20 mg, and some doctors even start as high as 40 mg. . . eight times higher than the dose needed by many people" (Cohen, 2012)!

Scary, isn't it?! This information helps us realize once again that we must question, question, question—even the experts. A good place to start questioning when listening to or reading a news report in regard to a recent study is this: What is the study measuring or comparing, and how? Does it compare sleeping 10 hours per night vs. 5 hours, or does it just discuss 5 hours as not enough time to rest? Who/what organization funded the study? If the study concludes that coffee drinking is healthy, you can bet that the funding came from a company associated with growing or selling the product. How many subjects did the study include? A study containing one hundred subjects is not enough to convince me to change my eating or sleeping habits. How long did the study last? Was it a quick 5 question survey or was it a longitudinal study completed over 10 years? Who reported the results of the study and what were the conclusions? Sometimes local newscasters don't have all the information and only report on the university conducting the study and the conclusions drawn, without any other identifying information. Are there other variables that possibly interfered (or could interfere) with the results? Perhaps those studies that claim that drinking two glasses of red wine per day can aid in prevention of heart disease have missed a dangerous connection between alcohol consumption and liver disease.

Question, research, question some more, talk to an expert or two, and then be your own expert. However, don't be your own consultant without following this process. You don't get all the knowledge you need from the Internet and not all of it is correct. Ask others who work in the field you are researching. Be prepared and humble enough to realize that your information and concerns may not be accurate and then search for further knowledge to clear up any misconceptions or inaccuracies.

Summing up the material covered in this chapter, be mindful of accepting or rejecting information based on face value: from people in general, ourselves in particular, advertising, news stories, and expert opinions. Critical thinkers recognize that there is more to the story and thus investigate more deeply before choosing a course of action or ascribing to a certain belief. As you can see, this pursuit can save you lots of money and a lifetime of heartache.

Part III
Demonstrating Critical Thinking Skills

Communicating: Do We Converse or Conversate? ■ *14*

> To talk without thinking is to shoot without aiming.
> —*English Proverb*

At this point, we've discussed many issues and factors involved with critical thinking. Maybe you are thinking, "I've got this down!" yet the response you get from others is still less than satisfactory. One possible reason for this dichotomy could be your communication style.

According to Loren Ford (2006, p. 14), there are four key elements of communication:

1. Reasons for communicating.
2. The process of communication.
3. How to be a good message receiver (listener).
4. How to be a good message sender (speaker).

The author goes on to emphatically discuss the famous quote by Ralph Waldo Emerson, who noted that "Who you are speaks so loudly that I cannot hear what you are saying." I would add that who we are can so greatly interfere with our ability to listen and speak to others that we don't recognize our effect on them, and thus, our relationships. Let's discuss who you are, that is, what is your communication style, what attitudes/biases/beliefs you possess and need to explore, and how we can begin (or continue) to pay attention to what we say and how it is said.

WHAT IS YOUR COMMUNICATION STYLE?

> Women are crazy, men are stupid; and women are crazy
> because men are stupid.
> —*George Carlin*

It has been argued for years that males and females have different ways of communicating, not just verbally, but non-verbally as well. In fact, non-verbal communication can be much more telling regarding a person's mood and attitude than the words they use. Think of it this way: someone you've known for years excitedly rushes toward you, squealing, "Hi! It's so good to see you!" Then that person (okay, usually women squeal . . .) reaches out to hug you while turning her face away and barely making contact with you. What the heck? Regardless of the reason for the contradiction (which could be infinite) between words and action, you are going to focus more on the action than the spoken words.

As an evolving critical thinker, it is time for you to observe the details of communication, beginning with yourself. We all seem to be experts at deciphering others' communication, but many of us are pretty clueless about our own style of interacting. As we have already discussed, some studies have shown that people tend to overstate their communication and social skills. We are surprised when others tell us that we seem aloof, yet we perceive ourselves as warm and friendly. Ford (2006 p. 15) noted that "The meaning of any communication is the response you get." He also stated that "It doesn't matter what you think you said; the response you get tells you how effective you were in communicating your message or what the receiver of the message heard."

So, what kind of communicator are you? Are you truly interested in hearing what the other person has to say or are you, like many people, busy thinking about how you will respond when it is your turn to speak? How often you do interrupt others? How often do you correct others? Are you concerned with trying to solve someone else's problems or just hearing what they have to say?

Here's where we could begin a diatribe on the differences between men and women when it comes to communication. We can drum up the tired arguments that women are more emotional, need to talk more than men, and need to vent vs. finding an immediate resolution to problems. Men, on the other hand, are said to be problem solvers who interrupt others often, and are devoid of emotion and the need for extended conversation. When we generalize about gender, research (and our own personal experience) has shown that these differences are sometimes present (Gray, 2012; Tannen, 1990), but the jury is still out on whether these differences are due to brain structure/organization or learning. However, as critical thinkers, we need to take individuals into account and we need to be responsible for our own communication styles, regardless of gender or past learning experiences. Hence, let's move away from the gender issue and toward better communication as individuals.

There are many theories and hypotheses regarding communication styles and each researcher or team of researchers develop their own spin, categories, and buzz words. A few that I really like (and you are more than welcome to research other hypotheses on your own) have to do with broad categories. The first and probably most widely recognized of these focuses on whether one is passive, passive-aggressive, aggressive, or assertive. A number of books explain the categories quite well. Among these are *Your Perfect*

Right: A Guide to Assertive Living, by Alberti and Emmons (1986), *When I Say No, I Feel* Guilty, by Smith (1975), *The Assertiveness Workbook: How to Express Your Ideas and Stand Up for Yourself at Work and in Relationships* by Randy J. Paterson (2000), and *The 5 Essential People Skills: How to Assert Yourself, Listen to Others, and Resolve Conflicts* by Dale Carnegie (2009).

Determining whether you are passive, aggressive, or assertive is a good place to start when observing your communication style. As with any theory with categories, understand that no one fits perfectly into any one category—thank goodness! Depending on the situation, you may be fit into any or all of these categories. Observe when and why you act in certain ways with certain people.

Passive people tend not to express their thoughts and feelings, especially when in conflict with others. They are concerned about disapproval from others and don't want to "make waves" or "rock the boat." Even when they need to and should stand up for themselves, they don't due to fear of conflict, hurting others' feelings, or fear of reprisal. In popular vernacular, the passive person is a "doormat." They're always fine, everything's okay, and it's frustrating to watch them give up their dignity in order to keep the peace.

It's probably safe to say that most of us have acted in a passive-aggressive way at some point in our lives. We don't want to rock the boat by saying no outright, so we agree, "Yes, Dear. I'll take out the trash in a little while," and then never do it. When the other person calls us on our contradictory behavior, we get angry and call that person a nag. This is one of the classic arguing points between husbands and wives. Wives ask (sometimes demand) husbands to accomplish some task, the husband tells her what she wants to hear in order to avoid an argument or responsibility, and then accuses her of nagging when she reminds him that he agreed to carry out the task. Passive-aggressive people have the best of both worlds, or so it seems to them: They can agree with someone or commit to something and then they can create a number of excuses for why they didn't get the job done. They forgot, they were busy, tired, or had a headache. They then feel they have the right to be indignant when they are confronted about their deal-breaking and accuse others of nagging or being controlling.

The opposite extreme is the aggressive person, who tends to bully his or her way into conversations and situations. These people are sarcastic, insulting, critical, and controlling. They interrupt often, usually to mock the other person's opinion or feeling. They'll tell you they're just kidding, and perhaps they truly believe this, but deep down, the other person feels hurt, angry, or confused. Aggressive people unconsciously enjoy those who are passive, because they don't fight back. The bottom line is that "Whether it is direct or indirect, aggressive behavior involves expressing thoughts, feelings, and opinions in a way that violates others' right to be treated with basic respect" (Ford, 2006, p. 71). The aggressive person needs to win, to be right, regardless of how he/she treats others. In fact, if their aggressive behavior is pointed out, they can become more aggressive in defending their reasoning and position! Hardly an example of critical thinking!

Last, but certainly not least, there is the assertive style of communication. Assertive people think about what they say before they open their mouths. They are concerned with solving a problem, not winning the argument. They do their best to treat others with respect and don't take it personally when someone else makes a mistake that affects them. They tend to begin a confrontation with "I" statements instead of the aggressive "you." When they need to complain or confront, they immediately take responsibility by starting with their feelings. "I am mad because you said you would pick up the dry-cleaning and you forgot." The aggressive person will typically begin that kind of expression with "You forgot to pick up the dry cleaning and now I have to do it!" Do you see the difference in approach? Starting with "I" defuses emotions because the speaker is stating that he/she has a part in the situation. Beginning the exchange with "You" leads to the recipient unconsciously "putting up their dukes," or preparing for an emotional and psychological fistfight. They are immediately feeling defensive and when that happens, listening and reasoning go out the window.

There is no guarantee, sadly, that being assertive will defuse a difficult situation or lead to getting what you want, but it is the most respectful way to communicate: it defuses each person's emotions, allows you to clearly state the problem and what you want, and it doesn't involve accusatory remarks or attempts to blame the other for the problem. Being assertive takes practice, always keeping the Golden Rule in mind. Pay attention to this in others when you hear a patron complaining about food, products, or service. Notice the approach the customer takes toward the employee as well as the employee's response. If that person continues to bark at the employee or manager, they will become more stressed and more likely to make further mistakes. You make mistakes too, so be gentle when others fall short. The squeaky wheel may end up getting the grease, but why make someone else miserable so that you can get an extra dollar or two off a product, use the expired coupon, or get a free meal? Be respectful and you will get much more; you might get the free meal, plus a free dessert thrown in because you are so nice and understanding. You will feel good about yourself and you will also earn respect. Maya Angelou once stated "I've learned that people will forget what you said, people will forget what you did, but people will never forget how you made them feel" (http://www.brainyquote.com/quotes/authors/m/maya_angelou.html).

LOSE THE 'TUDE, DUDE! IT'S NOT WHAT YOU SAY, BUT HOW YOU SAY IT!

> Our attitude towards life determines life's attitude toward us.
> —*John Mitchell*

Along these lines, I can't stress enough how one's attitude in approaching others and problems positively or negatively affects all of our relationships. Do you truly view others as your equal? I have witnessed so many people over the years treat salespeople and wait staff as if they were their personal slaves. Do you feel the need to correct even the most trivial of statements made by others? Do you communicate the same way with co-workers as you do with family or friends? We tend to be more polite to strangers and colleagues (and certainly the boss!) than we do with family. Conversing with friends can be completely different as well. Why is that? If we re-examine Freud's theory, he discussed defense mechanisms used by the ego in order to deal with anxiety produced by the conflicting demands of the id and superego. One particular defense mechanism is called displacement, in which we have strong, negative feelings about something/someone but don't feel safe expressing those feelings directly to the other person, so we dump our anger and frustration on someone in our way on the freeway, or we wait until we get home and walk in the door cranky at our spouse, who then yells at the kids, who yell at the dog. . . . It's an ugly cycle. The main idea is that we feel safer expressing strong, negative emotion with people we know aren't going to or cannot hurt us, so we unconsciously (sometimes consciously) "displace" our feelings to those people. As you can guess, this doesn't help strengthen our relationships with others, causing them to withdraw and creating the exact opposite of what we truly want and need: to vent our frustration, connect with, and be heard by the other person.

What does this mean for the person who wishes to be a better thinker and feel in control of their life? It means losing the attitude. You know, when you were a teenager living deep in your own personal fable, your parents would listen to your arguments and warn you about your "attitude." "Don't take that tone with me, young lady! "Do you talk to your friends the same way you talk to me?" Of course not! Your teen's friends would not put up with sarcastic, condescending words or tone of voice. They might decide to end the friendship. You, dear parent, are the "safe" person your teen can dump on in times of stress. However, while this is normal behavior, it doesn't mean anyone has to accept it unequivocally.

How do we "lose the 'tude?" First, we need self-awareness. You might be getting tired of the mantra "Know thyself," but you can't be an effective communicator if you are or act like you are completely unaware of your own emotions and thought processes. What do you **really** think of the person you are chatting with? Do they bore or irritate you? Do you agree or disagree with what they are saying? What are your biases in regard to their personality and communication styles, their beliefs, and what they are saying at the moment? You need to be honest with yourself, then listen to how you speak to that person. How do you treat him/her? When you anticipate talking with this person or about a particular subject, what are your precipitating thoughts?

In addition, we teach others how to treat us, so if you allow someone to speak or act disrespectfully toward you (and this includes any children you raise or work with), they will continue. Conversely, if you believe that others tend to be rude or mean to you, check your own behavior first. You might be getting back what you give.

My parents wisely taught my sister and me that it's not what you say, it's how you say it. Think about how you apologize (IF you do . . .) when you know you've hurt someone. Do you quickly mumble the words, barely looking at the other person? Do you say it without feeling, like you're reciting a grocery list? Do you have a touch of irritation in your voice, or do you actually look into that person's eyes and FEEL sad that you hurt them and tell them so? We pay more attention to actions than words, and we are constantly using intuition, logic, and emotion to decide if someone is being genuine. If your words and emotions don't match, people focus on the emotions. If your words, emotions, and actions don't match, others will focus on your actions, or lack thereof.

Say what you mean and mean what you say. Don't tell someone you miss them and want to have lunch with them and then never set a date. Don't be nice to anyone and then say hurtful things about them to others. Don't allow anyone to say anything hurtful to you without voicing your feelings. Do learn the difference between hearing and listening, as well as talking vs. conversing.

HEARING VS. LISTENING, TALKING VS. CONVERSING

> There is all the difference in the world between having something to say and having to say something.
>
> —*John Dewey*

We can hear without listening. Think about when you are driving and your favorite song is playing on the stereo system. You are hearing the music. Now focus on the words in the song and sing them. You are listening to as well as hearing the music. Try this in conversation now; you are hearing the other person speak but in your mind you are thinking about your response, noticing his/her eye color or what clothes he/she is wearing. We think that eye contact and an occasional head nod mean we are attentive, but there is much more to this special skill. Listening involves the ability to filter out the distractions of the mind and our other senses and truly focus on the other person's vocal inflection, emotion, and words, as well as observing their body language, choice of words, and their eye contact with us. We must realize that listening takes our whole being, which is why we sometimes instinctively stop what we are doing to give our full attention to the other person. When you no longer notice the blare of the television or the man chewing noisily next to you in the restaurant, you are fully present and engaging in conversation. When we are fully present and engaged, our critical thinking skills are at their sharpest. Make it a goal to be engrossed in discussions as often as possible and notice how others become drawn to you because you are respectful and caring.

Along the same lines, we can talk without conversing. Do you talk "at" others or "with" others? Talking "at" others is evidenced by telling your story without pausing to see if the other person is attending, interrupting others to tell your story or your opinion, or telling others what to do. Notice the word "tell" being used often in the preceding sentence. To tell means to give information to someone or to order or strongly advise someone to do something. As you can see, "telling" someone something involves one person speaking, and speaking in order to convey information, not to find out about the other person's thoughts, feelings, or opinions. Telling doesn't even require paying attention to the other person, which is why it feels like someone is talking "at" us; it feels like we are just a sounding board and not very important to the other person. The conversant might as well be talking to him/herself in the mirror.

Talking "with" others means including them in the conversation. We talk briefly, then let them talk, and vice versa. We want to hear what each has to say. We want to tell our story, but also listen to the experiences of others. We welcome questions and ask our own. Both parties constantly pay attention to each other's body language, facial expressions, eye contact, and tone of voice. In a conversation, we should also both be aware when we and the other person have had enough. These subtle—and sometimes not so subtle—characteristics are called **social cues**. Social cues are largely taught and tell us when to speak or not, what to say and how to say it, and when to begin or end a conversation.

> **social cues**—Aspects of social skills that are largely taught and tell us when to speak or not, what to say and how to say it, and when to begin or end a conversation.

According to Tanis and Postmes (2003), "A social cue is a verbal or non-verbal hint that guides conversation and other social interactions." Pickett, Gardner, and Knowles (2004) noted that social cues also influence our impression of each other, reduce ambiguity, and aid in message comprehension. Those who are "cueless" have difficulty interacting with others (Tanis and Postmes, 2003).

I'm sure you have known a person who just won't take a hint that you need to end a conversation. You say goodbye and they tell another story (there's that word "tell" again . . .). I knew a peer in college who was "cueless". He would walk me to my car after class, talking at me the entire time. He seriously never took a breath between sentences, so there were very few natural pauses where one could say, "Well, gosh, I have to get going." As we walked to my automobile I would tell him that I needed to get to work and he would just keep talking. Key ring out and jingling (and I had a LOT of keys), car door being unlocked, backpack shoved into the backseat, and he would launch into yet another story, always about him. I would finally have to interrupt him mid-sentence and get in the car in order for him to shut up and leave! I always felt so rude having to cut him off, but as he told me once, after he actually noticed that I was irritated by his lack of awareness, "I'm not very good at taking hints." No kidding, Captain Obvious! There are a few issues involved here. One, he either didn't learn or completely ignored social cues. Two, insecurity is part of this scenario. He didn't know how to listen or engage someone in conversation so he just kept talking to make himself more comfortable. Three, because of this insecurity, he was extremely needy. He needed to keep my attention by chattering away, all the while not realizing he was losing my receptiveness, and respect.

Don't allow lack of observation of social cues, insecurity, and subsequent neediness to interfere with your work or personal relationships. Learn to pay attention. Learn to be more independent. Learn to be an effective conversationalist. Learn to be quiet. Watch others who do this well and emulate them. Stop talking about yourself and ask the other person about themselves. Not one or two questions and then back to you; show a genuine interest in that person's life. If you can't be genuinely interested, then go back to step one and ask yourself how you feel about that person, or at least end the conversation respectfully. We all want to feel important, and when we talk at others, trying to "fix" them or their problems, talking more about ourselves than our conversation partners, and not paying attention to what they are saying both verbally and non-verbally, we lose valuable opportunities to connect with others, learn about them and ourselves, and practice collaboration in solving problems. You present as conceited, insecure, arrogant, and uncaring. I doubt that's the impression you want to give either professionally or personally.

In summary of this section, remember that attitude is everything when communicating with others, so we must understand our own feelings and motivation when conversing or arguing. Thus, the trick to finding your communication style is three-fold: understand your feelings and motivation going into a verbal exchange, be open to noticing what you say and how you say it, and be painfully aware of the other person's reaction. You will see a pattern in yourself and others and then you can work on changing your attitude and behavior. This, like everything else discussed so far, is a journey. Critical thinkers work on their communication skills their whole lives. They know that there will be many times that they will do well, and there will always be other times when emotion will get the best of them and they will hurt someone else's feelings, come across as arrogant or needy, or passively accept poor treatment. This is called being human.

Managerial Expertise, Employee Relations, and Soft Skills

15

> The truly great leaders are skilled at building healthy relationships
>
> —*Simeon, from James Hunter's book,* The Servant *(1998)*

We've discussed communication styles and skills; now let's put this knowledge to good use at work. Whether you are a CEO, manager, or "worker bee," everyone needs to observe and understand how to get along with others at our place of employment. Most of us obviously know that we cannot act or speak the same way at work that we do at home, yet ironically, some of us have more freedom to be ourselves at work than at home!

Even though this chapter is broken down into specific sections, the underlying issue throughout is one of leadership. Being a leader is not exclusive to the president of the company. A nice definition of leadership comes from the source of the quote above: "The skill of influencing people to work enthusiastically toward goals identified as being for the common good" (Hunter, 1998, p. 28).

THE NECESSITY OF SOFT SKILLS

> That some achieve great success is proof to all that others can achieve it as well.
>
> —*Abraham Lincoln*

Working with students so often, I have noticed over the years that they are so focused on getting good grades or choosing the right university that they forget about developing their communication and social skills. They are worried about getting their first "real" job after graduation and many believe that attendance at a prestigious university as well as a great, experience-filled resume will clinch the deal. Those aspects will most likely get your foot in the door for an interview, but your personality will be the deciding factor in whether you land the job (Morisey, 2008; Parsons, 2011). In case you are smugly thinking, "Yeah, well I graduated from (fill-in-the-blank) university, so I'll get the job over the person who has a degree from (fill-in-the-blank) college," I just want to give you fair warning that it isn't enough. You will be working with a group of people on a daily basis. That means you have to be like-minded and get along with them. You can accumulate all the prestigious degrees and awards in the world but if you can't function appropriately in a group setting and you aren't very productive when working on your own, you won't get or keep the job (Klaus, 2008; Morrow, 2013).

Don't believe me? Ask anyone who runs a business. I know you think you're fantastic (and everyone has told you so) because you have a degree from a very expensive, venerable university, but the people at the top who decide your fate have long gotten over being impressed by someone's detailed vita credentials. They want to see creativity, commitment, action, and results (Buckingham &Buckingham, 2012; Kern, 2010). What kind of work experience do you have? How can you benefit the company? What skills/talents do you bring? How do you deal with disagreement and conflict? Why should they hire you instead of anyone else? What are your short and long-term career goals?

Do you see where this is going? None of these questions has any connection to what college you attended. They are all centered on your personality, problem solving, social, and critical thinking skills.

The workplace is a very unique environment. There are many rules, regulations, policies, and personalities to deal with. Some environments are very formal, some more casual. Make sure you choose the right one for you, in the correct field for you. That's right, interviews are not just for your prospective employer; you must decide if you want to spend a large portion of your life in that particular setting with those particular people, dealing with a particular set of issues.

With all this said, one of the most valuable abilities one can have, professionally and personally, is a set of behaviors and attitudes called soft skills:

"Soft skills are personal attributes that enhance an individual's interactions, job performance and career prospects. Unlike hard skills, which are about a person's skill set and ability to perform a certain type of task or activity, soft skills are interpersonal and broadly applicable."

Soft skills are often described by using terms often associated with personality traits, such as:

- optimism
- common sense
- responsibility

- a sense of humor
- integrity

and abilities that can be practiced (but require the individual to genuinely like other people) such as:

- empathy
- teamwork
- leadership
- communication
- good manners
- negotiation
- sociability
- the ability to teach.

"It's often said that hard skills will get you an interview but you need soft skills to get (and keep) the job" (Parsons, 2011)

According to the Collins English Dictionary (2009), soft skills are "desirable qualities for certain forms of employment that do not depend on acquired knowledge: they include common sense, the ability to deal with people, and a positive flexible attitude."

Soft skills include your ability to recognize social cues. If you are not good at detecting social cues, whether you suffer from some social or behavioral disorder, a form of autism, like Asperger's syndrome, or you just didn't learn to pay attention to these relational indicators, now is the time to learn. No excuses, only solutions. Review the chapter on communication for ideas, read some books on the subject, and/or seek the help of a therapist. Remember, critical thinkers do seek help because they are focused on personal and professional growth.

Now the possibly painful question: How strong are your soft skills? Before you answer, please note that in a Psychology Today article from the 1990s, a survey was conducted to determine how realistically we view ourselves in a number of areas. Guess what? Almost 85% of those surveyed felt they were above average overall. When asked about their ability to get along with others, 100% felt they should be in the top half of the population, 60% rated themselves in the top 10%, and about 25% believed they would be in the top 1% of the population (Hunter, 1998). In a similar review, Tori DeAngelis (2003) reported on a series of studies (with mostly student subjects) conducted by David Dunning and colleagues at Cornell University regarding overestimation of various skills. He and Justin Kruger encountered the "Dunning-Kruger Effect," "in which poor performers in many social and intellectual domains seem largely unaware of just how deficient their expertise is. Their deficits leave them with a double burden—not only does their incomplete and misguided knowledge lead them to make mistakes but those exact same deficits also prevent them from recognizing when they are making mistakes and other people choosing more wisely" (Olson, Zanna, & Dunning, 2011).

In earlier studies, Kruger and Dunning (1999), Ehrlinger and Dunning (2003), and Epley and Dunning (2000) noted that "the least competent performers inflate their abilities the most" (DeAngelis, 2003). Furthermore, we overestimate our competence due to ignorance and long-standing beliefs about ourselves and our abilities. Epley and Dunning (2000) also noted that their undergraduate subjects consistently overestimated the likelihood that they would engage in generous or selfless acts.

Taking this research information into account, as well as your observance of social cues, are you thinking that you're in one of the top brackets of appropriate social skills? Think again. In fact, observe again and again and again. Just because no one has offered any constructive criticism about your various abilities doesn't mean you are doing a great job. Dunning also related that since people dislike giving negative feedback, we don't hear suggestions about how to improve our behavior or work performance (DeAngelis, 2003).

So, honestly answer these questions. How much are you talking vs. listening? Do you pay attention to the reaction of your colleagues when in conversation or when you verbally interrupt their flow of ideas? What facial expressions and body language are they demonstrating? What tone of voice are they using? Do you recognize the signals when someone else wants to end the conversation? Do you respect those signals or do you continue to talk? Do you talk so much that others have to abruptly interrupt you in order to end the conversation?

Another important question is this: Are you giving advice when it wasn't requested, or even worse, at the same time an authority figure is doing so? Students do this to me all the time. I will be talking to two students about graduate school choices and invariably the most confused, anxious person will start giving advice to the more confident one. If your own "house" isn't in order, don't advise anyone else. In other words, take care of your own life before you tell others what to do. There are people who believe that they are friendly and helpful, and truly strive to be, but they are impulsive in their statements and behavior, continually interrupt others, and they feel the need to convey instant answers to everyone within earshot. In reality, they are perceived as arrogant, disrespectful know-it-alls who are busy telling others how to handle work and personal issues but can't seem to pay attention to their own behavior or social cues when in conversation.

Furthermore, in group discussions, do you notice that you are doing a lot of the talking and brainstorming, and that the group ends up doing things your way quite often? Do you have a ridiculously passive, quiet group or are you overbearing and need to win? When the volume of your voice increases, you are trying to win. You are trying to be heard, you want to talk first, or you want the other person to agree with you instead of protest. Now take these casual communication skills into account and think about how you come across in an interview. I bet your style is very similar.

Soft skills are so crucial in today's workplace that companies teach soft skills training workshops, and books and articles are popping up all over the Internet and in book stores (Hunter, 1998; Morisey, 2008; Morrow, 2013; Parsons, 2011). There are too many books to mention; explore some titles through www.amazon.com and find the one that's right for you. It's painful to be truly aware of your mistakes, but it's infinitely more harmful to your psyche if you lose relationships (or fail to create them) or miss out on job opportunities and can't understand why.

AUTHORITY VS. POWER

Honor bespeaks worth. Confidence begets trust. Service brings satisfaction. Cooperation proves the quality of leadership.
—*James Cash Penney*

One of the most insightful, beautifully written books I have ever read about workplace/relationship skills is called *The Servant*, by James Hunter (1998). It's not a novel or how-to book; it's a story of a middle manager who is forcefully requested by his company to spend a week in a monastery with a small group of other professionals in order to improve his leadership and soft skills. A former business-leader-turned-monk named Simeon is the instructor. During the week, as the group processes various ideas about leadership, communication skills, and attitude, all come to realize what they were missing in both their personal and professional lives.

One of the many powerful sections in the book discusses the difference between power and authority, borrowing and expanding on ideas from Max Weber, one of the founders of sociology. James Hunter's (1998) Simeon described the differences thusly:

Power: The ability to force or coerce someone to do your will, even if they would choose not to, because of your position or your might. (p. 30)
Authority: The skill of getting people to willingly do your will because of your personal influence. (p.30)

Anyone can have power, but not necessarily authority. Some parents exert a lot of power over their children, but they are so demanding or abusive that they have no authority with their offspring. The kids will obey due to fear of reprisal, not because they respect their elders. Others may have gained respect and authority, but may not be in a position of power. Hunter's (1998) characters go on to state that "power can be bought and sold, given or taken away," but that authority "is about who you are as a person, your character, and the influence you've built with people" (p. 31). People in power rely on threats (or perceived threats) in order to get the job done. Those with authority rely on their relationships with others to complete tasks. People want to do well and please the person with authority because they respect and maybe admire that person. Having authority with others means that you are an excellent role model. You empower others by treating them as you wish to be treated. Having authority does not imply a lack of discipline; when others make mistakes, they still need reminding or gentle reprimanding. However, this type of discipline will lead to the person wanting to improve. Harsh words or threats of being fired from the person exerting power will lead to resentment and eventually, decreased productiveness from the employee.

According to Hunter (1998), having authority also implies that you should treat your employees as volunteers. I would expand this to our personal relationships or teacher-student connections as well. People don't have to work with or for you, enroll in your class, or be in a relationship with you. They have choices but they chose to be with you at one point in the process. They could work elsewhere, drop the class, or leave the home you share. Kids have choices too. They can stay or run away; they can also leave emotionally or psychologically. Certainly, when they reach adult status, they are free to go as well.

As parents especially, we do need to resort to power at times: raising your voice or even spanking a child. However, if you have no authority your power won't make an impression either, except to demonstrate that you are a bully who yells and threatens to get your way. Think of the boss you once had that everyone feared. Think about the work atmosphere at the company. When people are afraid of reprisal, they aren't mentally and emotionally free to be creative and brainstorm effective solutions. Competition and finger-pointing runs rampant as employees vie to be in the boss' good graces, and no one will challenge outdated, long-standing policies that hold the company (and its profits) back. I worked for a company like this once. I wasn't in the main office every day but when I was, I could feel the tension in the hallways and during meetings. I recall breathing a huge sigh of relief every time I left the building. I didn't feel comfortable expressing my professional opinions and always wondered if I was correctly adhering to company policies, since I rarely got any positive feedback from higher-ups. However, the slightest mistake (and I didn't make many!) meant a barrage of nastiness and threats of job loss, directed at me through my immediate supervisor, who also got verbally slammed for not keeping her employees in check.

My husband works for a company that has a nice balance of authority vs. power. Years ago, when the older gentleman who ran the company passed away, his sons took the reins. Before they did, there was more turn-over in employees who felt the need to move on. When the sons took over, they devised a system of financial incentives that increased morale, production, and profits while decreasing turn-over, and the need to continually train new people. Colleagues from various departments had to interact more often and solve problems more quickly. That meant less time for blaming and more time spent resolving issues. The new system works. Everyone has the opportunity to feel like an important part of the manufacturing process. Who would want to leave when they are being challenged, they feel important and respected, and they receive monetary rewards for being more productive?

DECISION MAKING AND EMPLOYEE SATISFACTION

"In all our contacts it is probably the sense of being really needed and wanted which gives us the greatest satisfaction and creates the most lasting bond.

—Eleanor Roosevelt

I knew early on in my career that I needed a more informal environment with few restrictions on how I spent my workday (aside from requisite meetings). I do best when I am given broad parameters about what is expected and when, and then given the freedom to meet these expectations and deadlines. The one time that I worked for a company with tighter restrictions, I paid the price, and so did my clients. This place of business had very strict times of the day for making phone calls, having client interactions, and even eating lunch. When it was decided that we should go out for lunch, everyone was expected to attend, even if you brought lunch from home. It didn't help that I was much older than my supervisor and the other employees, I was the only married person, and I had a tighter financial budget. I would bring lunch, then be pressured to either leave it or bring it with me to whatever restaurant the cult . . . sorry, group . . . decided on. I absolutely would not humiliate myself (and the eatery) and bring a sack lunch to a sit-down restaurant, so I would stay behind and get some work done. As the group was leaving, I would always hear questioning whispers about why I wasn't tagging along.

Anyway, these "rules" and expectations were weighing me down so much that I began to get angry, depressed, and apathetic. I would cry almost every night while driving home, and I suffered from frequent headaches and digestive problems. I wasn't getting work done on time and wasn't meeting my clients' needs in a timely manner. I switched to part-time, thinking this would help. When it didn't, I finally quit and opened my own psychotherapy practice.

The main issue for me was that I was told when hired that I was being brought on-board in order to eventually help supervise and make program decisions, and almost immediately after I started on the job I got the message that my duties were to follow directions and not suggest any changes in program functioning. I wasn't even allowed to use tried-and-true therapy techniques. I was only permitted to use the same interventions that everyone else was using. This was incredibly frustrating because each therapist has different training, experience, and treatment orientation. Thus, each therapist brings many different viewpoints and therapy techniques to the treatment team. These different perspectives help clinicians view the client's presenting problems in many different lights, which aids the team in addressing all the client's needs by utilizing a number of different modalities of treatment. Curtailing a clinician's use of all possible resources stagnates the individual therapist, the clinical team, and the client's therapeutic progress.

In the end, I wasn't allowed to be part of the decision making process at the clinic, even with the clients assigned to me. I couldn't be me; I had no control over my work day, and no voice in regard to using my therapeutic skills.

There have been many studies done over the years (Black and Gregersen, 1997; Corsentino & Bue, 1993; Faiello, 2000; Kim, 2002; Ritchie & Miles, 1970) regarding the connection between participatory decision making and employee satisfaction. It has become clear that if employees are happy, they perform better. This would be true for anyone accomplishing anything in their lives. Satisfied employees are also more likely to remain with the company (Kaye & Jordan-Evans, 2001). It behooves organizations to keep their employees because the cost of replacing them is prohibitive. In fact, Kaye and Jordan-Evans (2001) found that the cost of replacing workers is 70 to 200 percent of each lost employee's annual salary. Plus, there is the cost of losing highly skilled employees to the competition. Therefore, if employees are allowed to be part of the decision making process, whether in their little corner of the world or in the larger company workings, they tend to be more productive and satisfied with their work. This is a win-win situation: Employees are happy, and companies make more money. Yet, there are many employers intent on making the work environment difficult. Some bosses want all the power (and have very little authority with their team or in their department) and all the glory. Work, like other areas of our life, needs to be meaningful and we need to feel important. Now some people are perfectly content being told what to do. They don't want the added responsibility of decision making at work. They want to do their job and go home, period. That's fine. I am addressing those people who want to make a difference at work. If you feel powerless in the place where you spend most of your waking hours, you won't be an effective, productive employee, you will feel worthless, and you will become depressed and angry.

If you are a boss or manager, take heed. Find out why people in your company or department are leaving or complaining. Some people just need to complain, but you know who those people are. They wouldn't be happy if you promoted them to president of the company. If you are losing good people, don't assume it's just because of money. People are willing to stay with their present company as long as they feel valued and important in the daily process (Kaye & Jordan-Evans, 2001; Kim, 2002), regardless of their salary.

If you are an employee, decide if your present job leads to you feeling valued and important. Watch for balance here; there are some decisions you are not going to be part of. That is someone else's job. However, if you feel unheard in your particular area of expertise, perhaps it is time to chat with your supervisor or seek other employment.

Those of you who are students, understand that the classroom is not a town-hall meeting or a democracy. With some exceptions, you don't get to decide how class time is spent, what topics of discussion are covered, how exams are constructed, or how your professors choose a grade scale for the course. Think of your instructors as your bosses. You wouldn't/shouldn't tell your boss how to run the company, so don't think that you can control what happens in the classroom. Just because you paid for a class does not mean that you have ownership of it or your professor. You are paying for someone's time and expertise, not control of the merchandise or the outcome. Don't tell anyone in charge what to do unless your assistance or opinion is requested.

If you are interested, check out the numerous books regarding career skills/strengths. One that has stood the test of time is *The 7 Habits of Highly Effective People (2004)* by Stephen R. Covey. Others include Dick Lyle's *Winning Habits (2004)*, and Marcus Buckingham's series focused on improving work performance: *First, Break All the Rules (1999)*, *Now Discover Your Strengths (with Donald O. Clifton, 2001)*, and *Go Put Your Strengths to Work (2007)*.

SEALING THE DEAL

You manage things, you lead people.
—*Simeon, from James Hunter's book,* The Servant *(1998)*

In summary, if you want to be a leader in any setting and/or improve your experience at work, you must observe yourself and others. Practice and learn from the following:

- Soft skills
- Social cues
- Authority vs. power
- Decision making and feelings of importance at work

All of these topics focus on the critical thinking requirements and goals of self-knowledge/awareness, communicating effectively, utilizing empathy, educating and teaching, questioning, focusing on relevant vs. irrelevant issues, and taking responsibility for the direction of your life.

If you want the job, be the right, <u>whole</u> person for the job. If you want to keep the job and move up in the company, continually practice the various skills and talents of a great critical thinker. Remember, actions speak louder than words. Be brave enough to ask those close to you how you are perceived. Then be even more courageous in listening to the truth and effecting change within yourself.

Everyday Uses of
Critical Thinking

16

So often times it happens that we live our lives in chains and we
never even know we have the key.

—*Eagles' song* "Already Gone"

We have discussed the definition, requirements, and goals of critical thinking, along with the inherent sense of personal responsibility, but how do
we put these skills and observations into daily practice? For some, making
effective decisions seems to come naturally. Others are constantly struggling
and constantly in crisis. As noted earlier, critical thinking skills are learned,
so we can change for the better. The deciding factor is the effort put into
learning, and isn't educating oneself one of the tenets of critical thinking?

First, you have to agree that you deserve to have less emotional stress
than you currently experience. Second, you need to focus on the decisions
you are currently making and the people with whom you spend time. Third,
you have to be willing to look at painful mistakes—past and present—and
make changes. This means dealing with feelings, which many of us don't
like or haven't been taught to do. There are also certain areas of our lives
that we need to concentrate on. These include social skills, personal relationships, job/career choices/colleague communication, our connection with
money, and intellectual laziness.

SOCIAL SKILLS

As I grow older, I pay less attention to what men say. I just watch
what they do.

—*Andrew Carnegie*

Regardless of the educational degree you earned in school, the university
or trade school you attended, or the size of your yearly salary, one aspect
of your life will most conspicuously advertise who you are: your command
of social skills, including attentiveness to social cues. Having an advanced
degree from a prestigious university does not guarantee a job. If you are bril-

liant but can't get along or work with others, you will continue to search the want ads on weekends (Hildebrand, 2009; Martin-Young, 1996).

Corporate America notices the little details about your personality before you get (or lose) the job. From the first contact by phone, email, or resume, to your Facebook or other social media status, to how you treat the receptionist, you are being studied (Hildebrand, 2009). Is your personality a good fit for the company? Do you treat others with respect? How do you deal with delays? I have even heard that some companies will keep you waiting in the reception area for a while before your interview in order to see how you handle anxiety or unpredictability. While you are waiting, do you sit down and immediately reach for your cell phone to check messages? Do you start to fidget and sigh, asking the receptionist when you will be seen? Do you smile, begin to work on something or otherwise use your wait-time wisely? Do you have an appropriate sense of humor? How you handle stress, conflict, and unpredictability say more about you than your resume and educational degree.

Scrutinizing our social skills can be difficult and painful. We have to realize that we aren't perfect. We don't always do or say the right or best thing. We don't want to be "too nice" because others will take advantage of us. However, we don't want to be so involved with ourselves that we never give to anyone else. Therefore, you must decide how much time and effort you are willing to invest to improve your communication and relational skills. This depends on how much motivation you have to evolve. If you believe that you are "built" a certain way and can't change, you close the door to the possibility of self-renovation.

Sometimes we measure social skills based on whether someone is introverted or extroverted. If you are introverted you tend to be shy in certain social situations. At times, shyness can be mistaken for apathy or aloofness; thus, poor social skills. Conversely, being extroverted involves being outgoing and comfortable socializing with others. Naturally, we tend to believe that those who are extroverted have better social skills. However, the shy person can be very observant, conversant, and a great listener once you get to know him or her. The extrovert may be so busy bouncing from person to person in the room (like Tigger) that they never stay put long enough to have an extended conversation with anyone. They can be too busy talking to give the other person a chance to get a word in.

Some people have difficulty with social interactions because they are hyper-aware, worried that every interaction with others will result in failure or accidentally hurting someone's feelings. They honestly don't know what is correct in terms of conversing with others, especially those they don't know well. This also has to do with "small talk." Many state that they hate small talk, because it seems phony and contrived. Small talk—the art of chatting about trivial topics with someone you don't know well—doesn't have to be phony and contrived. If you genuinely like getting to know people, it is evidenced immediately in your small talk. You convey interest in the other person, try to find some common ground, and you aren't so worried about how you come across that you become too emotionally paralyzed to speak. Small talk involves empathy. You see a stranger drop a load of papers and you rush over to help, joking about the last time you lost some papers in the wind as you walked to your car. You have found common ground, expressed empathy and interest, and made small talk. You don't know how the other person will respond and it doesn't matter, because you are treating that person the way you would want to be treated in a similar situation.

Another reason why social skills are difficult stems from early learning. Were your parents friendly people? Did they start up conversations or joke with strangers in public? Did they use manners in dealing with others (please, thank you)? Did they enjoy spending time with others? Did they tell you funny stories about their adventures with others? Did you have conversations about doing or saying the right thing? An observation I have continually made over the years has to do with nicknames. People I know who grew up with nicknames and/or gave nicknames to loved ones tended to be more outgoing—they had genuine interest in others and thus, extensive social skills. I remember affectionately calling a child "kiddo" in my son's grade school classroom. This was a very quiet Asian boy and I was trying to get him to warm up to me. He immediately and angrily asked why I called him kiddo and what did that mean? I explained it as a term of endearment, like a nickname, and asked if his parents had any nicknames for him. He replied that they did not; they called him only by his first name. Though it was obviously a cultural difference, I felt sad that this little boy's relationship with his parents might be so formal that they didn't banter and joke with each other. I don't know if that was the case, but I was sad nonetheless.

Still another reason for poor social skills is the egocentric attitude some develop. There is a sense of superiority present that constructs a wall between "me" or "us" and "them." There is a sense that one doesn't need to use please or thank you when requesting something. They aren't required to help another or make small talk, or even hold a door open for a few seconds because someone is behind them walking out of a store. These narcissists expect and demand attention and special treatment but don't believe they need to return the favor. Being in their presence is terrific enough. They need not do anything else to improve the situation.

Others are taught, either through experience or direct instruction, not to trust others. Being "nice" is viewed as a weakness. They learn to take what they can get from every situation and person, and not allow others to hurt them or get something better than they do. As Ricky Bobby's father stated in the movie Talladega Nights, "If you ain't first, you're last." We have all seen this attitude and behavior during the holiday season Black-and-Blue Friday sales where people are trampled heading into a store that advertised a ridiculously cheap bargain price on TVs, etc. The next time you go to a buffet-style restaurant, pay attention to people's behavior there too. Most people will take a little bit of whatever food they are scooping and leave some for others. Then there are the food hoarders who compulsively need to take all of whatever they reach for. Then they smile with satisfaction as they walk away with a plate piled high with food, as if they actually won some competition. It is really sad when kids follow their parents' lead on this. I remember standing behind a little boy, no more than 10 years old, whose family was becoming the butt of the buffet line joke because of their food greed. This kid was taking mini-donuts. Not one or two, five or six, with about 10 total in the bin before they would be replaced. Yes, I counted, because I wanted a few too. I jokingly asked him to leave some for the rest of us. He turned to look at me, took the rest of the donuts, and walked away noting that he got them all.

You may not care what others think of your behavior or you may assume that you can play the social game, say what others want to hear, and get what you want, but to reiterate, critical thinkers want to live with character and integrity and they recognize that they don't live in a vacuum. You share the world and its resources with others. If you want the "goodies" in life, you have a few choices. You can take, take, take and be reviled, or share and be respected. There are positive and negative consequences for each life-style. You choose what you are willing to live with. Find a middle-ground between being too nice and being self-centered. Pay attention to the emotional costs and don't whine when you don't get what you want. Change yourself and your situation and become a better person.

RELATIONSHIP CHOICES

He who knows others is learned; he who knows himself is wise.

—*Lao Tsu*

In no other area of one's life is it more important to know thyself, control emotions, and utilize appropriate social skills than in our personal relationships. It is said that we "always hurt the ones we love" but this does not have to be. Here it is crucial to remember two things we have already discussed: (1) We need to treat others the way we wish to be treated; and (2) We teach others how to treat us. I was wisely taught as a beginning therapist that in treatment, clients would only rise to the level of the therapist's psychological and emotional functioning. If the therapist was not handling life well, he/she subsequently would not be able to teach the client to function effectively. This rings true for teaching as well, or any profession or status in life in which one must be a mentor and role model (think parenting too). Conversely, if we are stuck at a certain developmental level or a specific emotional issue, we will continue to attract and be attracted to people who function at our same psychological level, and our children will be stuck there too. For example, if you grew up in your family-of-origin (the immediate family you were born into and lived with), at least one member was an alcoholic, and you had not engaged in any substantial introspection or received psychotherapy to become aware of the issues surrounding living with an alcoholic, throughout your life you would more likely be attracted to needy, dysfunctional people, alcoholic or not.

What I am attempting to say is that when we are not functioning well and making decisions that negatively affect us, we will have the same issues in relationships and we will be more likely to choose people at the level of our dysfunction. Now no matter how psychologically healthy we think we are, all of us have some dysfunctions—personality quirks—that make us unique. The trick is to continually observe oneself, understand one's childhood history and present emotions, and work at changing our attitudes and beliefs for the better. Look back at the huge list of questions in chapter one for more clarification about your "hot button" issues.

The more you grow as a person, the stronger you become, and the more likely you will "move up" psychological levels of functioning AND attract others at that higher level. You will no longer be attracted to abusive, needy, controlling, manipulative, jealous, substance abusing people. You will recognize their psychological and emotional games (i.e. manipulation) a mile away and you will know how to remain detached.

A further bonus of exploring oneself and one's childhood is that empathy and, subsequently, social skills increase. You will treat others the way you wish to be treated and you will not allow anyone to say or do anything to hurt you. You will speak up, you will leave, you won't even waste your time talking with anyone who makes you feel worthless. Then you will be free to seek and obtain the relationships you say you want. You will be the right partner, vs. trying to find the right partner. You will seek a relationship, whether love or friendship, because you WANT someone to share life with, not because you NEED to have someone in order to feel whole or not alone. When we search for someone to share our life with because of emotional need, we fall for the first person who is nice to us. We aren't as choosy and thus we may end up putting up with bad behavior. When you have done some soul-searching, let go of past pain, and are ready to allow someone to be part of your life, it is because you feel complete without that person already. You will be choosier and think more clearly about what that person brings to your already full existence. Their presence will <u>add</u> value to your life, not <u>give</u> it value.

As a therapist, I would always recommend to divorcing or separating clients that they wait at least 6 months before dating again (including sexual relations). Most of the time the client would be appalled. "Six months! That's a long time!" When we end a relationship, especially a long-term connection, we need time to be alone. We are needy, vulnerable, and scared, and we need time to adjust. We need to process our grief at the loss (even if you wanted to split up), figure out why the split occurred, and what role we played in the relationship and break-up. This last part is especially hard because no one likes to contemplate how they screwed up.

It's much easier to blame the other person, especially if you are the dump-ee vs. the dump-er. Countless times I saw clients, friends, and family alike dive right into another relationship, only to be quickly disappointed—and hurt—yet again. One client came to see me about every six months for a few years. He had tremendous childhood issues of loss and abandon-ment, and could never bring himself to explore these extremely painful issues. In the meantime, he had a continually volatile relationship with his ex-wife, who abandoned him and their daughters years before. As he sought new relationships, they all contained the same pattern of women who were highly dysfunctional and could never really have a close bond with him or his kids. Every six months or so he would present in therapy and attempt to describe the present woman and relationship as different from the previous one. The first was blonde and pathologically insecure. The next was petite, brunette, and stalked him mercilessly for months after he broke off their relationship. The present woman was tall, red-headed, extremely religious, and very alcoholic. He denied that they were similar. They looked different and they had separate issues, right? All were highly dysfunctional and incapable of truly relating to someone else because of their dysfunctions. He could then continue his pattern of being involved with women who could never really love him, leading to continual loss, like the kind he dealt with in childhood. To paraphrase what my therapist (thank you Sandi!) once said to me when I struggled with similar issues: Same Poop, Different People.

In summary, take note of who you are attracted to and whom you attract. If you have trust issues, it is not because others are untrustworthy. "Trust in others has so much to do with how much confidence and trust we have in ourselves," suggests Dr. Phil McGraw (2004). Basically, you don't trust yourself to make appropriate choices. Therefore, you are constantly hyper-vigilant about the possibility of getting emotionally hurt in a relationship. We can then unconsciously create what we don't want (rejection) by being controlling, suspicious, jealous, or even apathetic.

Self-trust is about listening to your thoughts, feelings, and gut reactions (i.e. intuition). If you don't trust your choices, how can you be an effective critical thinker? If you are always afraid of getting rejected, how can you grow as a person and truly educate others?

Furthermore, follow the Golden Rule and speak up when someone says or does something that leads you to feel unimportant. Understand your personal issues and how you affect others. Take responsibility for your suc-cesses and failures, and recognize that others have equally valid thoughts, opinions, emotions, and beliefs. It bears repeating that this is a journey, not a destination. If you need the help of books, friends, or therapists, seek it. Critical thinkers recognize the need for and ask for assistance. I saw a won-derful quote in Julie Andrews' book entitled *Home* (2008). Julie's mentor said this to her when she was a budding songstress: "Remember, the amateur works until he can get it right. The professional works until he cannot go wrong" (p. 117).

ON THE JOB

> Life isn't about finding yourself.
> Life is about creating yourself.
> —*George Bernard Shaw*

I always question the unemployment numbers each month, for a number of reasons. There are many variables involved in the reason for unemployment and as a psychotherapist and educator, I often wonder how many of these people without jobs are actually unemployable due to their lack of critical thinking and/or social skills. I have spoken to many ethnic and minority students over the years who are preparing for careers in corporate America or internationally, and they complain that their friends and family have accused them of being "whitewashed" because they have adopted proper business attire, attitude, and manner of speaking. Let's face it, whether we like it or not, we can't address our boss—of any race or ethnicity—like this: "Yo, Bro, wassup?" Part of having a job or career is learning how to interact with people of all cultures, races, ethnicities, age groups, and customs. Unless you own your business, you have to fit into the business culture. In fact, even if you own a business, you still must conform somewhat to professional courtesies and social norms. This isn't about being white or any other race; it's about speaking and acting professionally. If you can't or don't wish to play the game, find another field of work. I knew early on that I could not work in corporate America, wearing suits and pantyhose every day and working the same hours each week. I also don't like being micro-managed. I need to know the guidelines and regulations of my profession and workplace, and I need the independence and trust from management to carry out my duties. I also need to have a flexible schedule that doesn't dictate lunch times or coffee breaks. Therapy and then teaching have been ideal in this regard. In fact, when called upon to dress the part and speak in a professional tone utilizing psychological terminology, I become anxious, insecure, and shy. When allowed to speak casually about my profession, you can't shut me up!

Knowing which occupation and work environment are best for you is crucial to your happiness and decision-making skills. It takes time to figure out the perfect fit, but this is part of personal and professional growth. Once you know how you work best, you must deal with colleagues, underlings, and superiors. I know, my choice of employee descriptors isn't politically correct, but I want to emphasize that you will be interacting with people at all levels of status in the company (and life in general) and you must learn how to treat them all with respect. I naturally gravitated to the secretaries everywhere I worked. This wasn't a brown-nosing ploy on my part; I have always had a great deal of respect for support staff, like secretaries, receptionists, and nurses in doctors' offices, because they have to deal with the everyday stresses and difficulties of running a business and interacting directly with clients or patients. They also know how to obtain what you need and how to get around the system when there is a crisis of some sort. They work their fannies off to make the office run smoothly and I know there were many days when their job was a lot harder than mine, and I was treating severely emotionally disturbed children and their parents! Long story short, how you treat the people who support you or work underneath you says volumes about your character, integrity, and people skills, three characteristics that help you land and keep your job.

On the flip side, your boss, whether you like him/her or not, deserves your respect too. That person works very hard to maintain a professional atmosphere, bring in new business, and maintain all the employees' standard of living, including salary and benefits. Your attitude is crucial here. Your boss and the company don't owe you anything. You owe it to them to do the best job possible, compromise with colleagues, and work toward company goals. Quite frankly, if you are going to spend a majority of your life working, make sure you do something you love, give 110% every day, and work in a place and for people who respect and value you and the work you do. Don't bring your personal problems to work, don't look for dates or a mate there, watch your language, including off-color sexual comments or jokes, and don't gossip about anyone. Always dress appropriately, even at the yearly holiday party. How you behave at work should not be the same as you behave with friends or family. Have some fun at work, definitely, but pay particular attention to what you say, how you say it, and to whom you say it.

DOLLARS AND SENSE

Balancing your money is the key to having enough.
—*Elizabeth Warren*

Getting back to the opening sentences of this section, many of us, because of our culture of narcissism, we think that we deserve more than we have or get, and don't believe that we need to treat colleagues with respect, let alone support staff, and then we wonder why we are fired, why we can't land a job, or don't get raises and bonuses. I remember reading a question and answer forum in the local paper about a year or two ago, at the height of our 2008 economic woes. The woman asking was wondering if she made a mistake turning down a job in which she was offered $75,000 per year. She previously had a job making $80,000 per year and felt that $75,000 was not enough, that she would take a big financial hit. I can only imagine the forum supervisor's shocked and disgusted response (as well as her prospective employer's) as he explained that after taxes that the woman was only giving up around $300 per month and that she would more than likely have made up the difference in pay raises and bonuses after a few years. Instead of $75,000 per year, down from $80,000, she was still getting temporary unemployment wages. What was this woman thinking?! She was inflexible. She had a set dollar amount in her head, as well as a set prestige/status level to live up to as well. These narcissistic image factors interfered in her ability to make a wise career/financial decision.

I have known several people over the last few years that, due to the economy, lost very good jobs. These were people with careers who had great difficulty finding another job in their chosen profession. Apart from the depression and worthlessness they felt, they still had a sense that the only job they would take would be in the same pay range and/or level of seniority. Psychologically, they were trying to re-create themselves and didn't want to start over at the bottom, so they were only looking for prestigious jobs comparable to what they left, but they were continually disappointed.

In such cases, we must put pride and other strong emotions aside—I've been there, I know how hard that is—and look for and accept the job that might feel a bit beneath us. I had to do this at the workplace I mentioned earlier and I hated every minute of it. My skills were not being used and when I volunteered them, I was told I didn't have enough seniority in the company to basically do what I was licensed and experienced to do! I struggled with constant physical symptoms, I cried, I got angry, and then started to plan what I really wanted, which was a private practice. I was terrified that I wouldn't have enough clients to make a living and pay the office bills, let alone those at home, but as I inquired more and more, I found that I would have enough clients at first to sustain a very modest income and that there was tremendous room for growth. After six long, awful months working for a company that was poorly managed (they bounced paychecks a few times, even with money steadily coming in) and downright unethical at times, I happily opened my practice close to home with an insurance company that I worked with for many years, which sent me the bulk of my clients. I had my own hours, my independence, and my sanity. I became more confident as a therapist and businesswoman and this newfound comfort later led to organizing and presenting seminars, which led to the job I have loved the most, teaching. The moral of the story? Put your pride aside and be open to new possibilities. You can't always be at the top and being at the bottom can give some perspective and hunger to do and be more. Your anxiety can be harnessed to either feel sorry for yourself or push you to concentrate on other opportunities.

While we are on the subject of money, and whether there is an economic "crisis" or not, we all need to be responsible for our finances. I am astonished by the number of people who don't know where their money goes each month. How do you not keep track of how much money you bring home, how much you pay in bills, and how much leftover, or discretionary cash you have to save and play with? With my salary changing every semester, I regularly list what our average monthly bills are, how much we save, and how much we can spend. We adjust our finances accordingly and make sure we are not spending more than we have. We take out a set amount of money in cash from my husband's paycheck each week and that is what we both use to have lunch out and pay for a few errands. If we need more, we let each other know. We have joint checking and savings accounts that we can both access at any time. We discuss what we will spend money on and make decisions together on larger items like cars, furniture, repairs, and vacations. This all seems very sensible to me and part of the partnership called marriage. Others have different viewpoints. Some have trust issues and don't want or feel they need to share their salary with a spouse. Those of you saying you trust your spouse BUT you want the finances separate are fooling yourselves. Money is about control and control is about trust. Listen to friends who argue over which one will pay for dinner that night or whose salary will pay for the mortgage vs. the car. It's one thing to have separate play money accounts, but I'll tell you, the married clients I saw in therapy and those I know now who don't have at least one joint account to pay their mutual bills did not/do not have close bonds with their spouses. I know one couple in which he does not know how much money his wife makes and she does not share her money with him. He has his money, she has hers, and large purchases are made—I'm talking automobiles—without consulting each other. Their monetary relationship (okay, their marriage in general) is akin to two 5 year olds who don't want to share their toys.

Money is about control, and it is also about power. It feels good to see your name on a paycheck and then be able to spend that money any way you please. Spending money can bring us psychological comfort, like eating junk or comfort food. I love to buy soft or sweet-smelling things for myself when I am feeling down. However, I know when to stop. As we saw in the great real-estate-economic-bust in recent years, many of us got carried away with spending for comfort. We quickly found out, as author Spencer Johnson (1984) so wisely stated, "The joy of toys never lasts forever."

We can blame the government, the banks, other mortgage lenders, the moon being full, but in reality, individuals are to blame for their own financial ruin. We put our trust in others to tell us what to do and we don't research the issue ourselves. Yes, the banks and mortgage lenders all invited us to get cheap, short-term home loans that would get us into the McMansion of our dreams, with the promise of an ever-growing economy with ever-growing salaries and many of us, in our greed and narcissism, sucked it up like chocolate milk through a straw. We worked <u>hard</u> for a living and we <u>deserved</u> to have a huge house, a gigantic, gas-guzzling vehicle, and $7,000 per year grand vacations! Everyone else was doing it, why couldn't I? I knew people who were taking equity money out of their new homes to build a pool, landscape their property like they were living in a swanky hotel, and buying fancy cars. Having a brand new mortgage and then immediately increasing your debt with a second mortgage in order to build that pool and spa in your backyard is financial suicide for many, as far as I'm concerned. Using coupons for groceries, clothes, or restaurants was quietly considered gauche, cheap. God forbid anyone should be frugal. The image of wealth and prosperity had to be upheld at all costs. Then the housing bubble burst, as all bubbles do, and people lost jobs, cars, homes, and their dignity. All of a sudden, frugality and self-sacrifice are "in." I believe there are at least two parts to this problem: (1.) Lack of education and comfort in dealing with stress/emotions and (2.) Lack of education in handling and understanding money.

Let's begin with lack of education and comfort in dealing with stress/emotions. We have continually discussed the importance of emotion in our lives: being comfortable acknowledging and expressing emotion, and how emotion drives our decision-making skills.

Since money brings us control and power over our lives, sometimes it may feel like the only indicator of how we are doing in life. It is measurable, unlike doing good deeds for the sake of doing good deeds. Spending money can instantly make us feel happy, comfortable, and carefree. Quite heady emotions for the simple act of buying a cup of coffee, or something on a grander scale. Let's face it, it's no fun to always be frugal, having to watch what you spend and even agonize over the most minor monetary decisions. I never liked shopping with girlfriends if I didn't have some money to spend. It's fun to help someone else spend money, but at the end of the day, I wanted something to take home too, to make me feel strong and independent. I have noticed throughout my life that those who are comfortable with themselves and in dealing with emotion usually are doing well financially. I'm not talking about being "rich," whatever that means, but handling their money in healthy ways and not succumbing to societal trends or the ever-present need, largely created by companies in conjunction with the media, to buy things and have the latest equipment. Self-esteem and financial well-being go hand in hand. This is something to think about if you are serious about becoming an excellent critical thinker.

In regard to lack of education in handling and understanding money, again, our recent societal financial crisis made everyone acutely aware (or should have) that we are sorely lacking in teaching our children and ourselves how to manage money. How many of us really understand how "simple" interest works, whether it involves savings accounts, mortgage interest, or credit card debt?

When I was in high school, there was a special math class for the kids who weren't taking geometry, trigonometry, or calculus in order to attend a four-year college. It was not so lovingly and mistakenly called idiot math, and the kids who were going to college weren't allowed to enroll in the course. The class taught all the practical applications of finances: how to understand mortgages, simple interest, credit cards, and balancing a checkbook. I would have given my right arm to take that class instead of trig. Luckily, I had parents who taught me financial basics well, including the very practical advice of living within your means and always knowing how much money you have, whether it's what you are carrying in your wallet or how much was stashed away in the savings account at the bank. This understanding of very basic, real-world math is lacking in our younger generations today, as well as their parents. I have some students who can't even figure out their present grade in the class based on the points already recorded. Either they are lacking in simple math skills, or intellectual laziness is the main culprit. I believe both factors are to blame.

INTELLECTUAL LAZINESS

"What's the use you learning to do right when it's troublesome to do right and ain't no trouble to do wrong, and the wages is just the same?

—*Huck Finn*

Over the past few years, I have become aware of a growing phenomenon with some of my students, and even my own children: intellectual laziness. My husband has noticed this in certain middle-aged colleagues as well. I define intellectual laziness as the unwillingness to explore options and seek necessary information on one's own. Again, here's another issue that comes down to personal responsibility for one's success or failure. Students won't add up the number of points they have in order to obtain their present grade in a course, nor will they attempt to use a calculator. They'll ask me. They won't spend five bucks to buy a mini-stapler to bind papers together for a report; they'll come to class and ask if I have one.

I can't tell you how many times students will ask where a particular topic is in the course textbook. Do they search one of the current chapters we are studying or consult the index in the back of book? Nope. They email me. In rare cases, the material isn't readily available, but the majority of the time the information is right at their fingertips. They don't search on their own, they want the answers—now, please! If I can't (or don't) help in time, they will turn in an assignment with missing data, stating that they tried to email me because they couldn't find it in the book. It becomes, to them, my fault that points will be deducted from their score. Those of you already whining that the student is correct are the perpetrators I am talking about. The answer is simple: attempt to do the work before you ask for help. Don't spend 5 minutes, but don't agonize for 5 days either. You know what a satisfactory effort entails. When you don't attempt to solve your own problems, you appear weak, needy, inefficient, and irresponsible. When you are confronted about your lack of persistence, you will end up feeling humiliated or even angry at the person who challenged your carelessness.

My own kids will have to look up a definition of a word in the dictionary and one of them will immediately ask me what the word means. I don't mind doing this once, but after the third time I remind my offspring that we not only have an actual tome called a dictionary, but we have an ever-present Wi-Fi connection too. The response I get? "It takes too much time to look it up!"

With the Internet and information on any topic at our disposal 24/7/365, there is no excuse for this intellectual laziness. If we don't know specific information about a political, religious, or lifestyle topic, we can get the facts from our phones while having lunch (granted, though, this is not the best time). Intellectual laziness is not just about seeking information. It also involves the opinions and beliefs we hold so dear. Remember, when we think we have enough information, we stop looking for answers. We become comfortable with our opinions and beliefs and forget where they came from, or when (Ruggiero, 2012).

When this comfort and eventual laziness transfers to one's career, it can slow the work environment, lower employee morale, and lead to continual conflict. If you aren't willing to solve your own problems or help in the process with others, you will be the employee everyone loves to hate. "Oh geez, Harry will be at the meeting? All he does is blame others for his department's mistakes, and then he demands that other employees solve the problems." Yet again, narcissism rules: I don't make mistakes. I don't have to apologize. I don't have to answer to anyone. I don't care what others think of me. Understand and express responsibility for your errors, fix the problems, learn from them, and move forward. You will gain respect and maybe even a bonus or pay raise for being a forthright, trustworthy employee. Translate this into your personal life as a spouse, lover, friend, parent, or relative and it's a win-win situation.

Those Opposed to Critical Thinking

17

It makes sense if you don't think about it.

—Anonymous

Over the years, as I have assisted clients in increasing self-awareness and their ability to solve their problems, as well as teaching in both community college and university settings, I began to realize that not everyone supported the requirements and goals of critical thinking. I know, pretty naïve of me, but learning/the pursuit of knowledge have always been passions of mine and when I was younger it never occurred to me that others felt differently. Why would knowledge of self, others, and the world be a negative thing? We were born with incredible brains that have amazing creative capacity. Why shouldn't we use what we were gifted to its full extent?

Remarkably, there are people and groups, some we know and live with, who believe that higher-order thinking is detrimental, even evil. Some are concerned that questioning may lead to doubt, which might result in modifying or abandoning one's religious beliefs (Gervais & Norenzayan, 2012; Grewal, 2012). Yes, that does happen. However, if one is questioning in the first place, then that person's convictions really aren't his or hers; they have been absorbed from someone else and followed, but not truly what one accepts as true. Remember, if your beliefs aren't explored, if they aren't firmly established in your heart, then they weren't your beliefs to begin with. If our tenets are well-established then they should stand up to any amount of scrutiny and even solidify our stance, as long as we have rational answers and reasons for our convictions, usually supported by facts or very convincing, analyzed faith. Thus, we must employ higher order thinking skills (HOTS) in order to enhance effective thinking and decision making:

"Higher order thinking skills include critical, logical, reflective, metacognitive, and creative thinking. They are activated when individuals encounter unfamiliar problems, uncertainties, questions, or dilemmas.

Successful applications of the skills result in explanations, decisions, performances, and products that are valid within the context of available knowledge and experience and that promote continued growth in these and other intellectual skills" (King, Goodson, & Rohani, 2012).

However, there are some individuals and groups who are opposed to teaching HOTS in K-12 schools, and most certainly in higher education. These individuals and groups fear that secular instruction including HOTS will turn students away from faith and religion. Therefore, in this chapter we will explore reasons for opposition to critical thinking, along with some warning signs to be aware of as you encounter this population of detractors.

INDIVIDUALS

To the man who is afraid everything rustles.

—Sophocles

Those of you who are currently students, as well as those of you who long since graduated from college or another type of higher order thought training probably know someone who is vehemently opposed to higher education or critical thinking in general. Some people just don't believe that critical thinking is useful and see this training as a waste of time. Some parents feel this way about college. Why spend time thinking, reading, and questioning when you should be making money instead? Some don't know the experience of college or understand that these years are not just about learning a trade to assist in paying the bills. This makes sense to me; this has to do with lack of knowledge about or valuing the learning process. Not everyone should attend a community college or university in order to find their life's work, but we all need to think for ourselves. Oh wait; there are some who don't want that either. They feel uncomfortable with this concept and learned early on to trust authority figures to tell them what to do, how to think, and how to lead their lives. Whether those authority figures were one's parents, doctors, teachers, political or religious leaders, they follow along, not allowing themselves to question these authorities' decisions and reacting to the world instead of responding in a reasoned fashion. These people tend to take information at face value; they don't seek information for or against ideas because they believe the authority figure's perception. They don't wish to be questioned and when they are, they avoid having to think about their beliefs by becoming angry, withdrawn, or simply leaving the room.

In developmental psychology, we discuss identity development, something we all deal with at various times in our lives, but especially during adolescence, when it is our job as teenagers to start exploring who we want to be, what our creed is, and how we want to live our lives. Identity, according to Erik Erikson (1950, 1968), is important in becoming a productive adult. It is a time to begin to separate both physically and emotionally from one's parents. This can bring conflict between parents and children as kids push for independence and parents must gradually let go of control of their offspring. As parents, when we don't allow our kids to think for themselves and we don't encourage verbal discourse on personal and world events, not only do we miss out on our kids' burgeoning cognitive processes, we also stunt their growth as individuals. Some may decide to rebel and others may take on the parents' belief system without further question. The direction depends on the parents' openness to their kids' way of viewing the world, along with each child's temperament.

For those kids who take on their parents' beliefs without question, James Marcia (1980) would state that they were in a state of identity foreclosure. This means that one has "committed to a set of values or goals without exploring alternatives" (Berk, 2013, p. 479). As we get older and more experienced we may feel more comfortable exploring new ideas, stop caring altogether and have no direction, or just transfer our foreclosure to a spouse and believe what he/she espouses without question. You can probably guess how life turns out for those who don't fully explore and consciously choose their values and priorities and always follow the crowd, or those who purposely don't commit to any goals or values and wander from job to job and relationship to relationship with no plan for the future.

GROUPS

> The mind of the bigot is like the pupil of the eye; the more light you pour upon it, the more it will contract.
> —*Oliver Wendell Holmes, Jr.*

Some individuals opposed to critical thinking also belong to groups who share their viewpoint. This is an instance where ethnocentrism comes into play. Dr. Scott McLeod (2012) is one person who noted the sad irony of one such group:

The Republican Party of Texas states in its official 2012 political platform:

"We oppose the teaching of Higher Order Thinking Skills (HOTS) (values clarification), critical thinking skills and similar programs that are simply a relabeling of Outcome-Based Education (OBE) (mastery learning) which focus on behavior modification and have the purpose of challenging the student's fixed beliefs and undermining parental authority" (http://txdemocrats.org/2012/platform.pdf).

In response, Dr. Scott McLeod, blogger on www.dangerouslyirrelevant.org, responded:

"This is astounding since most everyone else in America seems to understand that our educational graduates and our employees need greater, not less, development of critical and higher-order thinking skills in order to be effective citizens, learners, and workers in our hyperconnected, hypercompetitive global information society" (2012).

The Texas Republicans' charge of "challenging the student's fixed beliefs" is a preposterous misnomer. Beliefs are not fixed; people's perceptions are (or can be). Our beliefs are not always accurate and thus need to be refined and redefined as we gain knowledge. Remember, the quality of your life is determined by the quality of your thoughts and decisions (Schick and Vaughn, 2014), so if our thoughts are inaccurate, we will make some serious mistakes! And "undermining parental authority"? Since when do parents own what their children think? Just exposing a child to certain situations or ideas (e.g. religion or politics) does not lead to that child having strong beliefs in favor of those ideologies. Talking the talk does not necessarily lead to walking the walk, as we have seen in ourselves and others countless times. Discussion and reflection lead to solid belief. This must include discussion of ideas contrary to one's beliefs as well. This is what some individuals and groups are really afraid of. It's like allowing sex education in the schools or talking with your own children about sex. There is great concern for some that the more we tell our kids, the more they will want to have sex. This thought process goes on to claim that the less we tell them, the better off they are. Then we wonder why 12 year olds are having babies. Even though study after study has shown that the more open we are about sex and sexuality, the more likely kids will wait to have their first sexual experience and the more likely they will use birth control and be responsible for themselves and their partner (Henrich, Brookmeyer, Shrier, & Shahar, 2006; Kirby, 2002), some people refuse to read, let alone believe this research.

Other groups that may dislike and discourage higher order thinking are certain strict religious organizations. Again, the official stance of an organization may be one thing, but the practices of its participants may be completely different, so try not to stereotype the beliefs of individuals in these groups as being all-encompassing. Think of your own religious beliefs (or lack thereof). You don't follow every edict of your chosen creed, nor (very likely) does anyone else.

With that said, one particular religious group that tends to oppose critical thinking and higher education is the Jehovah Witnesses. In their official Watchtower newsletters, they warn against the temptation of higher education. "Although Jehovah's Witnesses are encouraged to do well at school, the Watchtower speaks against advanced education. It is described as a waste of time since the end is near, a place where dangerous ideas form, and pursued by people interested in power and wealth above spirituality" (Grundy, 2012). For example, in the September 1st, 2008 newsletter, scenarios of temptations were presented, including this one: "A well-intentioned teacher urges you to pursue higher education at a university" (Grundy, 2012). Other listed temptations included cigarette smoking, drug and alcohol use, posting your profile on the internet, or watching a movie containing violence or immorality.

Some other religious groups include some evangelical Christian churches, Orthodox Jewish sects, and some stringent Islamic organizations. The perception is that higher education, i.e. questioning, takes one away from God and true worship of Him, which means that at some point someone might decide to turn away from the religion. Yet, why would an organization want members who don't truly believe in the teachings being espoused? They would be living a lie. This is where cynicism regarding religion comes into play; more members equal more money, which equals a bigger organization and more power to influence political agendas. Belief should come down to what is in one's heart, not how much money is put in someone else's pocket. If that is the case, then religion would be doing exactly what it accuses non-religious critical thinkers of doing: pursuing material gains instead of spiritual growth.

There are other fringe groups that discourage higher order thought. In fact, in 2007, a website called Family Security Matters (FSM) listed the 10 most dangerous organizations in America. That list included universities and colleges, with a rank of #2 (www.familysecuritymatters.org; www.democraticunderground.com). FSM also produced an occasional list of the 10 most dangerous college courses. To be fair, after reading the latest list, some of the courses described seemed inappropriate, but I would hardly call them "dangerous." Although the author, Jason Rantz (2009), claimed that:

"Clearly the term "dangerous," in this context does not mean after a student takes a course, they will become violent activists that take to the street in arms; the term simply refers to the dangers of churning out students who are not capable of thinking for themselves."

So Rantz is concerned that college students won't be taught to think for themselves, but here are his comments in regard to a class at Brown University entitled "Introduction to Gender and Sexuality Studies":

"Gender and Sexuality Studies, whether here at Brown or elsewhere, is where confused students with a chip on their shoulders (usually hard-core Feminists and gay-rights activists) go to vent and get a degree which will not prepare them for the real world or help them get a job. An angry Gender and Sexuality Studies graduate with no job? Look out—that's dangerous."

Wait, I'm confused. Universities and colleges are among the most dangerous organizations in this country because they disallow students from thinking for themselves, yet taking a course regarding the study of gender (which is much more in-depth than Mr. Rantz realizes) in which students can and do express their independent viewpoints, is useless?

Still more contradictory and ironic, the FSM organization includes contributing writers who are currently or have been university professors. In addition, based on the dramatic word use employed, these writers are hardly objective about opinions with which they disagree, but that can be said for any group on the far left (i.e. liberal) or far right (i.e. conservative) of any issue.

Bear in mind that these examples remind us to "consider the source" when choosing a stance on political, religious, educational, or even daily decisions we make or beliefs we ascribe to. Identify the slant in terms of descriptive word use and the emotional appeals evoked.

Bottom line, in academia, as in other professions or organizations, there are great role models and there are poor ones. There are those who express their thoughts more objectively, some more subjectively. No one is 100% objective, but the question here is whether that person or organization is willing to allow discourse for all opinions and whether there is openness to changing one's viewpoint after considering evidence both for and against one's position.

As uncomfortable as it may be, examine both extremes and then analyze the middle ground, where you will undoubtedly find more gray areas, more complexity, and fewer knee-jerk reactions. Be aware of the confirmation bias (remember from chapter 1?) at work; are you searching for information that agrees with your viewpoint or are you truly attempting to investigate all sides of an issue? When you have a preponderance of information from diverse perspectives, only then can you truly think for yourself and make an educated (pun intended) choice.

WARNING SIGNS

A great many people think they are thinking when they are merely rearranging their prejudices.

—*William James*

So how do you know if someone or a particular group is opposed to critical thinking? After all, they may welcome you to the fold and ask about your credentials, but something might seem amiss. Check your gut feeling—your intuition. Do you feel like no one really wants to discuss both sides of an issue, even if they say or act like they do? If there is no openness to new ideas, or you are mocked because you see things differently, you are facing opposition. I have to honestly state that due to past experience, my personal bias is that when I meet someone who is either devoutly atheistic or devoutly religious, I tread lightly. In fact, anyone that leans way to one side or the other and has that either/or mentality regarding any line of thought tends to be closed to different viewpoints. I do not try to change that person or poke them intellectually in order to start a verbal and psychological battle. However, if they continually attempt to challenge me, I will respond in kind.

Recently, I went to pick up my daughter at the home of one of her friends, who happens to be Islamic. When I arrived, I found the friend's mother in deep conversation with another parent, who happened to be devoutly Christian. I love to learn about others' religious viewpoints, so I was all ears. I listened for a while as each woman explained her religion's beliefs and teachings and each found that they were very similar. They were genuinely interested in each other's faith. However, the Christian woman began to sweetly but firmly quote Bible scripture on the "correct" version of events to believe. She then turned to me for support, assuming I was also Christian. I attempted to lighten the situation by exclaiming that I was raised Jewish and how we now had the "holy trinity" in the room! She continued to question my beliefs, but in such a way that she tried to use my knowledge (and lack of it) to convince me that Christianity was The Way. So much for a great conversation in which we could all accept and educate each other. This gal was obviously uncomfortable with other viewpoints and she persisted as she began to discuss other topics, like homosexuality and teaching of evolution in public schools. She attempted to support her arguments with facts but what she claimed made no sense to me, as it was all one-sided and based on information from devoutly religious organizations; her information had no basis in science. In fact, she derided science and scientists to the point where I felt the need to interrupt and ask where she was getting her version of biological and physiological information about how the human mind and body function. She didn't answer.

Minutes later when I was asked about the topics of my university teaching, the Islamic woman was appalled that I would invite my students to explore their personal beliefs and ask questions, even about the very existence of God. She stated that this type of investigation was not the responsibility of individuals; this was the job of religious clerics/leaders. Untrained individuals alone, according to her, were not capable of making such important decisions.

Neither of these women was wrong, in my eyes. These examples are not being presented in order to prove anything or humiliate certain groups. For me, this was a lesson in humility and understanding, as well as being open to different viewpoints without having to defend one's (or one's group) beliefs or attack another's. I did walk away feeling frustrated as well; not because we didn't agree, but because we didn't agree to disagree and just listen.

The moral of the story here is to be patient with those who are different. Be open to learning from them as much as you want them to learn from you. If the conversation turns into a competition or argument, gently, respectfully excuse yourself. Don't argue or try to win. It's not worth the aggravation and it will only end in someone saying something hurtful, which never helps anyone.

What Now? Moving Forward

18

"A wise man knows his own ignorance. A fool knows everything."
—*Charles Simmons*

Congratulations! You are now reading the final chapter of this book. I hope along the way you have learned much about yourself, as well as how to understand and communicate with others. You certainly will have some new critical thinking skills at your disposal. Perhaps you have some questions or concerns about where and when to use these skills. There are times to speak and act, and other instances where silence is best.

HOW AND WHEN DO I USE MY NEW SKILLS?

"If I am going to be an effective critical thinker, shouldn't I be using my skills with everyone, all the time?" This is a question that I hear occasionally. It's a valid inquiry. As you have learned throughout this book and life in general, there are some people you can talk to and some you can't. In professional situations, such as business meetings and conversations with colleagues, absolutely. When you are involved in heated discussions about controversial topics, of course. When you are trying to influence a peer or your parents, especially on trivial or mundane topics . . . maybe not.

The most important thing to keep in mind is your own motivation. Self-awareness, one of the requirements of critical thinking, is key. Why are you reviewing or arguing a particular point? Are you truly attempting to educate self, other, and/or find the truth or are you trying to win? If you have answers for nearly everything that is said to you, then you are unconsciously trying to build up your ego and feel good about yourself. If you are arguing about insignificant issues, such as which brand of ketchup is best, you are trying to win. Listen to the tone of your voice, the words you use, and how your messages are received. Don't use finding the truth as an excuse to bully or badger everyone with whom you converse. How do you know if you are bullying or badgering? Simple; you have an answer (usually sarcastic) for everything and you won't stop talking long enough to listen to the other person. You find yourself thinking of ways to counter the other person's arguments instead of keeping your mouth shut and your ears open. The other person will let you know how you are doing too because they will become irritated with you, fidgety, maybe even sarcastic and loud. Remember, critical thought does not include having all the answers.

Always use your CT skills to question and investigate. Understand that this does not necessarily mean verbally. No one wants to know everything that goes on inside your mind. Practice another requirement of critical thinking: the ability to recognize relevant vs. irrelevant information. Choose your battles wisely and take responsibility for your role in conversations, relationships, and events. Furthermore, be aware of psychological issues (yours and others') that interfere with critical thinking:

- Control
- Insecurity, Neediness
- Low or over-inflated self-esteem
- Lack of trust
- Lack of Coping Skills
- Denial of Responsibility: Feelings, Thoughts, Actions
- Poor Social/Communication Skills
- Drug Use
- Fear, Anger, Grief

Finally, know that your critical thinking skills are only as good as your overall functioning on a given day, so be aware that feeling ill, tired, hungry, stressed, angry, depressed or even deliriously happy will interfere with your memory, cognitive, and emotional performance, and hence, your decision making. Always treat others the way you wish to be treated and be the change you wish to see in the world.

WHEN NOT TO USE YOUR NEW SKILLS

For some people, knowing when to be quiet is fairly easy. For others, especially those without a seven-second delay between the brain and the mouth (meaning: impulsive), knowing when to zip your lip is a lot more difficult. To reiterate, CT is a lifelong journey, not a destination, so education needs to be a constant goal. Learn from your mistakes; understand what you did and why, and generate and follow through on a plan to conduct yourself differently.

There are some definite times and reasons not to demonstrate your CT skills. These include any instance where your safety might be in jeopardy. When your airline trip has suddenly turned into a cruise, you wouldn't argue with the flight attendant about whether or not you should wear a life vest as you disembark the airplane. Along the same lines, if someone is pointing a gun in your face and demanding your car keys, it's most likely not a good time to reason with the fellow about why he wants your automobile.

Be careful about how you communicate with your boss or other authority figures. You may think you are being respectful or feel that you have the right to question that person's practices because you have great ideas, but your supervisor or instructor may not agree. In fact, that person will be angry about your egotistical fantasy that you can and should dictate how they run their company or decide on classroom policies. One of my husband's colleagues lost his job for this very reason.

Furthermore, pay attention to how often you correct others. Every once in a while I encounter students who feel the need to constantly correct my statements (even when I am joking). They don't quite understand that sometimes others speak a certain way in order to make a point, exaggerate a story, or provide basic information about a very complex topic. Perhaps it involves impulsivity; they feel compelled to speak. Maybe they just want to set the record straight in order to feel in control. Whatever the reason, people who engage in this practice of correction appear arrogant, condescending, and annoying to others. I have noticed that some of these students briefly recognize when others are irritated with them and they look defeated for a moment…until they find another idea to repair. To reiterate, no one enjoys working with a know-it-all. Because effective critical thinking involves self-awareness, you would be wise to detect other people's reactions and change your behavior. Otherwise, you will lose out on valuable personal and professional opportunities. Then again, you might be so busy believing that you know more than others or that they need your instruction that you won't even notice the loss.

As another example of when not to use your CT skills (or even believe you possess them), there was a judge in Florida who sentenced an 18 year old woman to a 30 day jail sentence along with a $10,000 fine because she cursed at him and flipped him off as she walked out of the courtroom (Vinclauv, 2013). Good job, Your Honor! Granted, this "adult" was not using CT skills at all, though she possibly believed she was because she was questioning authority.

We may not always agree with the rules and regulations, but we need to follow them in order to stay physically safe and get along with others. If you decide that you are above the law and you can ignore the rules, then be prepared to face and be accountable for the consequences.

One more instance in which CT skills may not be helpful is when you are dealing with someone who thinks in absolutist terms. CT is all about finding and defining gray areas and absolutists don't believe there are shades of gray. For them, the world and decisions are black and white. You're either Republican or Democrat; Black, White, or some other racial group; gay or straight; good or evil. These folks don't want to discuss anything contrary to their rigid views. Follow their lead and keep quiet. Don't try to educate these dictators; you'll just end up in a very obnoxious, loud quarrel. Use the same caution in dealing with someone spewing hateful rhetoric. Keep in mind that you can't teach someone who doesn't want to learn. My interpretation of this plays with a variation of an old saying . . .

"You can lead a fool to knowledge but you can't make him think."
—*Unknown*

Here's another way of looking at this:

"A man convinced against his will is of the same opinion still."
—*Benjamin Franklin*

KEEP ON KEEPING ON

Keep on questioning
Keep on learning
Keep on growing
Keep on yearning

I didn't write this book because I am a perfect critical thinker. I certainly am not. Each day I experience successes, commit errors, and realize something new about myself. Each semester I am grateful for what my students teach me about whom they are, who I am, and who I wish to be. I practice critical thinking skills as a part of my daily routine. I know where these skills have taken me so far and how much more I need to discover. It is my hope that you will begin (or continue) your personal journey of better self-awareness, healthier life choices, and a happier, less stressful life. As far as we know, we only live on Earth once. Make the best of it, for yourself and others.

I would like to conclude this manuscript with a beautiful, insightful passage from the movie, *The Curious Case of Benjamin Button (2008)*, about a man who ages backwards. I share the character's sentiments.

In a letter to his daughter, Benjamin wrote:

For what it's worth: It's never too late or, in my case, too early to be whoever you want to be. There's no time limit, stop whenever you want. You can change or you can stay the same, there are no rules to this thing. We can make the best or the worst of it. I hope you make the best of it. And I hope you see things that startle you. I hope you feel things you never felt before. I hope you meet people with a different point of view. I hope you live a life you're proud of. If you find that you're not, I hope you have the strength to start all over again.

References

Alsop, R. (2008). *The Trophy Kids Grow Up: How the Millennial Generation is Shaking Up the Workplace*. San Francisco: Jossey-Bass.

American Heart Association, (2012). 2011 Statistics on Obesity in the U.S. Retrieved February 11, 2012, from http://www.americanheartassociation.org

Anderson, C. A., Carnagey, N. L., & Eubanks, J. (2003). Exposure to Violent Media: The Effects of Songs with Violent Lyrics on Aggressive Thoughts and Feelings. *Journal of Personality & Social Psychology, 84*(5), 960-971. doi: 10.1037/0022-3514.84.5.960

Anderson, C. A., Funk, J. B., & Griffiths, M. D. (2004). Contemporary issues in adolescent video game playing: Brief overview and introduction to the special issue. *Journal of Adolescence, 27*, 1-3.

Andrews, J. (2008). *Home: A Memoir of My Early Years*. New York: Hyperion.

Andy Warhol quotes. Retrieved February 11, 2013, from http://www.brainyquote.com/quotes/authors/a/andy_warhol.html

Article on Cindy Crawford (January 11, 1993). *People magazine*.

Armario, C. (May 14, 2009). For Some in Florida, Hurricane Season Is Time to Party. Retrieved February 11, 2012, from Wells Media Group, Inc http://www.insurancejournal.com/news/southeast/2009/05/14/100493.htm

Bandura, A. (1977). *Social Learning Theory*. Englewood Cliffs, N.J.: Prentice Hall.

Bandura, A. (1986). *Social foundations of thought and action: A social cognitive theory*. Englewood Cliffs, NJ: Prentice Hall.

Bandura, A., Ross, D., & Ross, S. A. (1961). Transmission of aggression through imitation of aggressive models. *Journal of Abnormal and Social Psychology, 63*, 575-582.

Bandura, A., Ross, D., & Ross, S. A. (1963). Imitation of film-mediated aggressive models. *Journal of Abnormal and Social Psychology, 66*, 3-11.

Baumeister, R. F., & Leary, M. R. (1995). The need to belong: Desire for interpersonal attachments as a fundamental human motivation. *Psychological Bulletin, 117*, 427-529.

Bell, J. H., & Bromnick, R. D. (2003). The Social Reality of the Imaginary Audience: A Grounded Theory Approach. *Adolescence, 38*(150), 205-219.

Bell, S. M., & Ainsworth, M. D. S. (1972). Infant crying and maternal responsiveness. *Child Development, 43*, 1171-1190.

Berk, L. E. (2006). *Child development* (7th ed.). Boston: Pearson/Allyn and Bacon.

Berk, L. E. (2009). *Child development* (8th ed.). Boston: Pearson/Allyn & Bacon.

Berk, L. E. (2013). *Child development* (9th ed.). Boston: Pearson Education.

Berninger, V. W., Abbott, R. D., Augsburger, A., & Garcia, N. (2009). Comparison of Pen and Keyboard Transcription Modes in Children with and Without Learning Disabilities. *Learning Disability Quarterly, 32*(3), 123-141.

Bickle, M. (February 6, 2012). The power of super bowl advertising. from http://www.forbes.com/sites/prospernow/2012/02/06/the-power-of-super-bowl-advertising

Black, J. S., & Gregersen, H. B. (1997). Participative decision-making: An integration of multiple dimensions. *Human Relations, 50*(7), 859-878.

Blum-Kulka, S., Snow, C. E., & Aukrust, V. (2002). 'What Did You Do in School Today?' Speech Genres and Tellability in Multiparty Family Mealtime Conversations in Two Cultures (pp. 55-83).

Blumenthal, A. (August 20, 2012). Trophy kids at work. Retrieved from Public CIO website: http://www.govtech.com/pcio/Trophy-Kids-at-Work-Opinion.html

Bly, R. (1996). *The sibling society*. New York: Addison-Wesley.

Bolles, R. N. (1971). What Color is Your Parachute? Berkeley, Calif.: Ten Speed Press.

Bounds, G. (October 5, 2010). How Handwriting Trains the Brain. Retrieved from The Wall Street Journal website: http://online.wsj.com/article/SB10001424052748704631504575531932754922518.html

Bourne, L. (November 4, 2007). How children benefit from adult conversation. Retrieved from http://www.blog.montessoriforeveryone.com/how-children-benefit-from-adult-conversations.html

Bowlby, J. (1969). *Attachment and loss: Vol. 1 Attachment*. New York: Basic Books.

Brazelton, T. B. (1992). *Touchpoints: Your Child's Emotional and Behavioral Development*. Reading, Mass.: Perseus Books.

Brehm, S. S. (1992). *Intimate relationships* (2nd ed.). Boston: McGraw-Hill.

Brown Holt, L. (June 21, 2006). Religion vs. Spirituality. Retrieved from http://www.religiousscholar.com/religion-vs-spirituality-terms/

Buckingham, J., & Buckingham, M. (September 28, 2012). Note to Gen Y Workers: Performance on the Job Actually Matters. Retrieved from Time: Business and Money website: http://www.business.time.com/2012/09/28/note-to-gen-y-workers-performance-on-the-job-actually-matters.html

Bushman, B. J., & Anderson, C. A. (2002). Violent video games and hostile expectations: A test of the General Aggression Model. *Personality and Social Psychology Bulletin, 28*, 1679-1689.

Calaprice, A. (Ed.). (2010). *The Ultimate Quotable Einstein*. New Jersey: Princeton University Press.

Carlin, G. (2001). *Napalm & Silly Putty*. New York: Hyperion.

Carlin, G. (2004). *When Will Jesus Bring the Pork Chops?* New York: Hyperion.

Carter, T. J., & Dunning, D. (2008). Faulty Self-Assessment: Why Evaluating One's Own Competence is an Intrinsically Difficult Task. *Social and Personality Psychology Compass, 2*(1), 346-360. doi: 10.1111/j.1751-9004.2007.00031.x

Cizek, G. J. (1999). *Cheating on Tests: How to Do It, Detect It, and Prevent It.* Mahwah, N.J.: L. Erlbaum Associates.

Coady, D. (2011). An Epistemic Defence of the Blogosphere. *Journal of Applied Philosophy, 28*(3), 277-294. doi: 10.1111/j.1468-5930.2011.00527.x

Cohen, M. D., Jay. (2012). Drug Overdosing: How to Avoid Medication Side Effects. *Life Extension News.* Retrieved from Life Extension website: http://www.lef.org/protocols/prtcls-txt/t-prtcl-165.html

Corsentino, D., & Bue, P. (1993). Employee involvement. *FBI Lmv Enforcement Bulletin, 62,* 10-11.

DeAngelis, T. (2003). Why we overestimate our competence. *American Psychological Association Monitor, 34*(2), 60.

DeBecker, G. (1997). *The Gift of Fear.* New York: Dell.

Definition of common sense. (2013). Merriam-Webster, Inc.

Definition of euphemism. (2013). www.freedictionary.com

Definition of logic. (1989). Webster's Encyclopedic Unabridged Dictionary of the English Language

Definition of narcissism. (2012). www.dictionaryreference.com

Definition of reason. (1989). Webster's Encyclopedic Unabridged Dictionary of the English Language

Definition of religious (2012). Merriam-Webster, Inc.

Definition of soft skills. (n.d.). *Collins English Dictionary—Complete & Unabridged* (10th ed.).

Definition of spiritual. (2012). Merriam-Webster, Inc.

Dickerson, S. S., Gruenewald, T. L., & Kemeny, M. E. (2009). Psychobiological Responses to Social Self Threat: Functional or Detrimental? *Self & Identity, 8*(2/3), 270-285. doi: 10.1080/15298860802505186

Dohnt, H., & Tiggemann, M. (2006b). The Contribution of Peer and Media Influences to the Development of Body Satisfaction and Self-esteem in Young Girls: A Prospective Study. *Developmental Psychology, 42*(5), 929-936. doi: 10.1037/0012-1649.42.5.929

Dohnt, H. K., & Tiggemann, M. (2006a). Body Image Concerns in Young Girls: The Role of Peers and Media Prior to Adolescence. *Journal of Youth and Adolescence, 35*(2), 141-151.

Dunning, D. (2007). Self-Image Motives and Consumer Behavior: How Sacrosanct Self-Beliefs Sway Preferences in the Marketplace. *Journal of Consumer Psychology, 17*(4), 237-249.

Dunning, D. (2012). Confidence Considered: Assessing the Quality of Decisions and Performance (pp. 63-80). New York, NY, US: Psychology Press.

Durham, M. G. (2008). *The Lolita Effect: The Media Sexualization of Young Girls and Five Keys to Fixing It.* New York: The Overlook Press.

Ehrlinger, J., & Dunning, D. (2003). How Chronic Self-Views Influence (And Potentially Mislead) Estimates of Performance. *Journal of Personality and Social Psychology, 84*(1), 5-17.

Eisenberg, N. (2003). Prosocial behavior, empathy, and sympathy. In M. H. B. L. Davidson (Ed.), *Wellbeing: Positive development across the life course.* (pp. 253-265). Mahwah, NJ: Erlbaum.

Eisenberg, N., Fabes, R. A., & Spinrad, T. L. (2006). Prosocial development. In N. Eisenberg (Ed.), *Handbook of child psychology: Vol. 3. Social, emotional, and personality development* (6th ed., pp. 646-718). Hoboken, NJ: Wiley.

Elkind, D., & Bowen, R. (1979). Imaginary Audience Behavior in Children and Adolescents. *Developmental Psychology, 15*(1), 38-44. doi: 10.1037/0012-1649.15.1.38

Engelhardt, C. R., Bartholow, B. D., Kerr, G. T., & Bushman, B. J. (2011). This is Your Brain on Violent Video Games: Neural Desensitization to Violence Predicts Increased Aggression Following Violent Video Game Exposure. *Journal of Experimental Social Psychology, 47*(5), 1033-1036.

Epley, N., & Dunning, D. (2000). Feeling "holier Than Thou": Are Self-serving Assessments Produced by Errors in Self- or Social Prediction? *Journal of Personality and Social Psychology, 79*(6), 861-875.

Erikson, E. H. (1950). *Childhood and society* (1st ed.). New York,: Norton.

Erikson, E. H. (1968). *Identity, Youth, and Crisis.* New York: W. W. Norton.

Evans, E. D., & Craig, D. (1990). Teacher and student perceptions of academic cheating in middle and senior high schools. *Journal of Educational Research, 84*, 44-52.

Evans, G. (2004). The environment of childhood poverty. *American Psychologist, 59*, 77-92.

Faiello, P. (March, 2000). Employee power. *CA Magazine, 133*, 45-46.

Fancher, R. (1996). *Pioneers of Psychology* (3rd ed.). New York: W.W. Norton.

Feldman, R. (2007). *Child Development* (4th ed.). Upper Saddle River, NJ: Pearson Prentice Hall.

Fletcher, D. (September 16, 2011). The Haitian Curse. *Time Magazine.* Retrieved from Time.com website: http://www.time.com/time/specials/packages/article/0,28804,1953778_1953776_1953804,00.html   #ixzz2I9f-06SPi

Fokkema, T., & Knipscheer, K. (2007). Escape Loneliness by Going Digital: A Quantitative and Qualitative Evaluation of a Dutch Experiment in Using ECT to Overcome Loneliness Among Older Adults. *Aging & Mental Health, 11*(5), 496-504. doi: 10.1080/13607860701366129

Ford, L. (2006). *Human Relations: A Game Plan for Improving Personal Adjustment (4th Edition)* (4th ed.). Upper Saddle River, NJ: Pearson.

Fraser, A. M., Padilla-Walker, L. M., Coyne, S. M., Nelson, L. J., & Stockdale, L. A. (2012). Associations Between Violent Video Gaming, Empathic Concern, and Prosocial Behavior Toward Strangers, Friends, and Family Members. *Journal of Youth and Adolescence, 41*(5), 636-649.

Freud, S. (1974). *The ego and the id.* London: Hogarth (Original work published 1923).

Friedman, M. (September 16, 2011). God's Wrath Caused Katrina. *Time Magazine*. Retrieved from Time.com website: http://www.time.com/time/specials/packages/article/0,28804,1953778_1953776_1953796,00.html

Gale Encyclopedia of Public Health. (2013). [S.l.]: Gale, Cengage Learning.

Garner, R. (April 3, 2006). How art of conversation between children and parents has died. *The Independent*. Retrieved October 22, 2012, from http://www.independent.co.uk/news/education/education-news/how-art-of-conversation-between-parents-and-children-has-died.html

Gaylin, J. (1985). For Crying out Loud. *Parents (1978)*, *60*, 80.

Gentile, D. A., & Anderson, C. A. (2003). Violent Video Games: The Newest Media Violence Hazard. In D.A. Gentile (Ed.), *Media Violence and Children*. Westport, CT: Praeger Publishing.

Gentile, D. A., Anderson, C. A., Yukawa, S., Ihori, N., Saleem, M., Ming, L. K., . . . Sakamoto, A. (2009). The Effects of Prosocial Video Games on Prosocial Behaviors: International Evidence from Correlational, Longitudinal, and Experimental Studies. *Personality & Social Psychology Bulletin*, *35*(6), 752-763. doi: http://dx.doi.org/10.1177/0146167209333045

Gervais, W. M., & Norenzayan, A. (2012). Analytic Thinking Promotes Religious Disbelief. *Science*, *336*(6080), 493-496. doi: 10.1126/science.1215647

Ginsberg, A. (2007). The Personal Fable and Risk-Taking in Early Adolescence. *Journal of youth and adolescence*, *36*(1), 71-76.

Goldman, A. (2008). The social epistemology of blogging. In J. v. d. H. a. J.Weckert (Ed.), *Information Technology and Moral Philosophy*. Cambridge, MA: Cambridge University Press.

Golodryga, B., & Singh, N. (2012). Bullied 14-Year-Old Girl Gets Plastic Surgery to Fix Ears, Nose, Chin. Retrieved from Good Morning America/Yahoo News website: http://gma.yahoo.com/blogs/abc-blogs/bullied-14-year-old-girl-gets-plastic-surgery-fix-1103228.html

Gottfried, D. S. (June 18, 2012). Cortisol Switcharoo: How the main stress hormone makes you fat and angry. Retrieved March 12, 2013, from http://www.huffingtonpost.com/sara-gottfried-md/cortisol_b_1589670.html

Gray, J. (2012). *Men are from Mars, women are from Venus*. New York: HarperCollins.

Green, D. (2013). Freshmen Dropout: How to help them during this transition. Retrieved from Yahoo Voices website: http://voices.yahoo.com/shared/print.shtml?content_type=article&content_type_id=1029628

Greene, K., Krcmar, M., Walters, L. H., Rubin, D. L., Jerold, & Hale, L. (2000). Targeting Adolescent Risk-taking Behaviors: The Contributions of Egocentrism and Sensation-seeking. *Journal of Adolescence*, *23*(4), 439-461. doi: http://dx.doi.org/10.1006/jado.2000.0330

Gregory, A. (August 21, 2001). Cultivating employee loyalty. *Malay Mail*.

Greitemeyer, T., & Osswald, S. (2010). Effects of Prosocial Video Games on Prosocial Behavior. *Journal of Personality and Social Psychology*, *98*(2), 211-221. doi: 10.1037/a0016997

Greitemeyer, T., & Osswald, S. (2011). Playing Prosocial Video Games Increases the Accessibility of Prosocial Thoughts. *Journal of Social Psychology, 151*(2), 121-128. doi: 10.1080/00224540903365588

Grewal, D. (2012). How Critical Thinkers Lose Their Faith in God. *Scientific American, 306*(7), 26-25.

Grundy, P. (2012). Facts About Jehovah Witnesses: Advanced Education. Retrieved from http://www.jwfacts.com/watchtower/quotes/education.php

Henrich, C. C., Brookmeyer, K. A., Shrier, L. A., & Shahar, G. (2006). Supportive relationships and sexual risk behavior in adolescence: An ecological-transactional approach. *Journal of Pediatric Psychology, 31*, 286-297.

Hildebrand, D. (May 13, 2009). A Job Interview is More Than Just a Conversation. Retrieved from Suite 101 website: http://suite101.com/article/a-job-interview-is-more-than-a-conversation-a116765

homicidesquad.com. (2012). Kitty Genovese. Retrieved October 3, 2012, from http://www.homicidesquad.com/kitty_genovese

Hunt, J. (2012). A Baby Cries: How Should Parents Respond? *The Natural Child Project*. Retrieved March 14, 2013, from http://www.naturalchild.org/jan_hunt/babycries.html

Hunter, J. (1998). *The Servant*. New York: Crown Business.

Inhelder, B., & Piaget, J. (1958). *The growth of logical thinking from childhood to adolescence: An essay on the construction of formal operational structures*. New York: Basic Books.

Is the self-esteem movement running out of steam? (April, 2007). *Gale Schools—Article Archive*. Retrieved from Gale Cengage Learning website: http://www.galeschools.com/article_archive/2007/04/esteem.htm

Janis, I. L. (1972). *Victims of Groupthink: A Psychological Study of Foreign-policy Decisions and Fiascoes*. Boston: Houghton, Mifflin.

Johnson, J., Cohen, P., Smailes, E. M., Kasen, S., & Brook, J. S. (March 29, 2002). Television viewing and aggressive behavior during adolescence and adulthood. *Science, 295*, 2468-2471.

Johnson, S. (1984). *The Precious Present*. Garden City, N.Y.: Doubleday.

Kaye, B., & Jordan-Evans, S. (2001). Retaining key employees. *Public Management, 83*, 6-11.

Kelly, J. (November 12, 2012). TV, video games linked to obesity. *Pittsburgh Post-Gazette*. Retrieved from Post Gazette website: http://www.post-gazette.com/stories/news/health/tv-video-games-linked-to-obesity-661685/

Kemeny, M. E., & Shestyuk, A. (2008). Emotions, the neuroendocrine and immune systems, and health. In M. Lewis, J. M. Haviland-Jones & L. F. Barrett (Eds.), *Handbook of Emotions* (pp. 661-675). New York: Guilford Press.

Kennedy, R. F. (1964). *The Pursuit of Justice*. New York: Harper & Row.

Kern, F. (May 19, 2010). What chief executives really want. *Business Week*. Retrieved from Yahoo Finance website: http://finance.yahoo.com/news/pf_article_109596.html

Kim, S. (2002). Participative Management and Job Satisfaction: Lessons for Management Leadership. *Public Administration Review, 62*(2), 231.

Kimble, G. A. (1991). The spirit of Ivan Petrovich Pavlov. In G. A. Kimble, M. Wertheimer & C. L. White (Eds.), *Portraits of pioneers in psychology* (pp. 26-40). Washington, D.C.: American Psychological Association.

Kimmel, M. S. (2009). *The Gendered Society* (4th ed.). New York: Oxford University Press.

King, F. J., Goodson, L., & Rohani, F. (2012). Higher order thinking skills: Definition, teaching strategies, assessment *Assessment and Evaluation: Educational Services Program*: The Center for Advancement of Learning and Assessment.

Kirby, D. (2002). Antecedents of adolescent initiation of sex, contraceptive use, and pregnancy. *American journal of health behavior, 26,* 473-485.

Kirby, G. R., & Goodpaster, J. R. (2007). *Thinking*. Upper Saddle River, NJ: Pearson/Prentice Hall.

Kirk Cameron's 'Origin Of Species' Plan: Ex-Actor To Distribute 50,000 Altered Darwin Books. (November 22, 2009). Retrieved March 20, 2013, from http://www.huffingtonpost.com/2009/09/22/kirk-camerons-origin-of-s_n_294349.html

Klaus, P. (2008). *The Hard Truth About Soft Skills: Workplace Lessons Smart People Wish They'd Learned Sooner*. New York: HarperCollins.

Knorr, C. (November 19, 2010). Selling to kids tips. *Consumerism*. March 22, 2013, from *http://www.commonsensemedia.org/advice-for-parents/selling-kids-tips*

Kohlberg, L. (1981). *Essays on Moral Development*. San Francisco: Harper & Row.

Kohlberg, L., Levine, C., & Hewer, A. (1983). *Moral Stages: A Current Formulation and a Response to Critics*. Basel: Karger.

Kruger, J., & Dunning, D. (1999). Unskilled and Unaware of It: How Difficulties in Recognizing One's Own Incompetence Lead to Inflated Self-assessments. *Journal of Personality and Social Psychology, 77*(6), 1121-1134.

Kutob, R. M., Senf, J. H., Crago, M., & Shisslak, C. M. (2010). Concurrent and Longitudinal Predictors of Self-Esteem in Elementary and Middle School Girls. *Journal of School Health, 80*(5), 240-248.

LaPierre, W. (December 21, 2012). NRA Press Conference.

Lasch, C. (1979, 1991). *The Culture of Narcissism: American life in an age of diminishing expectations*. New York: W.W. Norton.

Latane, B., & Darley, J. M. (1968). Group Inhibition of Bystander Intervention in Emergencies. *Journal of Personality and Social Psychology, 10*(3), 215-221. doi: 10.1037/h0026570

Lazarus, R. S. (1991). *Emotion and Adaptation*. New York: Oxford University Press.

Lefcourt, H. M. (1982). *Locus of Control: Current Trends in Theory and Research.* Hillsdale, New Jersey: Erlbaum.

Linn, S. (Writer). (2008). The Commercialization of Children.

Lohmann, R. C. (March 30, 2011). Sexting Teens: A picture with consequences. *Psychology Today.* Retrieved from Psychology Today website: http://www.psychologytoday.com/blog/teen-angst/201103/sexting-teens

Ludwig, S. (2010). Beliefs About Overconfidence. *Theory and Decision, 70*(4).

Marcia, J. E. (1980). *Identity in Adolescence.* New York: Wiley.

Maris, D. (October 10, 2012). A drug recall that should frighten us all about the FDA. *Forbes magazine.* Retrieved from Forbes.com website: http://www.forbes.com/sites/davidmaris/2012/10/10/fda-recall-points-to-serious-problems-at-the-fda/

Mark Twain quotes. Retrieved January 9, 2013, from http://www.american-literature.com/quotes

Marketing to Tweens: Data, Spending Habits + Dos and Don'ts to Reach This Fickle Age. (June 19, 2008). Retrieved March 21, 2013, from http://www.marketingsherpa.com

Martin-Young, N. (March, 1996). Communication Skills in the Workplace: Employers Talk Back. *CEI Newsletter.* Retrieved from CEI website: http://www.nccei.org/newsletter/comskills.html

Maslow, A. H. (1970). *Motivation and personality* (2d ed.). New York: Harper & Row.

Matsuba, M. K., & Walker, L. J. (1998). Moral Reasoning in the Context of Ego Functioning. *Merrill-Palmer Quarterly, 44*(4), 464-483.

Maya Angelou quotes. http://www.brainyquote.com/quotes/authors/m/maya_angelou.html

McCabe, D. L., Butterfield, K. D., & Trevino, L. K. (2012). *Cheating in College: Why Students Do It and What Educators Can Do about It.* Baltimore: Johns Hopkins University Press.

McCabe, D. L., Trevino, L. K., & Butterfield, K. D. (2001). Cheating in Academic Institutions: A Decade of Research. *Ethics & Behavior, 11*(3), 219-232.

McCullough, D. (2012). "You're not special" graduation speech. Retrieved from Fox News Boston website: http://www.myfoxboston.com/story/18720284/2012/06/06/full-transcript-youre-not-special-speech.html

McGonigal, J. (2011). *Reality is Broken: Why Games Make Us Better and How They Can Change the World.*

McGraw, P. (2000). *Life Strategies: Doing What Works, Doing What Matters.* New York: Hyperion.

McGraw, P. (2004). Relationshiops/Sex: Changing Your Attitude, Changing Your Life Retrieved from Dr.Phil.com website: http://drphil.com/articles/article/145/

McLeod, D. S. (June 27, 2012). Teach students higher order or critical thinking skills? Not if the Texas Republicans have their way. Retrieved from http://dangerouslyirrelevant.org/2012/06/teach-students-higher-order-

or-critical-thinking-skills-not-if-the-texas-republicans-have-their-way. html

Mischel, W., & Liebert, R. M. (1966). Effects of Discrepancies Between Observed and Imposed Reward Criteria on Their Acquisition and Transmission. *Journal of Personality and Social Psychology, 3*(1), 45-53. doi: 10.1037/ h0022696

Moore, B., & Parker, R. (2004). *Critical thinking: Evaluating claims and arguments in everyday life.* Palo Alto, CA: Mayfield Publishing Co.

Morisey, M. (May 20, 2008). Skills beat out certifications in networking job market, study finds. *Search Networking.* Retrieved from Search Networking website: http://searchnetworking.techtarget.com/news/1314388/ Skills-beat-out-certifications-in-networking-job-market-study-finds

Morrow, P. (2013). Getting along with others. *Credit Today.* Retrieved from Credit Today website: http://www.credittoday.net/public/Getting_ Along_With_Others.cfm

Mosby's Medical Dictionary. (2012) (9th ed.). Mosby.

Olson, J. M., Zanna, M. P., & Dunning, D. (2011). The Dunning-Kruger Effect: On Being Ignorant of One's Own Ignorance (pp. 247-296).

Osofsky, J. (1995). The effects of exposure to violence on young children. *American Psychologist, 50,* 782-788.

Ostling, R. N., Dolan, B., & Harris, M. P. (1987). Raising Eyebrows and the Dead Oral Roberts Stirs Controversy with an Extraordinary Claim. *Time, 130*(2), 55-55.

Parsons, T. L., & Rouse, P. b. M. (April, 2011). **Soft skills.** Retrieved from SearchCIO website: http://searchcio.techtarget.com/definition/soft-skills

Phillips, D. (August 19, 2012). Rep. Todd Akin: A 'legitimate rape' victim's body can naturally stop pregnancy. Retrieved from Examiner.com website: http://www.examiner.com/article/rep-todd-akin-a-legitimate-rape-victim-s-body-can-naturally-stop-pregnancy

Piaget, J. (1965). *The Moral Judgment of the Child.* New York: Free Press.

Piaget, J. (1999). *Judgement and Reasoning in the Child.* London: Routledge.

Pickett, C. L., Gardner, W. L., & Knowles, M. (2004). Getting a Cue: The Need to Belong and Enhanced Sensitivity to Social Cues. *Personality and Social Psychology Bulletin, 30*(9), 1095-1107.

Portraits of Pioneers in Psychology. (1991). Washington, D.C.: American Psychological Association.

Prochaska, J. O., DiClemente, C. C., & Norcross, J. C. (1992). In Search of How People Change: Applications to Addictive Behaviors. *American Psychologist, 47,* 1102-1114.

Project, P. U. C. f. F. P. F. M. (2012). Family meals spell success. Retrieved March 14, 2013, from Purdue University http://www.cfs.purdue.edu/ cff/documents/promoting_meals/spellsuccessfactsheet.pdf

Pula, M. (March 26, 2011). Has social networking led to a decline in social skills? Retrieved from http://blog.mlive.com/kgazette/opinion_impact/print.html?entry=/2011/03/our_turn_column

Rabbi Schmuley Boteach. Shalom in the Home (2006).

Randi, J. (1987). *The Faith Healers*. Buffalo, N.Y.: Prometheus Books.

Rantz, J. (January 6, 2009). FSM's Third Annual 'America's Most Dangerous College Courses'. Retrieved March 28, 2013, from http://www.familysecuritymatters.org/publications/id.2190/pub_detail.asp#ixzz2OqtXsP8

Rape and Incest National Network (RAINN). (2009, January 9, 2013). Rape Statistics. from http://www.rainn.org/get-information/statistics/sexual-assault-offenders

Reifman, A. (February 1, 2012). Academic Dishonesty: Prevalent but Preventable. Retrieved from http://www.psychologytoday.com/blog/the-campus/201202/academic-dishonesty-prevalent-but-preventable.html

Right-wing front group Family Security Matters releases '10 Most Dangerous Organizations'. (October 25, 2007). Retrieved March 28, 2013, from http://www.democraticunderground.com

Ritchie, J. B., & Miles, R. E. (1970). An analysis of quantity and quality of participation as mediating variables in the participative decision making process. *Personnel Psychology, 23*(3), 347-359.

Roach, J. (May 28, 2003). Video games boost visual skills, study finds. *National Geographic News*. Retrieved from National Geographic website: http://news.nationalgeographic.com/news/2003/05/0528_030528_videogames.html

Rochman, B. (February 22, 2013). Hover no more: Helicopter parents may breed depression and incompetence in their children. *Time*. Retrieved from Time: Health and Family website: http://www.healthland.time.com/2013/02/22

Rockwell, R. (March 9, 2011). Does Stress Cause High Cholesterol? [Reviewed by Connie Bye, March 9, 2011.]. Retrieved from Livestrong website: http://www.livestrong.com/article/26614-stress-cause-high-cholesterol

Roger, V. L., A.S., G., Lloyd-Jones, D. M., Benjamin, E. J., Berry, J. D., Borden, W. B., . . . Subcommittee., S. S. (2011). Heart disease and stroke statistics—2012 update: a report from the American Heart Association. Retrieved from American Heart Association website: http://www.heart.org/idc/groups/heart-public/@wcm/@sop/@smd/documents/downloadable/ucm_319588.pdf

Romero, F. (September 16, 2011). Pointing Fingers Over 9/11. *Time magazine*. Retrieved from Time.com website: http://www.time.com/time/specials/packages/article/0,28804,1953778_1953776_1953796,00.html

Rotter, J. B. (1954). *Social learning and clinical psychology*. New York: Prentice-Hall.

Rotter, J. B. (1966). *Generalized expectancies for internal versus external control of reinforcement*. Washington: American Psychological Association.

Ruggiero, V.R. (2004). *Thinking critically about ethical issues* (6th ed.). New York: McGraw-Hill.

Ruggiero, V. R. (2008). *Beyond feelings: a guide to critical thinking* (8th ed.). Boston: McGraw-Hill Higher Education.

Ruggiero, V. R. (2012). *Beyond feelings: a guide to critical thinking* (9th ed.). New York: McGraw-Hill.

Schick, T., & Vaughn, L. (2014). *How to think about weird things: critical thinking for a new age.* (7th ed.). New York: McGraw-Hill.

Schiffrin, H. H., Liss, M., Miles-McLean, H., Geary, K. A., Erchull, M. J., & Tashner, T. (2013). Helping or Hovering? the Effects of Helicopter Parenting on College Students' Well-being. *Journal of Child and Family Studies.* doi: 10.1007/s10826-013-9716-3

Selye, H. (1956). *The stress of life.* New York: McGraw-Hill.

Selye, H. (1976). *Stress in health and disease.* Boston: Butterworths.

Shaevitz, M. H. (October 18, 2012). Video games can actually be good for kids. Retrieved from Huffington Post website: http://www.huffingtonpost.com/marjorie-hansen-shaevitz/video-games-good-kids_b_1974015.html

Shapiro, E., & Shapiro, D. (September 20, 2011). The Differences Between Religion and Spirituality. Retrieved from www.huffingtonpost.com/ed-and-deb-shapiro/religion-and-spirituality website.

Shelov, S. P., & Remer Altmann, T. (Eds.). (2009). *Caring for Your Baby and Young Child Birth to Age 5* (5th ed.). New York: Bantam Books.

Skinner, B. F. (1953). *Science and human behavior.* New York: Macmillan.

Sternberg, R. J. (1985). *Beyond I.Q.: A Triarchic Theory of Human Intelligence.* Cambridge: Cambridge University Press.

Sternberg, R. J. (1996). *Successful Intelligence: How Practical and Creative Intelligence Determine Success in Life.* New York: Simon & Schuster.

Tanis, M., & Postmes, T. (2003). Social Cues and Impression Formation in CMC. *Journal of Communication, 53*(4), 676-693.

Tannen, D. (1990). *You just don't understand.* New York: Ballantine.

Tannenbaum, L. (2002). *Catfight.* New York: Perennial.

Teenage Consumer Spending Statistics. (2012). Statistic Brain Retrieved March 22, 2013 http://www.statisticbrain.com

The importance of family dinner. (2012). Retrieved from Menu Planning Central website: http://menuplanningcentral.com/articles/family-dinner.html

The Top 10 Most Dangerous Organizations in America. (2007). from http://www.familysecuritymatters.org

Tracy, B. (2010). *No Excuses!: The Power of Self-Discipline.* New York: Perseus Books Group.

Trunk, P. (July 18, 2006). Social skills matter more than ever, so here's how to get them. Retrieved from http://blog.penelopetrunk.com/2006/07/18/social-skills-matter-more-than-ever-so-heres-how-to-get-them.html

Vaughn, L. (2008). *The Power of Critical Thinking*. New York: Oxford University Press.

Vinclauv, A. (February 5, 2013). Teen gives judge the finger. receives $10,000 fine, 30-day jail sentence. Retrieved from Examiner.com website: http://www.examiner.com/article/teen-gives-judge-the-finger-receives-10-000-fine-30-day-jail-sentence

Viviano, J. (November 28, 2012). Survey: Fewer U.S. high school students are cheating, lying, stealing. Retrieved from http://www.dispatch.com/content/blogs/the-compass/2012/11/student-ethics.html

Warhol, A., & Colacello, B. (1980). *Andy Warhol's Exposures*. New York: Andy Warhol Bools/ Grosset & Dunlap.

Warren, R. (2002). *The Purpose-driven Life: What on Earth Am I Here For?* Grand Rapids, Mich.: Zondervan.

Weber, D. E. (September 22, 2008). The Brain on Cortisol. Retrieved March 12, 2013 http://www.brainleadersandlearners.com/general/the-brain-on-cortisol

Weiten, W. (2008). *Psychology: Themes and Variations* (8th ed.). Belmont, CA: Wadsworth: Cengage Learning.

West, L. Antibiotics Resistance—Is Excessive Use of Antibiotics Creating Super Bugs? Retrieved from About.com. Environmental Issues website: http://environment.about.com/od/healthenvironment/a/superbugs.htm

Wistrom, E. (February 8, 2012). Why do students drop out of college? Retrieved from BrightHub website: http://www.brighthub.com/education/college/articles/82378.aspx

Wyatt, J. M., & Carlo, G. (2002). What will my parents think? Relations among adolescents' expected parental reactions, prosocial moral reasoning and prosocial and antisocial behaviors. *Journal of Adolescent Research, 17*, 646-666.

Yarrow, M. R., Scott, P. M., & Waxler, C. Z. (1973). Learning Concern for Others. *Developmental Psychology, 8*(2), 240-260. doi: 10.1037/h0034159

YouthBeat: Youth and Parents Marketing Research Data Snapshots. (2013). Retrieved March 22, 2013, from C & R Research, Inc. http://www.youthbeat.com/data-snapshots

Zimbardo, P. G., Johnson, R. L., & Weber, A. L. (2006). *Psychology: core concepts* (5th ed.). Boston, MA: Pearson/Allyn and Bacon.